DATE DUE

AP25 '95			
MR1 0 '96			

Demco, Inc. 38-293

Books by Corliss Lamont

The Philosophy of Humanism, Seventh edition, Continuum, New York, NY, 1990.

The Illusion of Immortality, Fifth edition, Continuum, New York, NY, 1990.

Freedom of Choice Affirmed, Third edition, Continuum, New York, NY, 1990.

Freedom Is As Freedom Does: Civil Liberties in America, Fourth edition, Continuum, New York, NY, 1990.

Yes To Life: Memoirs of Corliss Lamont, Continuum, New York, NY, 1990.

Remembering John Masefield, Continuum, New York, NY, 1990.

A Lifetime of Dissent, Prometheus Books, 700 East Amherst St., Buffalo, NY, 14215, 1988.

Voice in the Wilderness: Collected Essays of Fifty Years, Prometheus Books, 700 East Amherst St., Buffalo, NY, 14215, 1974.

The Independent Mind, Horizon Press, New York, NY, 1951.

The Peoples of the Soviet Union, Harcourt, Brace & Co., New York, NY, 1946.

Russia Day by Day (Co-author with Margaret I. Lamont), Covici-Friede, New York, 1933.

Soviet Civilization, Second edition, Philosophical Library, New York, NY, 1952, 1955.

You Might Like Socialism, Modern Age Books, New York, NY, 1939.

Lover's Credo: Poems of Love, William L. Bauhan, Dublin, NH, 03444.

A Humanist Wedding Service, Prometheus Books, 700 East Amherst St., Buffalo, NY, 14215, 1970.

A Humanist Funeral Service, Prometheus Books, 700 East Amherst St., Buffalo, NY, 14215, 1977.

(Continued on last page of book)

FREEDOM IS AS FREEDOM DOES

Civil Liberties in America

CORLISS LAMONT

Foreword by Bertrand Russell
New Epilogue by the Author

HALF-MOON FOUNDATION, INC.

The Half-Moon Foundation was formed to promote enduring international peace, support for the United Nations, the conservation of our country's natural environment, and to safeguard and extend civil liberties as guaranteed under the Constitution and the Bill of Rights.

A Frederick Ungar Book
CONTINUUM • NEW YORK

1990

The Continuum Publishing Company
370 Lexington Avenue
New York, NY 10017

Fourth Edition

Copyright © 1956, 1972, 1981, 1990 by Corliss Lamont

Printed in the United States of America

Library of Congress Catalog Card No. 56-7820
ISBN 0-8264-0475-8

Cover photo: The author speaking on behalf of US aid to Soviets, 1942, at
Madison Square Garden meeting of National Council of American Soviet
Friendship. Thomas W. Lamont, financier and partner in J. P. Morgan &
Co., and father of the author, spoke in favor of US aid at the same event.

To my son Hayes

Freedom is recreated year by year
—JAMES RUSSELL LOWELL

CONTENTS

FOREWORD TO THE ENGLISH EDITION

BERTRAND RUSSELL

It is a pleasure to have the opportunity of introducing to the British public Mr. Corliss Lamont's book *Freedom Is as Freedom Does*. The book is an admirable epitome of the various forms of attack on personal liberty that have been taking place in America in recent years. So far as I am able to judge, Mr. Lamont is wholly reliable as to facts, and he has shown good judgement in selecting from an enormous mass of material. Every friend of freedom ought to lay to heart what he has to say. This applies not only to Americans, since there is no country where liberty may not be endangered.

All countries (except perhaps Holland and Scandinavia) are liable to waves of hysteria, though the extent of the damage caused by such waves differs greatly in different places. France had such a wave in 1793 and, in a lesser degree, during the Dreyfus case. Germany had it in the worst possible form during the time of Hitler. Russia had it under Stalin. And America has had it three times, in 1798, in 1919-20, and since the outbreak of the Korean War. Let us not flatter ourselves that Britain is exempt. From the accession of Charles I until the Revolution of 1688, hysteria of all kinds—left wing, right wing, religious, and economic—was rife. In reading what has happened in America since 1950, I constantly feel as if I were reading about England under the Stuarts. Congressional Committees are the counterpart of the

Star Chamber, and Senator McCarthy seems like a re-incarnation of Titus Oates who invented the Popish Plot. Nor is it necessary to go so far back. In the days of the French Revolution, when the mob sacked Dr. Priestley's house and the Government employed spies and *agents provocateurs* to ferret out sympathizers with the Jacobins, England was not unlike what America has been lately. The younger Pitt, if he found himself now in Washington, would feel quite at home. I think it important that English readers should remember such facts and should not react to what is amiss in America by smug national complacency. I think it also important to remember, in protesting against loss of liberty in America, that the loss in Russia was very much greater and that the defects of the American system afford no argument in favour of the Soviet dictatorship.

In spite of these provisos, I cannot deny that some of the facts about the anti-Communist hysteria in America are utterly amazing. Who would have guessed that the *Girl Scout Handbook*, a work intended to instruct what we should call Girl Guides in their duties, was savagely criticized because it praised the United States Public Health Service and spoke favourably of the United Nations, "the handiwork of that arch-traitor, Alger Hiss"? So severe was the censure that a correction had to be immediately issued omitting the offending matter.

Perhaps the most valuable chapter in Mr. Lamont's book is the one called "Police State in the Making." The Federal Bureau of Investigation (FBI) has been steadily building up its power and spreading terror far and wide. It has 130 million finger-print cards and a system of indexing them of which it is enormously proud. Only a minority of the population do not appear in a police dossier. Members of the FBI join even mildly liberal organizations as spies and report any unguarded word. Anybody who goes so far as to support equal rights for coloured people, or to say a good word for UN, is liable to be visited by officers of the FBI and threatened, if not with prosecution, at least with black-listing and consequent inability to earn a living. When a sufficient state of terror has been produced by these means, the victim is informed that there is a way out: if he will denounce a sufficient number of his friends as Communists, he may obtain absolution.

As in ancient Rome and modern Russia, this system has produced its crop of professional informers, mostly men who once were Communists and who now denounce others at so much a head. These are generally men over whom the Government holds the threat of prosecution for perjury for having at some time denied they were ever Communists. They are safe so long as they continue to do the dirty work demanded of them, but woe betide them if they repent. One of them, Matusow, after securing the conviction of a number of innocent people, went before a Federal judge and recanted. For this the judge said he would give him three years in prison. Although Matusow won this case on appeal, the Government currently is prosecuting him on another charge, that of perjury, for statements he made in his general recantation.

The police have, for many years, shown a complete disregard for the law and, so far as I can discover, no Federal policeman has ever been punished for breaking the law. The whole terrorist system would break down if one simple reform were adopted: namely, that criminals should be punished even if they are policemen.

The evils of the system have not failed to be condemned by some who cannot be accused of subversive opinions. This is true especially of the Federal judiciary. For example, as Mr. Lamont relates, the Federal Court of Appeals in San Francisco objected to the Government's "system of secret informers, whisperers and tale-bearers" and went on to say: "It is not amiss to bear in mind whether or not we must look forward to a day when substantially everyone will have to contemplate the possibility that his neighbours are being encouraged to make reports to the FBI about what he says, what he reads and what meetings he attends." On the whole, however, such protests from "respectable" citizens are distressingly rare. The persecution of minority opinion, even when not obviously connected with Communism, is a thing which has not been imposed from above, but suits the temper of most men and receives enthusiastic support from Juries.

At first sight, it seems curious that a great and powerful country like the United States, which contains only a handful of Communists, should allow itself to get into such a state of fright. One might have expected that national pride would prevent anything so abject, but such a view would be one which could only be suggested by a false psychology. We are all of us a mixture of good and bad impulses, and it is almost always the bad impulses that prevail in an excited crowd. There is in most men an impulse to persecute whatever is felt to be "different." There is also a hatred of any claim to superiority, which makes the stupid many hostile to the intelligent few. A motive such as fear of Communism affords what seems a decent moral excuse for a combination of the herd against everything in any way exceptional. This is a recurrent phenomenon in human history. Whenever it occurs, its results are horrible. There is some reason to hope that Russia is past the worst in this respect. When McCarthy fell into disfavour, it seemed as if persecution in the United States might diminish. So far, the improvement has been less than one might have hoped. But improvement has begun, and it would be no excess of optimism to think that it will continue, and reach a point where men of intelligence and humane minds can once more breathe an atmosphere of freedom. If this comes about, books such as Mr. Lamont's will have served an immensely important purpose.

INTRODUCTION

H. H. WILSON
Associate Professor of Political Science
Princeton University

One of the remarkable strengths of democratic societies has been their capacity for producing dissenting individuals, men of integrity and independence who have refused to pattern their thinking or behavior by popular standards. Sometimes, of course, these individuals have been merely anti-social, or anti-democratic, seeking to sustain their own personal interests, or the privileges of a class. Others have served as the true conscience-bearers of the society, reminding us of our traditions and declared values. In this category Corliss Lamont has achieved an honored position as one who dares to differ with majority opinion in politics, economics, and philosophy. Since his undergraduate years at Harvard, he has in classroom, in political campaign, and on the lecture platform devoted himself to challenging his fellow citizens to think about fundamental political and social questions. Life-long use of freedom has reenforced Dr. Lamont's devotion to democracy and his profound understanding of the philosophical basis for civil liberties. Abhorring violence and stupidity, he has persisted in his efforts to convince others that the best way of solving human problems is through the use of intelligence and reason. More than most men he has experienced the reality of Wendell Phillips' observation that "when a nation sets itself to do evil and all its leading forces, wealth, party, and piety, join in the career, it is impossible but that those who offer a constant opposition should be hated and maligned, no matter how wise, cautious, and well planned their course may be."

In this book he provides a panoramic view of the condition of civil liberties in the United States today. His approach is fundamentally both conservative and constructive. He presents not an encyclopedia of violations, but an analysis of a "general pattern of repression" which permeates the whole society. Stimulating and incisive discussion illuminates the situation as it exists in politics, education, business, government, communications, and the arts. In his discussion of the ideal of civil liberties Dr. Lamont examines the basic philosophy which undergirds these freedoms. There is need to communicate ideas, popular or unpopular, if there is to be civilization, for only through the constant search for truth and the stimulation of intelligence is progress possible. Only through the protection of freedom of speech and association, and their active use, is political democracy even theoretically possible. To offer alternative policies, programs, ways of organizing society is the right and responsibility of groups, as well as of individuals. Further, the democrat understands and must insist upon the right of people to read, hear, see, and consider. Otherwise we make mockery of the democratic principle that ultimately sovereign power rests with "we the people of the United States."

The social value of dissent, the need for critical intelligence has never been greater than it is today when science has presented society with the means to destroy itself. Ironically, in an era when society most desperately needs the creative stimulus of vigorous criticism and challenge to preconceptions, the threat to constitutional freedoms is graver than ever before in American history. A "multiplicity of moral, economic, legal and physical sanctions" curb the dissenter, the non-conformist. Constriction of freedom continues because so many of the techniques have been institutionalized and their application is generalized throughout the society. We have grown accustomed to the use of unconstitutional legislation by state and federal governments. We seem to have lost our capacity for what would once have been thought an in-

stinctual revulsion to professional informers. Now we demand
that even our teachers accept the function of informing on colleagues and students as a "moral" duty. Administrative agencies
issue orders listing organizations as "subversive," deny passports
and screen individuals for their thoughts and associations. Private initiative creates a commercial enterprise of blacklisting and
blackmail because industry, motion picture companies, radio and
television stations and educational institutions feel compelled to
test their employees for ideological purity which means, in operation, the avoidance of the controversial.

These developments should instruct Americans that the Constitution and the Bill of Rights do not safeguard the fundamental
liberties essential to a free society. Freedom cannot be preserved
for an apathetic or indifferent people by constitution or courts.
Many people are unaware of the extent to which repression has
gone. A whole generation is growing up conditioned to accept the
notion that only within narrow limits may one properly, or safely,
disagree with authority. One of the problems confronting any society is the tendency of people to acquiesce in change and then
to forget that change has occurred. In our passive acceptance of
eroding civil liberties one may discern something of the phenomenon Bryce characterized as the "Fatalism of the Multitude," the
belief that individuals cannot alter the course of events. Doubting
that "hysteria" among the people ever existed as a reaction to the
challenge of communism, Lamont insists upon a more serious consideration of why basic democratic principles are under attack.
Significantly he points out that the Constitution does not provide
for the economic implementation of civil liberties. There is a
problem of sheer financial inability to present minority opinions
because of the cost involved in printing and distribution, or in obtaining access to the mass media. Further there is no specific protection in the Constitution to provide an offset to the massive
propaganda of vested interests. There is, of course, potential
power if people decide to implement freedom of access to information. By legitimate constitutional means we could prevent the
maintenance of monopoly control over newspapers, radio and

television, and motion pictures. But such action requires a sophisticated understanding of the direct relationship between the free dissemination of opinions and the survival of political democracy. As a contribution to this understanding and a challenge to apathy and fatalism, Corliss Lamont has written this book.

He does not argue that the principle of freedom of expression is an absolute right. No man has a right to libel or slander another, incite to a breach of the peace, or commit contempt of court. But these specific actions, properly subject to regulation, are not a part of legitimate discussion and, therefore, do not constitute exceptions to the First Amendment. With Alexander Meiklejohn, Lamont would distinguish between "advocacy of action" and "incitement to action." Recognizing that the "clear and present danger" test has failed to work, he suggests the substitution of "a clear, direct and wilful incitement to the present commission of dangerous violence or some other serious and overt criminal act." This formulation would have the merit of depriving the legislatures of the power to prejudge individual cases and would compel the courts to examine the facts in each case. Some lawyers will have reservations concerning the use of "wilful" on the grounds that this would make prosecution almost impossible. Apart from this reservation it would appear that this standard is a far more precise formulation than the present indefinable phrase which has, since the Dennis case, become "a clear and *probable* danger."

Dedication to the use of reason and commitment to reliance upon empirical evidence militates against acceptance of the hoax of a Communist Party threat to American institutions. If subversion be understood to mean overturning or undermining institutions, the burden of proof is on those who would conjure up this fantasy. No Communist sits in any legislative body, holds any significant public office, controls any important media of communication, directs any military or police power, or has ever attained an influential role of social or political or intellectual leadership in the United States. There is no evidence to support the thesis that Communist ideology was ever successful in gaining substantial numerical support, even in the depths of the depression, and the rapid turnover and disillusionment of those who joined the Party should correct the contagion theory of communism. The extremely limited success of the Party existed only to the extent that it supported popular causes, or expressed the needs of distressed minorities. A case can be made to demonstrate that those who perpetrate the hoax element of this problem are accurately to be charged with subversion of our laws, institutions and basic philosophy. For they have truly undermined the foundations of a free society. By creating generalized suspicion, denigrating the use of reason, inculcating a "devil" or "plot" theory of history, and destroying the faith of people in the integrity of their leaders and the viability of their institutions they have lessened American capacity to provide example and leadership for the world.

In addition to providing a rationale for those who would suppress dissent, discourage questioning of our governors, or stimulate military solutions to international problems, emphasis upon subversion has detracted attention from that degree of reality which is to be found in the concept of espionage. So long as nation-states persist there will always be, from friendly or unfriendly nations, the possibility of intelligence or espionage activities. It is a legitimate, proper, essential and continuing task of all governments to protect themselves against such activities which may be potentially harmful to national interests. This is a difficult assignment at best because the nature of counter-intelligence and counter-espionage methods inevitably conflicts with democratic standards. The task, therefore, becomes one of protecting the nation without producing inhibiting fear, or instituting procedures disruptive of essential political and intellectual activities. In recognition of this problem, Dr. Lamont makes explicit what should be taken for granted, that "the government has the right and the obligation to prosecute anyone who commits specific acts of treason, sabotage, espionage and the like." In passing it is worthy of note that, despite the alarums of the last twenty years, no member of the Communist Party has been indicted or convicted for an overt act of violence against the Government and, despite elaborate efforts by Congressional committees to improvise it, there is little substantial evidence of espionage traceable to the Party. One is impressed in reading Dr. Lamont's invaluable analysis of "eight of the worst laws," including the Alien Registration Act (Smith Act), the Immunity Act, the Welker Act, the Labor-Management Relations Act (Taft-Hartley), that not one of these measures can be legitimately interpreted as strengthening the nation. Yet all eight make their contribution toward repeal of the Bill of Rights and legislating anti-democracy.

Contemplating the present state of our liberties leads one to ponder the long term implications of these developments. In speculating on "Is the Tide Turning?", Corliss Lamont replies with a qualified affirmative. There is no doubt that on the surface there has been some improvement in the last two or three years. Some relaxation of overt repression is suggested by the decline of McCarthy's prestige and the cessation of his tacit support by conservatives, the Administration's failure to get its wire-tapping bill out of committee, a slight lessening of arbitrary action by the Passport Division, a few favorable court decisions, and the positive affirmation of freedom by Chief Justice Warren and ex-Senator Harry Cain. Walter Lippmann hopefully, and perhaps prematurely, observes that ". . . the great majority of the leaders of American opinion are no longer willing to stand for the theory that espionage, sabotage, and subversion can be dealt with only by ignoring the Constitution, and by conniving at what is nakedly and simply lynch law."

Certainly one must hope that these developments mark a permanent change of direction and not a mere slackening of pressure reflecting a lessening of international tension. On the other hand one can't ignore a duality in the American tradition which tolerates pressure toward bigotry, repression, chauvinism and intolerance. This influence is as much a part of the American tradition as the idealistic, humane, democratic, and progressive current which many of us revere and consider to be *the* American spirit. And it tends to become dominant when the society is under attack, or is uncertain of its goals.

One may wonder to what extent the apparent relaxation is merely a function of an accomplished task. Quite possibly overt attacks on schools and teachers, for example, may cease, but does this represent an improved understanding of academic freedom, or an awareness that those involved in education have been housebroken and will never again challenge the verities? When scholars accept the premise, to quote the opening sentence from an influential college textbook, that "in economic organization and reform, the 'great issues' are no longer the great issues, if ever they were," pressure to enforce orthodoxy becomes superfluous. Robert Hutchins' comment on Congressional impact on the foundations underscores the same point: "If there ever was a foundation that was willing to be controversial, that was willing to take risks and venture capital in areas about which people have strong prejudices, it learned its lesson by the time Cox and Reece got through."

There is also the widespread phenomenon of a failure of nerve and lack of conviction on the part of those in a position to provide leadership. Publishers who are passionate in their defense of "freedom of the press" in any discussion of mail privileges, or wages-and-hours legislation, maintain an aloof silence when a radical editor is deported for his political opinions, and fail to report the news of Senator Eastland's thinly veiled attack on the independence of press and reporters. This lack of moral courage is further demonstrated by college presidents who instruct their faculties to "cooperate" with Congressional committees who violate the Constitution; great corporations that withdraw their sponsorship of "controversial" programs or individuals; and government officials who refuse to defend the integrity of their agencies from Congressional attack.

Where are we to find the replacements for the men of principle, the Thoreaus, Altgelds, Darrows, Meiklejohns, Holmeses who have provided examples of integrity and courage? We must recognize that several student generations have matured in an atmosphere which encourages conformity and the passive accept-

ance of the safe and orthodox. Our contemporary practice is to
stress the importance of being "a good member of the team;"
or, in Willy Loman's classic phrase, to insist that it isn't enough
to be liked, one must be well-liked. So there develops a tendency
to assume that we cannot afford or tolerate the disruptive potential of individual non-conformity, whether it be expressed in economics, politics, art, or science.

In any serious consideration of civil liberties one is ultimately
forced to examine the viability of political democracy in organized mass society. We are living today on the capital of ideas
and values accumulated over the past several hundred years.
Many of the values and attitudes to which we still pay lip service,
especially those related to civil liberties, derive from physical and
social conditions which existed in the eighteenth and nineteenth
centuries, but exist no longer. We are today, in fact, creating the
conditions, attitudes toward life, the purposes of society, and even
the kind of people who will shape this society for fifty and one
hundred years hence. Perhaps the dominant factor in forming
this society is the application of science, or technology. The fullest
exploitation of technology demands constantly expanding organization. This organization, originally limited to the production
of goods or services, reaches out almost inevitably to eliminate
chaos, disorder, or uncertainty in the society at large. In Roderick
Seidenberg's formulation, "the effective functioning of organization . . . rests upon a principle of predictability that inherently
demands the further organization of all contiguous regions of the
system. Order demands order." The result of the application of
the organizational principle is to push toward the ultimate col-
lectivization of society. As Lewis Mumford points out, mechaniza-
tion and regimentation "have been projected and embodied in
organized forms which dominate every aspect of our existence."
This development, with differences of degree, occurs whether the
political form be designated as democratic, socialist, fascist, or
communist. It becomes a problem only for those democratic societies that profess devotion to individual freedoms. Thus Adlai
Stevenson recently commented that "technology, while adding

daily to our physical ease, throws daily another loop of fine wire around our souls."

With this organizational revolution, individualism, however expressed, tends to be considered a disruptive element; and along with the discrediting of individualism, traditional concepts of civil liberty come to be thought of as having only dubious utility. In fact the suppression of heresy or dissent in a highly organized society becomes necessary when it is considered to be disruptive and non-productive, rather than potentially creative and productive. It is this extension of the organizational principle to all aspects of society, in an effort to mesh all institutions and individuals in the productive apparatus, that gives significance to apparently random cr unrelated attacks on scientists and State Department officials, on foundations, schools, colleges and churches. Scientists, like teachers, government employees, poets and sculptors must be disciplined and taught to do their bit as "members of the team." The coercion of technology is forcing the integration of what had been a haphazardly patterned "open society," and changes in the social structure of society do have an impact on cultural values. With the further extension of integration, of the organizational principle, there will be social changes as great as those which accompanied the earlier version of the industrial revolution.

"We do not imagine," as Mr. J. B. Priestley says, "that we are the victims of plots, that bad men are doing all this. It is the machinery of power that is getting out of sane control. Lost in its elaboration, even some men of good will begin to forget the essential humanity this machinery should be serving. They are now so busy testing, analysing, and reporting on the bath water that they cannot remember having thrown the baby out of the window."

If one is reluctant to accept passive surrender, there is justification for seeking to comprehend contemporary developments and to encourage others who share common values to search for alternatives to drift. What is involved is the task of restating the purposes and ends of life, a process which demands the re-examination of institutions and their supporting value systems. It is imperative that there be a re-examination of the premises on which political democracy has rested. Power in the society is concentrated, not dispersed; economic independence, in the traditional sense of owning productive property, is not feasible; modern communications tend to create a mass society, rather than a series of informed "publics," and there is constant pressure toward reliance on authority or on leaders to determine crucial politics. We cannot re-create the conditions which sustained independence in an earlier era. Instead we must devise methods which can be reconciled with our technology, our complex and integrated society, and our democratic aspirations. The challenge is to create a social system in which integration for some purposes does not frustrate individual initiative and creativity in other areas.

Dr. Lamont's book supplies massive evidence of the extent to which such initiative and creativity are obstructed by the drive against civil liberties, which restricts freedom of opinion, silences discussion, and moulds the individual to conformity. If American democracy is to survive, the way must be found to restore intellectual independence: freedom for the mind of man.

AUTHOR'S PREFACE

Ever since I was a student in Harvard College more than thirty years ago, I have been involved in the struggle for civil liberties. This book tells of the main battles in which I personally took part and at the same time tries to give an over-all survey of the onslaught against the American Bill of Rights since the end of the Second World War.

My first participation in a free speech battle occurred in 1924 when, as a Senior at Harvard, I actively supported a movement to have a few radicals invited now and then to address the undergraduates concerning economic and political issues. I and some of the other students had grown tired of hearing lectures (with lantern slides) on such subjects as "Wild Life in Darkest Africa," "Arctic Explorations of the Twentieth Century," and "The Flora and Fauna of the Amazon." We succeeded in liberalizing to some extent the program of outside speakers for Harvard.

In 1932 civil liberties became a definite field of concentration for me when I was elected to the Board of Directors of the American Civil Liberties Union (ACLU). Since then I have spent considerable time in working, speaking and writing in defense of the Bill of Rights. In 1934, when Boss Frank Hague had set himself up as the anti-labor dictator of Jersey City, I undertook a test case for the ACLU by peacefully picketing a factory where members of the Furniture Workers Industrial Union were on strike. Mayor

Hague's police arrested me for the high crime and misdemeanor of walking up and down in front of the plant in question and carrying an appropriate placard.

I was arraigned, fingerprinted and put behind the bars in a cell in the city jail for a few hours while bail was arranged. My case never came to trial because the issue over which I was concerned was soon settled when the higher courts, beyond the control of Boss Hague, reversed previous anti-picketing decisions in New Jersey and established the right of peaceful picketing in Jersey City on the grounds that it was a legitimate part of freedom of expression.

From 1934 on, I became increasingly involved in a direct personal sense in the struggle for civil liberty. Since my views on politics, economics, international relations and philosophy are for the most part unorthodox and unpopular, I have often been in trouble on account of them. As a teacher, writer and lecturer, I regard freedom of expression as a necessity for my regular work.

Many first-rate books have recently been published on some special aspect of the current civil liberties crisis. I refer to such excellent studies as those issued by the Cornell University Press during the past decade under the general direction of Professor Robert E. Cushman of Cornell. However, since the appearance of Osmond K. Fraenkel's *Our Civil Liberties* in 1944, there has been no volume that adequately presents a documented over-all survey of the drive against freedom in the United States. I am seeking to fill that gap and to alert as many of my fellow citizens as possible to the grave dangers which now confront American democracy.

In endeavoring to carry out this difficult task, I have had to sift and analyze an enormous amount of material. My method has been to select for discussion a limited number of laws, decrees, investigations, cases and incidents that illustrate the general pattern of repression. This study, then, is no encyclopedia of the all-but-numberless violations of civil liberties that have occurred in America during the past decade.

I do not attempt to cover, either, the important sphere of race relations, where there has been genuine though spotty progress towards civil rights since the end of the Second World War. In varying degrees all racial minorities in the United States have been subject to prejudice, discrimination and segregation: French Canadians in the Northeast, Mexicans in the Southwest; Orientals in the Far West; Puerto Ricans in New York City; Jews, Indians and Negroes wherever they live.

Since the 17,000,000 Negroes constitute by far the most numerous racial minority in America, their problems loom largest. The Negro people—and the white people as well—won a great victory for democracy when in 1954 the United States Supreme Court, in a unanimous decision, declared that racial segregation in the public school system is unconstitutional. But the background and consequences of this ruling, the notable role of the National Association for the Advancement of Colored People (NAACP) in fighting through the five cases concerned, and the full story of racial minorities in the United States lie outside the scope of this report.

In this book I am addressing not only liberals and radicals, but also conservatives who believe in democratic methods for the achievement of economic and social change. Amid the many bracing winds of doctrine stirring in America today all groups—except those which are opposed to democracy itself—ought to be able to agree on the necessity of defending the Bill of Rights. In the long run the best guarantee against the violence and revolution that have engulfed many countries in modern times is to maintain and expand freedom of expression. Belief in and support of civil liberties means peaceful transition in political affairs and an end to civil war.

Parts of this volume have appeared in pamphlet form in my series of Basic Pamphlets. Many individuals have helped me in the preparation of this study, and I am most grateful to all of them. I wish especially to thank Mrs. Olga Gellhorn, Mr. Jesse Gordon, and Miss Myra Jordan for their careful reading of the manuscript and for countless illuminating suggestions; Mrs. Lucille Milner, former Secretary of the American Civil Liberties Union, who gave me the benefit of her knowledge for my chapter on the ACLU; and, above all, Miss Mary Redmer, my editorial

assistant, whose critical and creative judgment was invaluable in
the development and production of this book.

New York City
December 1, 1955   C.L.

THE IDEAL OF CIVIL LIBERTIES

So long as the race of man endures and maintains organized communities, complete civil liberties and freedom of expression for all persons everywhere will be a universally valid ideal.

Thought remains a soliloquy unless men can communicate their ideas to one another; it is constant and meaningful communication between individuals and groups that makes possible the advance of civilization, the flowering of democracy, the creations of human culture. The greater the freedom of opinion, the greater is the flow of significant communication throughout every area of life.

The struggle to attain civil liberties and to establish them on a permanent basis has gone on in Europe and America for centuries. Throughout the Western World men and women have fought and died to bring about or to preserve political systems in which all groups and individuals have the right to free speech, due process of law and equality before the law. In 1791 the founders of the American Republic officially recognized this concept of freedom by adopting the Bill of Rights, the greatest of all state documents on civil liberties, as part of the United States Constitution.

But although these Rights are the written law of our land, at no time since their adoption 164 years ago have the American people been able to establish fully and securely freedom of speech, freedom of the press, freedom of assembly, freedom of religion, and the related provisions of the Constitution. On the other hand, Great Britain, which has no written constitution, has

probably come nearer to actualizing the fundamental principles
of civil liberty than any other country in the world. The lesson of
both past and present is that political principles do not defend
themselves, but require continuous support in the vigorous efforts
of the people.

Why, you may ask, has freedom of speech always been more of
an ideal than a reality? Perhaps because it is difficult for men to
be sufficiently civilized to let their fellow citizens freely express
ideas that seem dangerous and hateful. Those in authority frequently find it easier and safer to combat critics and dissenters
with violence and suppression than to compete with them in the
market place of opinion, answering their arguments and risking a
democratic decision.

Supporters of democratic government recognize that while a
self-governing people can, and frequently does, make serious mistakes, experience so far has shown that in the long run a democratic system best serves the interests of a nation. In such a society
freedom of speech, with its associated freedoms, is a transcendent
social and political value upon which rests, to a very considerable
degree, the welfare and progress of the community. To mutilate
or negate this freedom is to strike at the very heart of the democratic process. The most heated debate or abusive mud-slinging
political campaign is a thousand times better than resort to blows,
bullets or bombs.

In recent times there has been increasing agreement among
thinking men that the best way of solving human problems is
through the use of intelligence or reason in the form of modern
scientific method. The most pressing task of this era is to carry
over that method more effectively from the natural sciences into
the realms of politics, economics, sociology and international relations. But objective intelligence and the experimental procedures
of science can fully develop and play their proper role only in the
atmosphere of democratic institutions and freedom of opinion.

In such an atmosphere and under the American Bill of Rights,
all individuals and groups must be permitted to have their say.
Freedom of speech does not guarantee anyone support for his

ideas; it does guarantee him the opportunity to present his ideas to others. This means civil liberties for everyone: reactionaries and radicals, businessmen and workers, Catholics and atheists, Fascists and Communists, liberals, progressives, freethinkers and all the infinite variety of crackpots, fanatics, and self-appointed saviors of mankind. Whether an individual relies on religious dogma, mystic intuition, alleged revelations from the dead, the method of reason, the precepts of science or any other source of authority whatsoever, democracy gives him the right to express his views. As soon as we make exceptions in any direction, we are lost. *Civil liberties are indivisible.*

Thomas Paine, writing more than 150 years ago, was well aware of this principle. As he stated in his *Dissertation on First Principles of Government:* "He that would make his own liberty secure must guard even his enemy from oppression; for if he violates this duty, he establishes a precedent that will reach to himself."

Everyone is willing to grant the right of dissent on the many trivial or unimportant issues about which people may argue. But that is not the real test of civil liberties. As the late Supreme Court Justice Robert H. Jackson said, "Freedom to differ is not limited to things that do not matter much. That would be a mere shadow of freedom. The test of its substance is the right to differ as to things that touch the heart of the existing order." [1]

Thus in a truly democratic society daring new ideas, forgotten old ideas, unsound ideas that have been repeatedly exposed, ideas that seem ludicrous, obscene, obsolete or subversive to the majority, must all be allowed expression. In the United States we must permit even ideas that are considered "un-American," whatever that may mean, to have their fling. The so-called crackpot often turns out to be a trail-blazer; the genius frequently starts his career as a minority of one. As John Stuart Mill said in his classic essay *On Liberty:* "If all mankind minus one were of one opinion, and only one person were of the contrary opinion, mankind would be no more justified in silencing that one person, than he, if he had the power, would be justified in silencing mankind. . . . All silencing of discussion is an assumption of infallibility." The independent, non-conforming mind has been one of the glories of human history.

Until now, I have been talking primarily of individual dissent. Group dissent is, of course, just as important. In a free society and under a reasonable bill of rights, political, religious and other minorities should be scrupulously protected and assured the democratic opportunity of evolving into majorities. In the United States this means that not only the rights of political parties must be maintained, but also the rights of tens of thousands of voluntary organizations dedicated to one purpose or another. The manifold committees, councils, associations and societies functioning in America are a most important element in the development of democratic cooperation, the formation of public opinion and the achievement of basic reform and progress.

The right of persons or organizations to communicate certain ideas through the written or spoken word, through pictures or some other art form, is only part of what civil liberties mean. Just as important is the right of people to read, to hear and to see, whether the object of attention has its source in America or some other land. Neither the lifelong education of the individual nor the functioning of political democracy can proceed successfully unless everyone possesses full liberty to inform himself as he will on any subject in which he is interested. The citizen as voter cannot cast his ballot intelligently unless he has had the opportunity to ascertain the facts on the issues involved. The right, then, to seek and acquire knowledge is co-equal with any other right in the whole roster of freedoms.

The social value of dissent is perhaps greater now than ever before, because increased monopoly control of the mass media of communication—metropolitan newspapers, cheap magazines, motion pictures, radio and television—has fostered a lamentable conformity of opinion and cultural standards. The possession of something worth-while to say does not necessarily go hand in hand with the money to pay for its dissemination. Political and other minorities critical of official or orthodox views can hardly compete in the field of journalism with the big newspapers and magazines. And in America since the Second World War it has become more and more difficult for such minorities to obtain time on radio or television. Broadcasting and television companies, fearful of offending Washington bureaucrats and the well-organized pressure groups that are so vociferous from coast to coast, are reluctant to include dissenters in their programs or indeed "controversial" characters of any sort. Intelligent dissent on almost any issue is, therefore, more than ever a public service.

Yet today, as in the past, dissent is liable to be dangerous. Truth-seekers down the centuries have frequently paid a heavy price for giving utterance to their beliefs. Philosophers, teachers, scientists, religious prophets, poets and political innovators have again and again been ridiculed, reviled, dismissed from their jobs, exiled, imprisoned or done to death for their dissenting doctrines. We cannot expect that in the rough-and-tumble of human discord there will ever be an end to the denunciation of those who seek to upset the *status quo* in ideology or institutions. We can reasonably hope, however, that the guarantees of civil liberties will become so widely accepted everywhere that dissenters need not fear the loss of their jobs, violence on the part of public authorities or private vigilantes, or government prosecution. But this is a hope for the future.

In the United States at present the civil liberties crisis has reached such proportions that no citizen who believes in democratic institutions and procedures can fail to be alarmed. To be sure, we have had periods of hysteria before. The Alien and Sedition laws of 1798 resulted in many outrageous prosecutions until Thomas Jefferson's election as President in 1800. Repressive years followed the Civil War and the assassination of President Lincoln. And there were serious onslaughts on civil liberties during and after the First World War. But in my opinion the threat to constitutional freedoms is now far graver than at any time in the past, because the multiplicity of moral, economic, legal and physical sanctions that can be used against the dissenter is greater.

Today, instead of resorting to crude illegal procedures such as those sanctioned by Attorney General A. Mitchell Palmer in his violent raids against radicals in 1920, governmental authorities currently use unconstitutional legislation as a legal mask for their repressions. Thus through prosecutions and convictions under questionable Federal and State laws, they have jailed many progressive and radical leaders, deported others, and generally undermined the historic American tradition of freedom of political belief and association. Moreover, the U.S. Department of Justice to an unprecedented degree has relied in trials upon professional informers of questionable veracity; and has repeatedly disregarded the constitutional guarantee that a defendant is entitled to an impartial jury.

Apart from these legislative and judicial tactics, the Federal Government is violating both the letter and the spirit of the Bill of Rights in arbitrary administrative orders and rulings. These are responsible for the loyalty purge among approximately 2,300,-000 Federal employees; for the Attorney General's capricious listing of almost 300 organizations as subversive; and for the State Department's denial of passports to liberals, radicals and others on political grounds.

In another realm of official lawlessness, Congressional committees of investigation over the past decade have extended their activities and powers to include practically every aspect of political, cultural and intellectual life. The most dangerous of these committees have run wild in their unrestrained persecution of private citizens, Government employees and even Army personnel. These committees not only have constantly flouted the Bill of Rights, but have also consistently violated the three-way separation of powers in the American system of government by usurping the functions of the Judicial and Executive branches.

Meanwhile, in the unofficial sphere, vigilante groups and private business organizations have joined in the mid-century American witch-hunt to an alarming extent. The American Legion, the Daughters of the American Revolution and other such groups are everywhere on hand, attempting to intimidate those holding minority opinions and even those willing to give such opinions a fair hearing. Every Legion post throughout the country has its own

un-American activities committee ready to track down the slightest evidence of "subversion." The motion picture, radio and television industries, also following the lead of governmental authorities, have set up their own systems of censorship and purges; and
have actively cooperated with the Congressional Inquisition by
firing employees who refuse to answer questions on constitutional
grounds. Educational institutions, with some notable exceptions,
have surrendered to official pressures in the same way; and political discrimination in private employment has grown more and
more pronounced, with dismissal and blacklisting for dissent
spreading throughout business enterprise.

Behind all this sound, fury and tragedy is the alleged menace
of communism, which politicians and demagogues have bran-
dished in order to win elections and to bolster their political fortunes. It is true that after the First World War fear of communism
was also a potent factor in the widespread abrogation of the Bill
of Rights. Today that fear is greater and likely to retain a hold
indefinitely because Soviet Russia emerged from the Second
World War as a power rivaling the United States in strength and
influence; and because at the same time Communist regimes
gained control over most of Eastern Europe and, above all, over
vast and populous China. Hence, though the American Communist Party is at its lowest ebb, the McCarthys, the Brownells
and their followers, by recklessly exaggerating the threat of foreign communism to American domestic institutions, may be able
for a long time to continue whipping up the mass hysteria that
is so destructive of civil liberties.

The excuse for violations of civil liberty has traditionally been
that some crisis so menaces the security of the city, state or nation that it is dangerous to permit the unchecked flow of ideas.
Almost without exception this argument has been a mere pretext
for the suppression of freedom by the powers-that-be. In times of
emergency the basic freedoms are, if anything, even more essential than usual to the welfare of the community. For in such times
a nation or locality needs more than ever an alert, critical and
constructive public opinion that will help guide it through what-

ever dangers are threatening. Emergency abridgment of civil liberties is justified only when the machinery of representative government has so broken down that some of the established rules of democracy become temporarily irrelevant. Such could be the case during a disastrous flood, a vast earthquake or an armed invasion, any of which might result in the legitimate declaration of martial law.

Even in less critical situations we might sometimes agree that the abrogation of free speech could result in some limited social gain. But in the long run, the over-all dangers of such suppression, in setting evil precedents and rupturing the fabric of democracy, far outweigh whatever might be the short-run advantages. As Benjamin Franklin told his compatriots: "They who would give up essential liberty to purchase a little temporary safety deserve neither liberty nor safety." [2]

Inherent in my discussion of emergency situations, however, is the principle that freedom of expression, like other great human values, is not an absolute that should never be qualified if temporarily in conflict with other values. We must grant, for example, that at no time does a man have the right to indulge in libel or slander, or commit contempt of court. Moreover, government may legitimately control language used in purely commercial enterprises, as when the Federal Trade Commission issues a "cease and desist" order against fraudulent or misleading advertising.

It is also generally recognized that words are not protected by the Bill of Rights when they are an integral part of conduct violating a valid law, as when Davis and Brown talk over the specific means by which they intend to rob a bank. I suggest, in addition, that government has the right to curb freedom of expression when the language used constitutes a clear, direct and wilful incitement to the present commission of dangerous violence or some other serious and overt criminal act. It is not permissible, for instance, to hold forth with "fighting words" that tend to provoke a breach of the peace, or to call for someone's assassination.

The standard I have proposed seems to me more concrete and more susceptible to verification than the presently accepted rule that speech can be barred if it creates "a clear and present danger" of bringing about "the substantive evils that Congress has a right to prevent." * My suggested rule would cover not only crimes such as incitement to riot or murder, but also broader social dangers such as incitement to present acts of violent revolution against the state. Of course, government has the right and the obligation to prosecute anyone who commits specific acts of treason, sabotage, espionage and the like.

One of America's most respected jurists, Judge Learned Hand, has brilliantly summed up the current dangers to freedom in the United States. "Our nation," he declared, "is embarked upon a venture yet unproved; we have set our hopes upon a community in which men shall be given unchecked control of their own lives. That community is in peril; it is invaded from within, it is threatened from without; it faces a test which it may fail to pass. The choice is ours whether, when we hear the pipes of Pan, we shall stampede like a frightened flock, forgetting all those professions on which we have claimed to rest our policy. God knows, there is risk in refusing to act till the facts are all in; but is there not greater risk in abandoning the conditions of all rational inquiry? Risk for risk, for myself I had rather take my chance that some traitors will escape detection than spread abroad a spirit of general suspicion and distrust, which accepts rumor and gossip in place of undismayed and unintimidated inquiry.

"I believe that that community is already in process of dissolution where each man begins to eye his neighbor as a possible enemy, where non-conformity with the accepted creed, political as well as religious, is a mark of disaffection; where denunciation, without specification or backing, takes the place of evidence; where orthodoxy chokes freedom of dissent; where faith in the eventual supremacy of reason has become so timid that we dare not enter our convictions in the open lists to win or lose." [3]

This reasoned, eminently sane approach should provide at least

* For a more detailed discussion of the "clear and present danger" test, in connection with the Smith Act, see Chapter 5.

a partial answer to the main argument advanced by those who seek to curtail essential liberties in America today—that the Communists present a fearful threat to our free institutions. This whole argument is in my opinion arrant nonsense. As ex-President Truman has said, there are "only an eyeful" of Communists in the entire U.S.A. In all the anti-Communist furor of the past two decades, no member of the Communist Party has ever been indicted or convicted for an overt act of violence against the Government or even for advocating such an act. There is not a single Party member in any elective legislative body in the United States. And during more than thirty-five years of existence the best the Party could achieve in the way of public office was the election, in 1932, of the Mayor of Crosby, Minnesota, a town of approximately 3,500 population; and the election of two members to the New York City Council during the 1940's, for two and three terms respectively, at a time when proportional representation was in effect.

The notion of an over-riding Communist menace in America has all along been a hoax, played up by rightist and fascist elements to camouflage their anti-democratic aims; manipulated by yellow journalists and careerists of all types as a means of making money out of sensationalism; and utilized by Democratic and Republican Administrations alike as a way of gaining popular support for Cold War policies and as a political ritual designed to secure votes by alarming the electorate.

Only in such terms as these can we explain how America, with the wealthiest and strongest capitalist economy in the world and possessing one of the smallest, weakest and most unsuccessful Communist parties, has developed a deeper and more unreasoning dread of communism than any other country. By way of contrast, England, 3,000 miles nearer to the supposed threat of Soviet aggression and infinitely more vulnerable to military attack than the United States, suffers no hysteria, no witch-hunt, and hardly any of the pernicious folly about Communists which has stirred up such a frenzy in America.

Practically speaking, a democratic government will find it easier to keep track of and protect itself against radical groups if it does not drive them underground. It is far better for extremists to rant in public than to plot in private. Moreover, when a leftist or rightist group is deprived of its constitutional liberties, many other groups in the democratic community are endangered. If the state takes away freedom of speech and association from, for example, all known members of the Communist Party, then a further witch-hunt is sure to begin in order to ferret out the *secret* Communists and the so-called fellow-travelers. This is certain to engulf sooner or later many liberals, New Dealers and non-Communist dissenters in the community.

Justice Jackson well described the situation in his opinion of September 25, 1950, ordering the continuance of bail for eleven Communist leaders convicted in the lower courts under the Smith Act. He stated: "The right of every American to equal treatment before the law is wrapped up in the same constitutional bundle with those of these Communists. If in anger or disgust with these defendants we throw out the bundle, we also cast aside protection for the liberties of more worthy critics who may be in opposition to the government of some future day."

The lesson of history is that the level of liberty in any land tends to sink to that accorded its most unpopular minority. Scientists, teachers, writers, intellectuals of every variety, make no mistake about it! When the bell of suppression tolls, it tolls for thee!

In 1955, after a disgraceful decade, the hysteria began to cool somewhat; but despite improvement in the general atmosphere, and even on specific fronts, I think the years ahead will continue to prove a severe test for the American Bill of Rights. The forces making for repression are sinister, powerful and extremely adept at twisting the meaning of events to promote their own interests. While rarely resorting to outright violence, they have hamstrung liberals, progressives and radicals by compelling them to spend the greater proportion of their time, their energy and their funds on legal defense instead of on positive functions and programs.

In 1951 an enterprising reporter in Wisconsin supplied some interesting documentation on the present situation. John Hunter of the Madison *Capital Times* drew up a petition containing parts of the Declaration of Independence and the Bill of Rights and circulated it in a public park on the Fourth of July. The petition included the preamble to the Declaration, the first six of the ten articles in the Bill of Rights and the Fifteenth Amendment to the Constitution guaranteeing equal rights to all persons regardless of race or color.

Out of 112 individuals whom he approached, Mr. Hunter was able to persuade only one to sign. Almost all of the 111 others told him they were fearful of the consequences if they signed, and twenty asked him if he was a Communist. The first person to whom he showed the petition bluntly said: "You can't get me to sign that, I'm trying to get loyalty clearance for a government job." Another stated: "I can't sign that paper because I work for civil service." One man told Hunter to "get the hell out of here with that Communist stuff"; and still another commented, "I see you are using an old Commie trick—putting God's name on a radical petition." A woman who took the trouble to read the preamble to the Declaration of Independence asserted hotly: "That may be the Russian Declaration of Independence, but you can't tell me that it is ours." [4]

Chief Justice Earl Warren of the United States Supreme Court concentrated on the theme of the Bill of Rights in a speech in February 1955 at St. Louis: "A group of State employees—not in Missouri—charged with responsibility for determining what announcements could be posted on the employees' bulletin board refused to permit the Bill of Rights to be posted on the ground that it was a controversial document. . . . Only after the Governor in writing vouched for its non-controversial character was the Bill of Rights permitted to occupy a place along with routine items of interest to the State employees.

"And this happened in the U.S.A. on the 15th day of December 1954, the 163rd anniversary of our Bill of Rights, declared by proclamation of President Eisenhower to be Bill of Rights Day. It is straws in the wind like this which cause some thoughtful people to ask the question whether ratification of the Bill of

Rights could be obtained today if we were faced squarely with the issue. . . . My faith in the sober second thought of the American people makes me confident that it would now be ratified. On the other hand, I am not prepared to dispute with those who believe the issue would provoke great controversy." [5]

Henry Steele Commager, Professor of History at Columbia University, puts his finger on the peculiar character of our mid-century civil liberties crisis. It is "that laws, charges and investigations all address themselves to intangibles. They do not deal with acts, for the very good reason that there are already laws on the statute books that take care of all conceivable subversive acts. They deal, instead, with imponderable things like intentions, thoughts, principles, and associations, with that shadowy realm which has ever been the happy hunting ground of tyrants." [6]

I contend that whatever the dangers to American democracy from communism or any other movement, the best way to prevent dictatorship of either Right or Left is to re-establish the United States as a great bastion and continuing example of civil liberties and democratic rights for all individuals and groups. The Government can protect the nation against extremists of whatever variety by vigilantly exercising the recognized police powers of the state and taking the necessary coercive measures when ideas and words issue into illegal deeds. Again to quote Justice Jackson: "Only in the darkest periods of human history has any Western government concerned itself with mere belief, however eccentric or mischievous, when it has not matured into overt action; and if that practice survives anywhere, it is in the Communist countries whose philosophies we loathe." [7]

The Bill of Rights and the Constitution enunciate in specific and enduring form the underlying principles of freedom of speech. The trouble in the field of civil liberties has not been caused by defects in these well-known principles, but by the failure and unwillingness of individual citizens, private organizations and governmental authorities—national, State and municipal—to defend and uphold our fundamental constitutional guarantees. Even during "normal" times in the United States, when neither war nor economic depression threatened, there have been unceasing violations of the Bill of Rights.

The American Constitution does not of course provide for the economic implementation of civil liberties. It does not surmount the problems of citizens and organizations wishing to publicize a particular viewpoint but possessing insufficient funds to rent halls, print newspapers and pay for radio or television time. Nor does the Constitution deal with the dangers that arise when powerful economic interests with enormous financial means carry on such an overwhelming amount of propaganda that contrary views have little chance in the court of public opinion. Yet whatever the solution of these questions, it remains true that were the Bill of Rights enforced and actualized, the people of the United States would thereby make a portentous step forward.

Mere defense of the Bill of Rights, however, is not enough. "In the end, civil liberties cannot merely be defended. They must be exercised. They have no reality inscribed on fading parchment: they are sustained by no brooding omnipresence in the sky. They exist only to the degree that they are asserted by the action of men." [8] This compelling statement by Gerard Piel, Editor of *Scientific American,* points to the fact that initiative, courage and intelligence will always be prerequisites in the perpetual struggle for the liberation of the human mind.

2

CLASH WITH THE UN-AMERICAN ACTIVITIES COMMITTEE

During the decade following the death of President Roosevelt and the end of the Second World War, I found myself increasingly under attack and compelled more and more to defend my own civil liberties. I was a radical in economics and politics, in philosophy and international affairs, and—most unpardonable of all—an advocate of American-Soviet cooperation and of peaceful co-existence between the capitalist and Communist blocs.

Meanwhile in postwar America the Congressional committees of investigation, exercising limitless uncurbed powers, were spearheading the upsurge of the anti-democratic and narrowly nationalistic right-wing forces. I suppose it was inevitable that sooner or later one of these committees should seek my scalp. In due course two Congressional committees came after me, both of them because of my interest in the Soviet Union. I had lectured and written books on the subject of the U.S.S.R., and early in 1943 I had become Chairman of the National Council of American-Soviet Friendship. This was a non-partisan organization with the purpose of disseminating the facts about Soviet life and of trying to create better understanding between the American and Soviet peoples. The National Council had strong backing among liberal and conservative elements in the United States.

During the summer of 1945, after the surrender of Japan, I had resigned as Chairman of the National Council after serving in that capacity since the founding of the organization. Early in November 1945, before a new chairman was selected, the Council received a letter from the Un-American Activities Committee. Could the Committee send in an investigator to examine the Council's records? Scenting considerable trouble ahead, I agreed to re-assume my chairmanship of the Council in order to fight through the battle that was looming with the House Committee.

After the Council had made clear in several letters that it regarded the proposed investigation by the Un-American Activities Committee as entirely unwarranted, that Committee, in December 1945, served me with a subpoena to deliver over to it "all books, records, papers, and documents showing all receipts and disbursements of money by the said National Council of American-Soviet Friendship, Inc., and its affiliated organizations, and all letters, memoranda or communications from, or with, any person or persons outside and within the United States of America."

This meant, in effect, that the Committee wanted literally all the records and correspondence of the Council since its inception in 1943. Our Board of Directors objected to this sweeping demand on the ground that it disregarded the Fourth Amendment to the United States Constitution, which provides: "The right of the people to be secure in their persons, houses, papers and effects, against unreasonable searches and seizures, shall not be violated." The Board also directed Executive Director Richard Morford, as custodian of documents, to protect them to the best of his ability and within the limits of the law, according to the advice of counsel.

The Council contended that the Un-American Activities Committee's subpoena represented an illegitimate attempt to conduct a "fishing expedition" of the sort that American courts in the past had condemned in no uncertain terms. In 1936 a decision of the United States Supreme Court had quoted approvingly from a Circuit Court opinion: "A general, roving, offensive, inquisitorial, compulsory investigation, conducted by a commission without any allegations, upon no fixed principles; and governed by no rules of law, or of evidence, and no restrictions except its own will or caprice, is unknown to our Constitution and laws; and such an inquisition would be destructive of the rights of the citizen and an intolerable tyranny." [9]

Moreover, we of the Council were convinced that once the House Committee obtained possession of the hundreds of names of those who at one time or another had contributed financially to our work, it would start to harass and persecute these individuals, treating them as suspicious characters and no doubt handing over a list of their names to the Federal Bureau of Investigation.

When in 1938 the House of Representatives established its Committee on Un-American Activities, it is doubtful whether any of the honorable members of Congress foresaw the questionable uses to which the Committee would eventually be put. In its seventeen years of life, under the chairmanship successively of Martin Dies, Texas Democrat, John S. Wood, Democrat of Georgia, J. Parnell Thomas, New Jersey Republican, Harold H. Velde, Illinois Republican, and Francis E. Walter, Pennsylvania Democrat, the Un-American Activities Committee has unremittingly functioned to intimidate, discredit, and ruin the livelihood of liberals, progressives, radicals, trade unionists, intellectuals, educators—and in fact, all dissenters from the *status quo* in any field. The Committee has also served as the prototype for Federal and State Committees with similar goals.

The House resolution of 1945 which accorded the Committee permanent status, gave it far wider scope than any other Congressional investigating committee on record. "The Committee on Un-American Activities," reads the enabling resolution, "as a whole or by subcommittee, is authorized to make from time to time investigations of (i) the extent, character and objects of un-American propaganda activities in the United States, (ii) the diffusion within the United States of subversive and un-American propaganda that is instigated from foreign countries or of a domestic origin and attacks the principle of the form of government as guaranteed by our Constitution, and (iii) all other questions in relation thereto that would aid Congress in any necessary remedial legislation."

A broader license to meddle can scarcely be imagined. The Committee's mandate is clearly unconstitutional on its face. For the Committee's paramount purpose, namely, to investigate "un-American propaganda activities," necessarily negates the free speech guarantees of the Bill of Rights. The word "propaganda," used in a disparaging sense, is a synonym for the diffusion of *ideas* which you do not like. If you like the ideas which are being propagated, you probably call them "educational" or "construc-tive." The term "activities" in both the enabling resolution and the title of the Committee is a further disguise for the fact that the Un-American Activities Committee, in open violation of the Con-stitution, is directed to inquire into thoughts and opinions.

Besides this, the ambiguous phrase "subversive and un-Amer-ican" easily functions as an adjectival device for more encroach-ments on civil liberties, since Congressional committees use these further catchwords loosely to describe any ideas to which they happen at the time to be opposed. Certainly the Un-American Activities Committee has used these terms in that way, to investi-gate any individual or organization whose views its members happen to dislike.

When the House resolution authorizes inquiry into propaganda that "attacks the principle of the form of government as guaran-teed by our Constitution," it again invites the Committee to trample upon the Constitution. For to attack a political *principle* is to carry on a controversy within the realm of ideas; whereas it is precisely to permit free range for such controversy that is the very essence of American democracy. Moreover, "the principle" of our form of government is essentially indefinable, since polit-ical scientists as well as practical politicians disagree as to what this may be, or indeed, as to whether there is any one central principle in the American system of government. This part of the resolution, therefore, necessarily discourages free political dis-cussion in the United States and runs counter to the First Amend-ment.

The American Civil Liberties Union has well summed up the situation: "If the First Amendment is a restriction upon Congressional inquiry, and no one can doubt that it is—for Congress cannot by inquiry accomplish that which it is forbidden to do by legislation—then it is clear that an inquiry directed towards propaganda (which is after all nothing more than the exercise of free speech) is the most flagrant violation of the First Amendment which is possible by inquiry. For it takes courage in these days to exercise the right to speak freely, when one knows that—apart from the social consequences following in this day and age from voicing unpopular ideas—any expression of speech, or any association relevant to the exercise of free speech, may enable a Congressional committee to subpoena him and make him account for every chapter of his life." [10]

Such extraordinary and all-inclusive powers of investigation were surely not envisioned by those who wrote our Constitution. Congressional committees do have the right, and properly so, to make investigations for the purpose of preparing legislation and obtaining information relevant to that end. This permits them to look into certain specified fields, such as railroads, banking and currency, foreign relations, campaign expenditures and so on. But actually there is no specified field for the Un-American Activities Committee; and so it usurps any field that it chooses, calling before it individuals and organizations at will. The Committee, furthermore, has never officially adopted a precise definition of "subversive and un-American propaganda"; this constitutes an implicit admission that it does not know, and does not wish to say, where its legitimate scope begins and ends.

Finally, the vagueness of the Committee's mandate on the subject of "subversive and un-American propaganda" places witnesses in the impossible position of not knowing when they may properly refuse to answer a question put by the Committee. A Federal statute regarding contempt of Congress states that a witness who "refuses to answer any question *pertinent to the question under inquiry*, shall be deemed guilty of a misdemeanor, punishable by a fine of not more than $1,000 nor less than $100 and imprison ment in a common jail for not less than one month nor more than twelve months." [11] [Italics mine—C.L.]

In other words, a witness may decline to answer if a question is not *pertinent* to the specific subject being investigated. However, in the absence of definite criteria promulgated by either Congress or the courts, every individual summoned to a hearing of the Un-American Activities Committee must assume the burden of defining correctly "subversive" and "un-American." He must himself determine whether a question is pertinent as he understands those two key terms, which are epithets rather than legal standards; and must do this at the risk of being held mistaken and thereby prosecuted and punished for contempt.

For any individual to be put in jeopardy under such circumstances contravenes "due process of law," since it has long been established that a law must be formulated precisely enough so that it is possible for men of common intelligence to ascertain whether they are transgressing it. Many witnesses, rather than run the risk of contempt, will answer questions which the Un-American Activities Committee has no right to ask. All this militates against freedom of opinion, because it means that the safest course and the best way to avoid a Committee subpoena is to conform or remain silent on public issues, and to keep away from all controversial organizations and individuals.

Yet despite the fact that the House Committee on Un-American Activities is unconstitutional in its mandate and its operations, it has functioned almost without let or hindrance for close to two decades, riding roughshod over countless individuals and organizations in the United States, encouraging every reactionary force and in general turning the clock back on democracy. In 1954 under the chairmanship of Congressman Velde the Committee was spending the taxpayers' money at the rate of $275,000 a year and was employing a staff of no less than forty-one persons.

In conformance with the subpoena I had received, I went to Washington on January 23, 1946, and submitted all the pamphlets and other public materials of the National Council to the Un-

American Activities Committee, in order to try to convince it that an investigation of the Council was unjustified. I talked at length with the Committee's Chief Counsel, Ernie Adamson, a mild-mannered man of middle age, and suggested to him that if the Council were really "subversive" or "un-American," its leaflets, educational materials, pictorial exhibits and pamphlets containing the speeches made at its big mass meetings would surely prove the point. I also called his attention to the fact that among the 200 and more sponsors or Directors of the organization were many conservative and eminent American citizens, including several members of Congress; that high Government officials such as Vice President Henry A. Wallace, Secretary of State Edward R. Stettinius, Jr., Under Secretary of State Dean Acheson and Joseph E. Davies, ex-Ambassador to the Soviet Union, had spoken at our rallies; and that other prominent Government officials had sent messages to be read at such meetings.

My position was that disagreement with Government policies is by no means reprehensible, but that it was patently ridiculous to investigate the National Council of American-Soviet Friendship as "subversive" or "un-American" in view of the fact that its aims of American-Soviet understanding and of cooperation between the U.S.A. and the U.S.S.R. in both war and peace were also the official aims of the United States Government during the period under consideration.

In the material I turned over to Mr. Adamson was the text of the telegram sent by President Franklin D. Roosevelt to Mr. Joseph E. Davies, co-chairman of a National Council mass meeting in New York City on November 16, 1944. The wire read: "I am grateful to you and all those who are celebrating American-Soviet Friendship Day for the words of support and confidence I have received. There is no better tribute we can hold out to our Allies than to continue working in ever growing accord to establish a peace that will endure. The Dumbarton Oaks Conference was a step in this direction. Other steps will be taken. In line with this objective, such meetings as you are holding in Madison Square Garden and in other great centers throughout

the United States are of tremendous assistance and value." I also
cited the messages sent to the Council by President Harry S. Truman in May 1945, and by Dwight D. Eisenhower, then General in
the United States Army, in November 1945.

Ernie Adamson agreed to make a careful study of the many
documents I left with him, and the House Committee excused me
for two weeks. On January 31 Mr. Adamson wrote me a letter:
"Our staff has studied the literature submitted by you, and after
due consideration I have come to the conclusion that a substantial
part is political propaganda. I therefore request your attendance
before the Committee on February 6."

Even had Mr. Adamson's allegation about "political propaganda" been true, his statement stood as an admission that there
was no legitimate reason or constitutional ground for inquiring
into the Council's affairs. For literally tens of thousands of organizations in the United States, including the Democratic and Republican parties with all their numerous subdivisions, freely carry
on political propaganda under the American system. Such propaganda is the very lifeblood of politics in a democracy.

On the morning of February 6 I went to the Old House Office
Building in Washington with my lawyer, Charles A. Horsky of
the firm of Covington, Burling, Rublee, Acheson and Shorb, and
testified before the Un-American Activities Committee for about
an hour and a half. Ernie Adamson as Chief Counsel asked most
of the questions, all of which I answered. It was not he, but the
House members of the Committee who made a furor and attempted to intimidate me. Thus at one point when I was explaining the National Council's educational work for American-Soviet
understanding, John E. Rankin, Representative from Mississippi,
who looked like a shaggy, mean little lion, interrupted in a loud
ill-tempered voice:

"Why doesn't your Council tell the American people about the
wholesale rape carried on by the Red Army in Eastern Europe?"

"Well, Mr. Rankin," I said, "a lot of our material goes to school
children."

"The schoolteachers could take it," he snorted.

"In any case," I continued, "we don't issue as educational material extreme and doubtful charges of the kind you suggest."

Then Rankin shouted, "What does your Council think about communism and the subversive Communist Party in the United States that is attempting to overthrow our institutions?" I replied quietly: "Our Council takes no position regarding communism or any other economic or political system as such. Nor does it take a position regarding the Communist Party or any other political party."

Rankin pressed his point bitterly: "Do you mean to tell me that your organization refuses to take a stand on the Communist Party and revolution?" I repeated: "Such questions are not the business of the National Council, which is not concerned with domestic issues. We honestly stay within the provisions of our charter as an educational organization whose sole concern is presenting the facts regarding the Soviet Union and American-Soviet relations. We are glad to have the support of anyone who sincerely favors our work for American-Soviet cooperation."

It was here that Mr. Adamson interjected a question designed to trap me and the National Council. "Would you not agree," he asked with a bland look, "that the Council is in favor of the Soviet form of government and prefers it to the American form?"

"Mr. Adamson," I countered, "I certainly do not agree, and I challenge you to find a single statement in all our literature which implies such an attitude. Our organization does not take a position either for or against different forms of government."

Next Adamson mentioned the fact that contributions to the National Council were tax exempt and tried to tie this up with the right of the Committee to investigate our financial records.* My answer to that was: "If there's anything wrong with the Council's financial affairs in reference to tax exemption, we should be glad to have the proper department of the Government look

* In August 1955 the Un-American Activities Committee obtained the sinister power, through an Executive Order signed by President Eisenhower, to examine the income tax returns of individuals and organizations.

into the matter. That would be, in this case, the Treasury Department. You gentlemen must be aware that in the Constitution there is embodied a basic principle of the American Government known as the separation of powers."

At this, Representative Rankin leaped up from his chair and yelled at me: "Don't you know that the Congress of the United States is the greatest power in this land?" Then he angrily added: "I think we should cite this witness for contempt of Congress right now." In another moment he had stalked out of the room, looking very sullen and vindictive. I believe that Rankin, fortunately no longer a member of Congress, was the most arrogant and abusive public figure I have ever met.

Other Representatives who questioned me unpleasantly at this hearing were Herbert C. Bonner, Democrat of North Carolina; Karl E. Mundt, Republican of South Dakota, who was later elected to the Senate; and J. Parnell Thomas, Republican of New Jersey, who subsequently went to jail for swindling the Government by listing on his payroll employees who did not work and appropriating their salaries himself as "kickbacks." The Chairman of the Committee, John S. Wood, Georgia Democrat, did little more than swear me in and was courteous throughout.

Finally, Mr. Adamson came back to the question of whether I was going to provide the Committee with the complete correspondence and financial records of the Council for 1945. I answered that I did not have the power to bring these documents because I was only Chairman of the organization and not a dictator, and that I was not the Council's custodian of records. When he asked me who had this responsibility, I told him it was Mr. Richard Morford, the Executive Director.

The Committee members, distinctly annoyed at this information, made strenuous efforts to prove that I simply must have the power to hand over the subpoenaed documents. I kept repeating that the organizational set-up of the National Council gave specific officers specific responsibilities, and that we could not possibly agree to change our long-established methods of efficient functioning merely to satisfy the whim of some Congressional committee.

The upshot was that the Committee, frustrated and disgruntled, issued a subpoena for Richard Morford, who appeared before it on March 6. He of course did not bring the private records of the Council and repeated my argument that they were beyond the constitutional jurisdiction of the Committee. He also refused to answer a question as to what individuals were responsible for statements in the Council's bi-weekly publication, *Reporter on American-Soviet Relations*. To reveal these names, he claimed, would be to acquiesce in the violation of freedom of the press as guaranteed under the First Amendment.

Subsequently the Un-American Activities Committee voted that both Mr. Morford and I should be cited for contempt. At a session of the House of Representatives on June 26 the Committee Chairman, John S. Wood, moved my citation and read part of my testimony.. Congressmen Mundt and Thomas made the main speeches against me. Their entire emphasis was on the large number of alleged Communist fronts I had belonged to, and on my radical views in general. Thomas referred to me as "a darling of the Communist Party," while Mundt characterized me as "an adept artist in concealment" and a "buck-passer."

Representative Walter A. Lynch of New York, a Democrat, answered them in this way: "Every lawyer in this House knows there is not a scintilla of evidence before this House that could in any wise justify a grand jury in indicting this man for contempt of Congress. . . . We are sitting here today more or less as judges hearing only one side of the case and yet, even with that great advantage on the part of the Committee, we have seen an effort made to sway this House by passion and prejudice rather than by the cold facts of the case. For what purpose did the distinguished gentleman from New Jersey refer to the allegedly communistic connections of this man Lamont? They are not part of this record which is to be certified. . . . I do not care what Lamont's record is; I do not care whether he be the worst criminal in the world; I do not care whether he is a Communist or not.

I am concerned with the more important question, and that is whether a man can be held in contempt when he has answered the questions of the Committee and when he has told the Committee where they can get the information that the Committee desires." [12]

In spite of Mr. Lynch's forceful remarks, the House ringingly upheld what he called "passion and prejudice," and voted my contempt citation by 240-85. My case then went to the United States District Attorney in Washington who had the responsibility of obtaining my indictment by a grand jury. But the District Attorney was not enthusiastic about my case and in March 1947 dropped it altogether, having decided that it would not hold up in the courts.

At the same time, however, this same District Attorney persuaded a Federal grand jury to indict Richard Morford for the crime of contempt, the House of Representatives having voted a contempt citation against him in August 1946. Mr. Morford, a former minister of the Presbyterian Church, and a tireless worker for international peace, is a brave, public-spirited man. He went to trial in March 1948 and was found guilty of contempt of Congress a week later.

The presiding judge refused to admit as evidence for the defense the important constitutional points that the Un-American Activities Committee had exceeded its authority in subpoenaing the records of the National Council of American-Soviet Friendship and that it had violated the fundamental guarantees of free speech, freedom of the press and the right to be secure against unreasonable searches and seizures. When Mr. Morford made his final appeal to the United States Supreme Court on these issues, it refused to grant a hearing in the case. And Morford served out his three months' jail sentence in New York City during the fall of 1950.

During this same period the Un-American Activities Committee subpoenaed the financial records and correspondence of two other organizations, the Joint Anti-Fascist Refugee Committee, whose purpose was to provide relief to refugees from Franco Spain; and the National Federation for Constitutional Liberties, a group devoted to the defense of the Bill of Rights. The heads of these organizations took the same position as the National Council of American-Soviet Friendship, insisting that the House Committee was exceeding its powers and that in any case the Committee's mandate was unconstitutional.

Mr. George Marshall, Chairman of the National Federation, took the full responsibility for his organization, and was cited, indicted and sentenced to three months in the penitentiary for contempt of Congress. Unfortunately, in the case of the Joint Anti-Fascist Committee, responsibility for custodianship of documents rested in the entire Executive Board, instead of one official. Hence twelve members of this Board became involved in contempt citations, were found guilty and went to jail. The courageous Chairman, Dr. Edward K. Barsky, received a six months' sentence,* and the eleven other directors, three months.

As in the case of the National Council, the Supreme Court of the United States declined to hear appeals from the leaders of the Joint Anti-Fascist Committee and the National Federation for Constitutional Liberties. Nor would it grant certiorari to the motion picture actors and directors, "The Hollywood Ten," who in 1947, standing on the First Amendment, refused to answer the Un-American Activities Committee's question as to whether they were members of the Communist Party. These ten men served the maximum contempt sentence of one year in jail. They, Richard Morford, George Marshall and the members of the Anti-Fascist Board all deserve the gratitude of civil libertarians for their principled action in challenging the "Un-American Committee" on constitutional grounds. Although they did not achieve their ends, they set a splendid example and helped to educate the American people and the courts as to the true meaning of the Bill of Rights.

It is essential to remember that when the U.S. Supreme Court refuses to hear an appeal, that does not mean that it is passing on

* See Chapter 11 for the further consequences of Dr. Barsky's involvement in this matter.

the merits of the case in question or may not later take some
similar case and decide on the main principles involved. It seems
likely that today, after years of scandalous behavior on the part
of Congressional investigating committees, the Supreme Court
would grant a hearing on the appeal of an individual who had
invoked the First Amendment in refusing to answer questions before a legislative committee.

In May 1955 the Supreme Court, in an opinion condemning a
Congressional committee's abuse of the Fifth Amendment, gave
hope that it might uphold the First Amendment against Congressional violations. In Chief Justice Warren's words: "The
power to investigate, broad as it may be, is also subject to recognized limitations. It cannot be used to inquire into private affairs
unrelated to a valid legislative purpose. Nor does it extend to an
area in which Congress is forbidden to legislate. Similarly, the
power to investigate must not be confused with any of the powers
of law enforcement; those powers are assigned under our Constitution to the Executive and the Judiciary. Still further limitations
on the power to investigate are found in the specific individual
guarantees of the Bill of Rights, such as the Fifth Amendment's
privilege against self-incrimination which is an issue here." [13]

As Chief Justice Warren makes plain, Congressional committees have no right to go beyond their legal authority and
arrogate to themselves powers violative of the United States Constitution. This, however, is precisely what the Un-American Activities Committee has been doing since its inception. It is high
time that the courts and public opinion forced this Committee
to conform to the rules of American democracy and to the standards of elementary ethics.

3

MY CHALLENGE TO McCARTHY

My clash with the House Committee on Un-American Activities proved to be only a prelude to my most outstanding battle in the field of civil liberties. That began in 1953 when, through no choice of mine, I had a head-on collision with the Senate Permanent Subcommittee on Investigations,* of which Joseph R. McCarthy, Republican of Wisconsin, was then Chairman.

Senator McCarthy first tried to bring me before his Subcommittee in the summer of 1953 after his agents had made the horrible discovery that a book of mine, *The Peoples of the Soviet Union* was in some of the U.S. State Department overseas libraries. This work, published by Harcourt, Brace in 1946, was a specialized study of the Soviet racial minorities and took no position on the Soviet economic and political system. During the last week of June, McCarthy announced that he was subpoenaing me and twenty-two other authors whose books had been found in United States libraries abroad.

I had already gone away for the summer to the pleasant island of Martha's Vineyard off the Massachusetts coast. Feeling that

*This is a subcommittee, functioning since 1946, of the larger Committee on Government Operations, formerly designated the Committee on Expenditures in the Executive Department. McCarthy headed both the subcommittee and the parent body. Throughout this chapter and this book I frequently refer to the subcommittee as the McCarthy Committee.

every American has the right to freedom of vacations, I did not inform the McCarthy sleuths of my whereabouts. During July the Subcommittee succeeded in tracking down and subpoenaing for hearings only a few of the writers named. It did not locate me; and so I was able to go through the summer in relative peace.

But shortly after I had returned to New York City, from my vacation, McCarthy was on my trail again. On the morning of Tuesday, September 22, I was working in my study around the corner from Columbia University, and was actually writing the first chapter of this book when the apartment phone rang and an unknown person announced that he had a subpoena for me from the McCarthy Committee. So I went down to the front hall of the apartment house and accepted service of the subpoena. It summoned me to appear before the Committee the very next day at 2:30 p.m. at the United States Court House in Foley Square.

It was disturbing to realize that I had only a little more than twenty-four hours to get ready for the ordeal. A witness should be given at least three or four days between the serving of the subpoena and his appearance at a Congressional hearing. It was typical of McCarthy's unscrupulous tactics to try to catch his victims off guard and allow them no adequate time to prepare.

Since the events of the summer, I had expected that the McCarthy Committee would probably tap me eventually, and had been thinking on and off about possible courses of action. I had been especially impressed by a brilliant article in *The Nation* some months before, entitled "How to Stop the Demagogues," by Philip Wittenberg, a New York attorney; and had talked briefly with him about the new approach he recommended. He had informally agreed to take my case if I were called before a Congressional committee.

Fortunately for me Mr. Wittenberg was in town when I received my subpoena and I immediately dashed down to his office in a taxi. I had three long conferences with him before my Wednesday deadline. We settled the general principles on which I would stand, and went over a number of probable questions and the type of answer or refusal to answer I should make to them.

UNITED STATES OF AMERICA
Congress of the United States

———

To ___CORLIS LAMONT___

___450 RIVERSIDE DRIVE; N.Y, N.Y.___

_____, *Greeting:*

Pursuant *to lawful authority,* YOU ARE HEREBY COMMANDED *to appear before the* ___SENATE___ ~~COMMISSION~~ PERMANENT SUBCOMMITTEE ON INVESTIGATIONS OF THE SENATE COMMITTEE ON GOVERNMENT OPERATIONS *of the Senate of the United States, on* Wednesday, Sept. 23, 1953, *at* ___2:30___ *o'clock* P. *m., at their committee room* = 128 United States Court House, Foley Square, New York, New York, *then and there to testify what you may know relative to the subject matters under consideration by said committee.*

_____

_____

_____

Hereof fail not, *as you will answer your default under the pains and penalties in such cases made and provided.*

To ___JAMES N. JULIANA___

to serve and return.

Given *under my hand, by order of the committee, this* ___21st___ *day of* ___September___, *in the year of our Lord one thousand nine hundred and* ___fifty-three___

_____
                    Sub Joseph R. McCarthy, Chairman
Chairman, Committee on __Investigations of the__
                    Committee on Government Operations

The reason for McCarthy coming after me this time was surprising. He had uncovered the remarkable fact that the United States Army had included my book, *The Peoples of the Soviet Union,* in a bibliography. The listing had appeared, without my knowing about it, in an Army manual entitled *Psychological and Cultural Traits of Soviet Siberia,* published in 1953 by the Military Intelligence Section of the U.S. General Staff. On the basis of the mere listing of this volume, McCarthy widely asserted that the Army document "quoted heavily" from me, although in fact it used no quotation whatsoever from my work.

On September 9 Senator McCarthy had given the press excerpts from the Army pamphlet and made the absurd claim that it was Communist propaganda. On September 11 the Army disclosed that McCarthy had failed to release passages hostile to the Soviet Union and to reveal that the purpose of the pamphlet was to develop among the United States Armed Forces "an understanding of the Soviet people which will be militarily useful in case of war." [14] The Army stated that only 100 copies of the manual had been printed, with some forty distributed to high Army officials; and that since the document had a secrecy classification as "restricted," McCarthy's unauthorized release of much of it constituted a violation of the espionage law. The Army then proceeded to declassify the pamphlet from its restricted status "as a result of prior disclosures" on the part of McCarthy.

With these facts in mind, Mr. Wittenberg and I appeared before the McCarthy Committee at the Federal Court House early Wednesday afternoon, September 23. Senator McCarthy was presiding as chairman and was the only member of the Committee present. He had announced this hearing as a closed executive session, which is supposed to be strictly private. Hence I was surprised to see about a dozen spectators, men and women, sitting in one corner of the room. In another part, by himself, sat the ever loquacious and pliant witness Louis Budenz, whom I recognized from his newspaper photographs. He was present, I felt sure, for the primary purpose of intimidating me.

McCarthy did all the questioning himself, constantly pacing

back and forth at the end of a long table. Throughout the hearing he was neither abusive nor impolite, but suave and persistent in asking his outrageous questions. Although somewhat arrogant in manner, his personal behavior was far more restrained than that of the shouting, table-pounding members of the House Un-American Activities Committee—particularly Representatives John E. Rankin and J. Parnell Thomas—who had questioned me in Washington back in 1946.

I took my most decisive step at the very start when I asked permission to read a prepared statement objecting to the jurisdiction of the Committee. Since an objection to jurisdiction is absolutely basic and takes precedence over everything else, McCarthy had to allow my statement to be put into the record. In this three-page document, which had been drawn up by Mr. Wittenberg in precise legal terminology rather than in eloquent language about the Bill of Rights, I challenged the legal and constitutional power of the McCarthy Committee to inquire into my political beliefs, my religious beliefs, my associational activities, or any other personal and private affairs. I advanced four main grounds for this position.

First, I referred to the protections of the First Amendment to the American Constitution and cited the unanimous decision of the United States Supreme Court in 1953 reversing the conviction of Dr. Edward A. Rumely, Executive Secretary of the right-wing Committee for Constitutional Government, for contempt of Congress. Dr. Rumely had been indicted for contempt because in 1950 he refused, at a hearing of the House Select Committee on Lobbying Activities, to disclose the names of persons who had bought books in amounts of $500 or more from his organization. I quoted from the concurring opinion of Justice William O. Douglas in this case: "The power of investigation is also limited. Inquiry into personal and private affairs is precluded." [15]

In addition, I emphasized the First Amendment's guarantee of freedom of the press and urged that since Congress could not pass laws interfering with this vital freedom, and since a Congressional committee can only make inquiries relevant to con-

stitutional legislation, McCarthy had no right to ask me questions
about the origin, content and purposes of my writings. Several of
the Senator's questions were designed to disclose my sources of
research and the precise persons with whom I had discussed
problems pertaining to my book. Such inquiries constitute attempted interference with freedom of research and of scholarship.

Second, I relied heavily on the three-way separation of powers
in the American Government by which the Legislative, Judicial,
and Executive branches possess definite and limited functions.*
Thus I asserted that McCarthy's Committee would be trespassing
upon the powers of the Judiciary—from the Department of Justice through the courts and down to grand juries and trial juries
—by inquiring into my personal beliefs and personal affairs.

Third, I claimed that Public Law 601, establishing the Senate
Committee on Government Operations (parent committee to
McCarthy's Subcommittee) so limited the scope of both the Committee and any Subcommittee as to debar the investigation of me
as an author. For I was a private citizen who was not and never
had been in the employ of the Federal Government; and the listing of my book in an Army publication took place without my
prior knowledge or any consultation with me.

No Congressional committee is or can be authorized to summon
a writer and quiz him about his literary work and personal associations merely because one of his books is listed by a U.S. Government agency. For in that case the author of every book copy-
righted and then automatically placed in the Library of Congress
would be subject to Congressional investigation. And the impact
on freedom of opinion would be very severe indeed.

Fourth and finally, I argued that at the time of my hearing
the McCarthy Subcommittee was not a competent tribunal, because all of its Democratic Party members had resigned and had
deprived the Committee of its competency to act until properly
reconstituted. These three Democrats—Senators Henry M. Jackson
of Washington, John L. McClellan of Arkansas, and Stuart Sy-
mington of Missouri—formally withdrew in July 1953 as a protest

* See Chapter 4.

against McCarthy's insistence that as Chairman of the Committee he had the exclusive power to hire and dismiss staff members.*

Also in my opening statement I volunteered the information that I was not and never had been a member of the Communist Party. This I did in order to throw McCarthy off balance and to forestall his customary allegations to the press about an uncooperative witness surely being a dangerous Communist. Realizing that a large part of McCarthy's effectiveness was in the voluminous newspaper publicity he received, I wished to set the stage so far as I could for favorable counter-publicity on my side and the side of civil liberties. And I aimed, by disposing of the Communist issue in advance, to help clear the way for an impartial court test in the event my case ever went to trial.

After receiving my statement in silence McCarthy launched into a long series of questions. I answered a few concerning recorded facts. Yes, I had published a book about the peoples of Soviet Russia; had written a chapter for *U.S.S.R., a Concise Handbook*, edited by Professor Ernest J. Simmons and published by the Cornell University Press; and had sent a letter to *The New York Times* criticizing the decision of the United States Supreme Court in holding the Smith Act constitutional.

But most of McCarthy's inquiries I refused to answer, giving as my reason each time the objections expressed in my initial challenge to the jurisdiction of the Committee. Almost every question the Senator asked was loaded, as, for example: "Did you know that Mr. A. who wrote a chapter in this book used by the United States Army, was a member of the Communist Party?"

* This issue arose concerning the case of Mr. J. B. Matthews, Executive Director of the Committee, who had created a storm of controversy over his public charge that the Protestant Church in the United States had been widely infiltrated by Communists. The Democrats on the Committee believed that Matthews's accusation was so reckless that it undermined his usefulness as head of the staff. Senator McCarthy, on the other hand, defended Matthews and asserted that he would retain him, although Matthews had already offered to resign. Within a few days, however, the pressures had become so great that McCarthy accepted the resignation. See p. 79.

"Did you know that Mr. B. was a member of the Communist conspiracy?" and "Do you know any member of the Communist Party who to your knowledge engaged in either espionage or sabotage?" Instead of declining to answer, I should have preferred to say "No" to all such questions; but that would have weakened my legal position. And there was always the possibility, too, that McCarthy was trying to trick me into a response that, revealing some slip of memory, would lay the basis for a perjury charge.

Chairman McCarthy continued with his grilling for about an hour and then brought the hearing to a close. He said that I could not obtain a copy of the record because this session was "strictly executive." At the same time he ordered me to appear at a public hearing the following Monday, September 28, in Washington. At this point McCarthy, having taken the position all along that my Wednesday hearing was an executive session and therefore "closed," suddenly announced that he was going to give a resumé to the press.

Accordingly he called the reporters in and talked to them for some thirty minutes, informing them that I was guilty of contempt on at least two dozen counts. As McCarthy made public his version of the hearing, I gave out to the newspapermen copies of my statement objecting to the jurisdiction of the Committee, and discussed briefly the reasons for my stand. The press gave me excellent coverage; but usually McCarthy's tricky device of giving publicity to *his* version of a so-called private hearing from which reporters are barred is most disadvantageous to the witness. As Telford Taylor, reserve brigadier general and chief prosecutor at the trial of the Nazi war criminals, has said: "It is an outrageous procedure, obviously designed for the sole purpose of publicity." [16]

On Friday afternoon, September 25, a telegram came to my home from Senator McCarthy stating that my Monday hearing had been postponed. The wire added, "However, you are under continuing subpoena and both you and your counsel will be notified when your appearance is required." McCarthy went ahead with his public session Monday morning and examined other witnesses. To my astonishment the transcript of this hearing showed that at the very beginning the Honorable Senator had asserted: "Mr. Lamont has not been subpoenaed. He was notified that he could come today and purge himself of the contempt of failure to answer last week. Is Mr. Lamont here?" "There was no answer," the transcript recorded.[17]

Of course McCarthy had sent me no such message and had said in his own telegram that I was still under subpoena. He also knew perfectly well that I was not in the hearing chamber. Apparently he thought that the cancellation of my hearing might be interpreted as a retreat on his part and felt obliged to give the false impression that the responsibility for my not appearing rested with me.

At the same time the Senator used his two misstatements and the calling of my name as an excuse to make public the complete minutes of the "private" executive session at which I was examined on September 23. I immediately protested against this whole procedure and in particular against certain parts of the record. On October 24 Mr. Francis B. Carr, Executive Director of the Subcommittee and former head of the FBI in New York City, wrote me to say that the passages to which I had objected had been deleted from the record. This correction, however, did not offset the altogether erroneous impression given originally to the press and the public by McCarthy's unprincipled conduct.

Each person summoned by a Congressional committee must make his own decision, taking into consideration all the particular circumstances in his case, as to the policy he will pursue. I believe, for instance, that dependence on the Fifth Amendment in not answering questions may be fully justified and that we must defend the right of witnesses to stand upon it without any penalties from either public or private authorities. However, since a contempt case will not hold against an individual who uses the Fifth Amendment correctly, we must turn to reliance on the First Amendment or the separation of powers in seeking a court test to halt the excesses of Congressional committees. What I was trying to do through my case was not to cripple the power of

Congressional investigations, but to have them reasonably and specifically limited in scope and methods, according to the principles of the Constitution.

From the moment when I decided to challenge the McCarthy Committee on constitutional grounds I was determined to carry my case up to the United States Supreme Court if I were indicted for contempt and lost in the lower courts. I knew that should the Supreme Court also decide against me, the penalty would be from one to twelve months in the penitentiary. But I felt, without any sense of martyrdom, that such a jail sentence would be a small price to pay for the value to democracy of my fighting through this test case and for the personal satisfaction of having upheld the cause of civil liberties against McCarthy.

The course I followed before the McCarthy Committee was the same in principle as that taken by two well-known authors, Harvey O'Connor and Leo Huberman, whom McCarthy subpoenaed in July 1953 after he discovered that books written by them were in the U.S. State Department overseas libraries. These courageous writers led the way in the new type of challenge to the Congressional witch-hunt on the basis of the separation of powers as well as the First Amendment. Both men talked back to McCarthy in a spirited manner and insisted on reading their statements of constitutional defiance into the Committee record. Mr. O'Connor alone, however, was cited for contempt by the Senate. He was indicted in October 1953 by a grand jury in Washington, D.C.

McCarthy phrased his main question to O'Connor, who twice refused to answer it, in a way that was significant and disturbing. The Senator asked: "At the time you wrote the books which were purchased with taxpayers' money and put in our Information libraries throughout the world, at that time were you a member of the Communist conspiracy?" This question was obviously designed to trap the witness. If the witness answered "Yes," he would be incriminating himself to a dangerous degree. If he said "No," he would be running the risk of a perjury indictment. For the term *Communist conspiracy* is such a vague catch-all that unscrupulous Senators and district attorneys might well claim that a liberal who had once attended a single meeting of a so-called "front" organization had thereby taken part in the alleged conspiracy. The sensible and principled course for a witness under such circumstances is reliance on the First Amendment.

Since McCarthy dragged me into the picture in connection with alleged subversion in the United States Army, it is relevant to note that his investigations of the Army were a complete farce. With much fanfare the Senator announced in the fall of 1953 that he was going to reveal dangerous sabotage and espionage in the Army Signal Corps Laboratories at Fort Monmouth, N. J. His charges were never sustained. Instead, wrote Walter Millis in the *New York Herald Tribune* of December 8, 1953, "this really vital and sensitive military installation has been wrecked—more thoroughly than any Soviet saboteur could have dreamed of doing it —by the kind of anti-communism of which Senator McCarthy has made himself the leader and champion. The Fort Monmouth situation is truly scandalous."

Furthermore, McCarthy's Fort Monmouth excursion carried him far outside the jurisdiction of his Committee, which had no authority to investigate subversion in the Army, and constituted a usurpation of powers belonging to the Executive arm of the Government. In Walter Lippmann's words, the Senate as represented by McCarthy was not investigating at Fort Monmouth "anything that was its business as a legislature which makes the laws and then inquires into whether they are faithfully and efficiently and honestly administered and enforced. The Fort Monmouth cases were entirely within the prerogative and the responsibility of the Executive branch of the Government." [18]

Senator McCarthy also went after the man who had primary responsibility for the publication of the Army manual which listed my book in its bibliography. This was Major General Richard C. Partridge, Army Chief of Intelligence. General Partridge testified that the manual constituted "an honest attempt to deal with a very difficult subject" and refused to apologize for it. The Senator called the General "completely incompetent" and said,

"Why put a man in this job who doesn't know the first thing about communism?"[19] Shortly afterwards the United States Army, which was at that time still trying to appease McCarthy, transferred General Partridge from his Washington post to Europe.

It is significant that my challenge to the McCarthy Committee received wide support from conservative as well as liberal and radical sources. I talked with a number of Republicans who were bitterly opposed to McCarthy and who firmly backed me in my battle with him. These included many of my classmates and fellow-alumni of Harvard College. Conservatives for the most part, they had become increasingly anti-McCarthy because of the Senator's unfair and intemperate attacks on Harvard and its new President, Dr. Nathan M. Pusey.

Editorial comment on my case was also most encouraging. *The New York Times* stated: "The action of Corliss Lamont in defying the McCarthy Committee on the ground that the latter is unconstitutionally violating the personal rights of private citizens raises again the interesting and important question of how far Congressional committees can properly go. . . . Many citizens who have no use for communism are disturbed over the degree to which these committees are threatening an incursion into the domain of private rights and constitutional guarantees. . . . The ultimate disposition of this case may help define the area in which privacy of the individual is still protected."[20]

The Washington Post said in an editorial that I had "challenged the jurisdiction of Senator McCarthy's Government Operations Committee on substantial and significant grounds. . . . The basic issue, of course, is whether the courts, which have been understandably reluctant to impose broad, general checks upon the power of Congress to investigate, will be more willing to impose checks upon individual committees attempting to exercise powers which Congress has not conferred upon them."[21] In the Middle West the *St. Louis Post-Dispatch* editorially asserted that: "If the Senate should vote a contempt citation against Mr. Lamont, it would undoubtedly produce a test case that would go all the way to the United States Supreme Court where demagogues fare less well than they do in Congress. . . . Many Americans will applaud Corliss Lamont for having, in effect, spoken up for them and their right to be secure in their thoughts and their personal lives." [22]

In August 1954, almost a year after my original hearing before the McCarthy Committee, the United States Senate voted 71 to 3 to cite me for contempt of Congress. The three Senators who supported me were William Langer, Republican of North Dakota; Herbert Lehman, Democrat of New York; and Dennis Chavez, Democrat of New Mexico. Senator Langer led the debate against my contempt citation and repeatedly exposed the dishonest and unscrupulous tactics that McCarthy had used against me. In yielding to McCarthy's demand that I be cited, the Senate as a whole missed an excellent opportunity to help curb the excesses of the McCarthy Committee and to go on record in favor of proper limitations for Congressional investigations.

Shortly after my citation for contempt, the Senate Select Committee to Study Censure Charges against McCarthy asked the Senator why he had refused to answer questions put to him about his financial affairs in 1952 by the Senate Subcommittee on Privileges and Elections. McCarthy answered that the Subcommittee had exceeded its lawful powers. Senator Francis Case of the Select Committee was quick to point out that this was precisely my own argument against the McCarthy Committee. At this point, according to Murray Kempton of the *New York Post,* "There was a faint snicker around the room, and McCarthy looked as though he had been hit with a club." [23] In December 1954 the Senate voted 67-22 to condemn McCarthy for his contemptuous and obstructive attitude towards the Subcommittee.

On October 14, 1954 a Federal grand jury in New York City indicted me for contempt of Congress. It also indicted Albert Shadowitz, an engineer, and Abraham Unger, a lawyer, both of whom had also stood on the First Amendment in refusing to answer questions before the McCarthy Committee. In the statement which I issued concerning my indictment I said that the American Bill of Rights "is our proudest possession. Each generation must defend it anew. As part of this continuing struggle, I gladly enter into the legal battle that now confronts me."

The day after my indictment I was arraigned at the Federal Court House in New York, pleaded not guilty and was released on bail of $2,000. Assistant U.S. Attorney Lloyd F. MacMahon requested the presiding judge, Sylvester Ryan, to order me photographed and finger-printed. In his argument Mr. MacMahon referred to me as "a man of fine family who comes here with a silver sickle in his hand." [24] Judge Ryan sustained the objection of my attorney, Philip Wittenberg, to my being "mugged and printed."

Early in November, I filed a motion for the dismissal of the indictment, citing the constitutional arguments I had already propounded in my original statement of objections to the jurisdiction of the Committee. The brief which Mr. Wittenberg drew up on behalf of this motion included a new point, namely, that neither the Senate nor the Senate Committee on Government Operations had ever passed any resolution or minute formally and legally establishing the McCarthy Subcommittee.

Mr. Wittenberg argued: "Neither Public Law 601 nor Senate Resolutions referred to in the introduction to the indictment refer to the appointment of 'The Permanent Subcommittee on Investigations of the Committee on Government Operations.' That Subcommittee has no apparent legal existence. The indictment must therefore fall since there is no Subcommittee duly authorized to take testimony. . . . Nowhere in this indictment or resolutions is there a single word which authorizes this Subcommittee, or indicates its formation, its constituency or its authority."

Mr. Wittenberg then explained why this anomalous situation existed: "Had a Subcommittee been appointed it would have been necessary to assign such Subcommittee some authority. That authority would have served as a limitation on its power to investigate. Senator McCarthy pursuing a lawless course did not want any limitations on authority." Without such stated limitations, added Wittenberg, the McCarthy Committee felt free to roam far afield, investigating subjects clearly outside of its scope and within the jurisdiction of some other Congressional committee.

Judge Edward Weinfeld of the United States District Court, Southern District of New York, heard pleadings on my motion to dismiss at the end of November 1954. At the same time similar motions were argued on behalf of defendants Shadowitz and Unger. Judge Weinfeld did not hand down his decision until eight months later, on July 27, 1955, when, in a carefully reasoned opinion, he granted all three motions.

The indictments were defective, he said, because they failed to allege, first, "that the committee before which the alleged refusal to answer occurred was duly empowered by either House of Congress to conduct the particular inquiry, setting forth the source of this authority"; second, "that the inquiry was within the scope of the authority granted to the committee"; and, third, "that the witness' refusal to answer was wilful, or deliberate and intentional." [25]

Judge Weinfeld's first two points in effect upheld my claim that the McCarthy Committee from start to finish had no legal authority to carry on inquiries. The Weinfeld opinion stated: "No committee of either the House or Senate, and no Senator and no Representative, is free on its or his own to conduct investigations unless authorized. Thus it must appear that Congress empowered the Committee to act. . . . One vainly examines the Public Law and Senate Resolutions set forth in the indictment to find any reference to the Permanent Subcommittee, let alone any delegation of power to it." [26]

An old antagonist of mine, Republican Senator Karl E. Mundt, promptly wrote Attorney General Brownell and asked him to assign "the best talent of the Department of Justice" to drawing up a new indictment against me. Early in September, however, the Government gave notice that it would carry the Weinfeld decision to a Federal Appeals Court. This move indicated that the Justice Department had been unable to find any document granting the McCarthy Committee legal power. For had it done so, in all probability it would have followed Senator Mundt's suggestion and re-indicted me.

Meanwhile, in the fall of 1955, Harvey O'Connor went on trial in Washington, D.C., for contempt of Congress and pleaded in his defense the First Amendment and the same points on which Judge Weinfeld had dismissed my indictment. Federal Judge Joseph C. McGarraghy ruled against O'Connor on all of these issues and found him guilty, sentencing him to a year in jail and imposing a fine of $500. The Judge, however, apparently recognized the moral quality of O'Connor's challenge to the McCarthy Committee and suspended sentence on the prison term. O'Connor is appealing Judge McGarraghy's contempt conviction.

In 1956 a Federal Appeals Court in New York State upheld unanimously the Weinfeld decision that the so-called McCarthy Committee had no right to conduct an investigation of me because it had never been legally constituted.

From then on persons called before the McCarthy Committee were able to defend themselves successfully by citing my case. The U.S. government did not appeal this ruling.

4

THE CONGRESSIONAL INQUISITION

The three most pernicious Congressional committees of investigation are the House Committee on Un-American Activities, of which Representative Francis E. Walter, Democrat, and co-sponsor of the McCarran-Walter Immigration Act, is the present chairman; the Senate Subcommittee on Internal Security,° of which Senators Patrick A. McCarran, Democrat, William E. Jenner, Republican, and James O. Eastland, Democrat, have been successive chairmen; and the Senate Permanent Subcommittee on Investigations, of which Senators Joseph R. McCarthy, Republican, and John L. McClellan, Democrat, have been the chairmen. Another committee more limited in scope, but also sinister in its functioning has been the Special Committee to Investigate Tax-Exempt Foundations and Comparable Organizations,† of which Representatives Eugene E. Cox, Democrat, and B. Carroll Reece, Republican, have been the chairmen.

Unconstitutional behavior on the part of Congressional committees goes back at least as far as 1859 and 1860, the years immediately preceding the outbreak of the Civil War. In 1859, *after* John Brown had been tried, found guilty and hanged, the Southern majority in the Senate set up a Select Committee to investigate his assault on the town of Harpers Ferry and the extent to which persons not present during the raid were implicated. It soon be-

° This is a subcommittee of the larger Senate Judiciary Committee.
† I defer discussion of this committee to Chapter 9.

came evident at the hearings that the actual purpose of the Committee was to discredit the anti-slavery movement in general.

In 1860 a witness by the name of Thaddeus Hyatt, a New York merchant, was arrested at the behest of the Committee and brought before it. He refused, however, to take the stand. Haled before the Senate itself, Mr. Hyatt declared in a sworn statement: "The undersigned would respectfully observe that, while admitting the justice and propriety of investigating committees . . . he is constrained to regard [the] committee as . . . a tribunal with powers such as were never known before or contemplated in this Republican government; powers that are inimical to freedom, subversive of liberty; and in violation of the fundamental laws of the land." [27]

The Senate ordered Hyatt thrown into jail. But the Committee's Republican minority agreed with the prisoner that the Committee had gone beyond its proper bounds. The minority report contended that the Committee had made inquiries concerning subjects in relation to which Congress had no power to take action. The report asserted: "Witnesses and especially those known or suspected of ultra-abolition sentiments, have been freely examined as to their personal sentiments, theories, purposes, conduct, charities, contributions, lectures and speeches." [28]

In more recent times, after the turn of the century, Congressional committees were clearly guilty of exceeding their mandates, treating witnesses unjustly and violating the Bill of Rights. I recall, for example, that in 1933 a Senate Subcommittee on Banking and Currency, with Ferdinand Pecora, later a prominent judge, as Counsel, distinguished itself for headline and name-calling techniques. This Committee subpoenaed my late father, Thomas W. Lamont, and my elder brother, Thomas S. Lamont, both officers of J. P. Morgan & Co. In questioning them it went beyond its legal powers and was patently unfair in its newspaper releases regarding the hearings.

At one point the Committee took the unusual step of permitting a non-member, Senator Huey P. Long of Louisiana, to interrogate my father. In his questions the Senator, the leading American demagogue of his day and a predecessor of Joseph McCarthy, roamed far outside the sphere of banking and currency. Long's whole intent was to try to show that my father, through his investments in certain publications, was an active participant in a deep-dyed plot to discredit him. Throughout these proceedings my father maintained an attitude of good-natured contempt towards Senator Long.

The problem, then, of how to restrain Congressional committees has long been with us, although at all times relatively few of them have refused to stay within constitutional limits. Only during the past two decades, and notably since the establishment in 1938 of the House Un-American Activities Committee, has the problem of Congressional investigations become one of first magnitude in the political life of the United States.

As to the Un-American Activities Committee, *New York Herald Tribune* columnist Walter Lippmann declared in its early stages that its procedure constituted "a violation of American morality: It is a pillory in which reputations are ruined, often without proof and always without the legal safeguards that protect the ordinary criminal; it is a tribunal before which men are arraigned and charged with acts that are, as a matter of fact, lawful." [29] Mr. Lippmann's statement applies with equal force to the Senate Subcommittee on Internal Security and the Senate Permanent Subcommittee on Investigations; and it brings out the fact that all of these committees continually usurp both the Executive function of detecting and prosecuting crime and the Judicial function of holding trials and imposing punishment. The committees act as if they were prosecutor, judge and jury all combined.

The United States Constitution clearly defines the tripartite separation of powers in the American Government. Article I states: "All Legislative powers herein granted shall be vested in a Congress of the United States, which shall consist of a Senate and House of Representatives." Article II states: "The Executive power shall be vested in a President of the United States of America." Article III states: "The Judicial power of the United States shall be vested in one Supreme Court and in such inferior courts

as the Congress may from time to time ordain and establish."
These provisions set the stage for the "checks and balances" that
have always been an integral part of the American political system.

When in 1952 the Truman Administration instead of Congress
decreed the Government seizure of certain steel companies, the
United States Supreme Court declared the action unconstitutional precisely because it violated the three-way separation of
powers through the Executive branch assuming a function of the
Legislative branch. The Supreme Court rendered this decision
although the Korean emergency was still acute. Later, in November 1953, ex-President Harry S. Truman, in his letter to the House
Committee on Un-American Activities refusing to testify before it
regarding the Harry Dexter White case, maintained that the Committee was invading the rights of the Executive branch of the
Government by subpoenaing him. He thus took his stand on the
doctrine of the separation of powers.

In February 1954 the McCarthy Committee, representing the
Legislative branch of the Government, endeavored to take over
Executive prerogatives when it questioned Brigadier General
Ralph W. Zwicker of the United States Army about the honorable
discharge of Major Irving Peress, a dentist in his command who
had invoked the Fifth Amendment in refusing to answer McCarthy's questions. In a closed executive session of the Committee,
General Zwicker declined to divulge detailed information about
this matter on the grounds that he would be violating Army regulations by doing so and that in any case he had simply been putting into effect orders from higher up.

When the General took this entirely sound position, Senator
McCarthy became most abusive. "General," he said, "let's try and
be truthful. . . . I cannot help but question either your honesty
or your intelligence. . . . Don't you give me that double-talk.
. . . Anyone with the brains of a five-year-old child can understand that question. . . . General, you should be removed from
any command. Any man who has been given the honor of being
promoted to general and who says, 'I will protect another general

who protected Communists' isn't fit to wear that uniform." [30] McCarthy then proceeded to release publicly the full transcript of the Zwicker hearing without paying any attention to his Committee's own rule that testimony at an executive session must not be made public without a majority vote of the Committee.

Secretary of the Army Stevens promptly entered the fray, at first backing General Zwicker, but in the end unfortunately compromising with McCarthy. In September 1954 the Senate Select Committee to Study Censure Charges against the Wisconsin Senator, of which Senator Arthur V. Watkins, Republican of Utah, was Chairman, reported that "the conduct of Senator McCarthy toward General Zwicker in reprimanding and ridiculing him, in holding him up to public scorn and contumely, and in disclosing the proceedings of the executive session in violation of the rules of his own Committee, was inexcusable." [31] Senator Watkins's Committee recommended that the Senate should censure McCarthy for this behavior; but the Senate finally dropped the matter.

In a lead editorial *The New York Times* outlined the basic constitutional issue in the Zwicker case, explaining that there is a serious invasion of the Executive power "when the Legislative branch attempts to interfere with the legal and proper actions of subordinate executive officers carrying out their assigned functions. If there are objections to the way they do their duty, there is just one person in each agency who is responsible, and that is the head of the agency." [32] Later President Eisenhower commented on the episode by asserting: "The ultimate responsibility for the conduct of all parts of the Government rests with the President of the United States. That responsibility cannot be delegated to another branch of Government." [33]

In general, it is the powers of the Judiciary upon which the Congressional committees have trespassed most frequently and flagrantly. For in most of their hearings they act as if they were veritable courts of law. As Senator Wayne Morse has expressed it, "We have reached such a point in the conducting of Senate investigations, which go into the question of the innocence or guilt of persons under investigation, that it is a legal fiction to argue that, in fact, such persons are not standing trial." [34]

One of the provisions of the Fifth Amendment is that "No person shall be held to answer for a capital or otherwise infamous crime, unless on a presentment or indictment of a Grand Jury." The Congressional committees, however, nullify this guarantee and take over the functions of grand juries by asking witnesses accusatory questions about their alleged crimes and trying to build up a case against them. While grand juries, moreover, deliberate in secret session, the committees frequently trumpet criminal charges against an individual to the entire world. The committees also encroach upon the duties of district attorneys by seeking to develop evidence against witnesses for use in criminal prosecutions. And the committees assume the powers of courts by finding the "defendants" guilty and bringing about their punishment.

In these legislative "trials" Congressional committees deny to witnesses the legal safeguards long established in the administration of justice in English-speaking countries. One of those safeguards is written into the Sixth Amendment to the Constitution and reads: "In all criminal prosecutions, the accused shall enjoy the right . . . to be confronted with the witnesses against him; to have compulsory process for obtaining witnesses in his favor." This establishes the right of the defendant to have hostile witnesses cross-examined and his right to have witnesses subpoenaed in his own defense.

These rights the committees under consideration have never granted, with one exception. That was when Senator McCarthy demanded and won the right to cross-examine at the time he himself was a witness before his own Subcommittee on Investigations in 1954. This was during the hearings in regard to the pressures the Senator and Chief Counsel Roy M. Cohn had brought to bear on the U.S. Army to give preferential treatment to Private G. David Schine, special staff consultant to the McCarthy Committee.

Congressional committees do not ordinarily inflict punishment directly, except when they initiate contempt proceedings against their victims. However, a witness who is merely questioned—let alone one who refuses to answer questions—may suffer heavy penalties through the wide publicity given to defamatory charges against him or through losing his job and being put on a blacklist that makes future employment most difficult. "He is not imprisoned, but he is made a pariah. . . . He is not fined, but his income may diminish almost to the vanishing point. In addition, his social standing in the community, his familial relationships, his own mental well-being—all these are severely injured." [35]

Just as the medieval Inquisition of the Christian Church found heretics guilty and then handed them over to the secular authorities for punishment, so the Congressional Inquisition finds the heretics of today "guilty" and turns them over for punishment to some educational institution, business corporation or Government department where they are employed. Generally the "crime" is refusal to answer, on constitutional grounds, the questions put by Congressional committees; and the punishment is usually dismissal, whether the individual is working in the Federal, State or municipal service or in some sector of private enterprise.

When a Congressional committee, as has often been the case, brings pressure on a department of the Federal Government to oust an employee, we have another example of Congressional intrusion upon the administration of a Government office and interference with the functions of the Executive branch.

Many teachers, government employees, actors and others have been summarily dismissed, not because of their own testimony, but because of being put under a cloud of suspicion by unproved and lurid accusations aired by others before some Congressional committee and then recklessly released by it. The committees keep in their files a vast amount of raw, unevaluated material about individuals and groups, some in the form of newspaper clippings and much in the form of malicious "information" sent in by vigilante volunteers. According to the National Council of the Churches of Christ in the U.S.A., "Sometimes persons of ill will have been able to send things in for the files, receive back the items as official releases of 'information from the files of the House

Committee on Un-American Activities,' and distribute them as such." [36]

Over a period of almost seven years this Committee intermittently released from its records charges most harmful to the reputation of Bishop G. Bromley Oxnam of the Methodist Church. At a special hearing before the Committee which the Bishop finally obtained to refute these charges, he asserted: "The preparation and publication of these 'files' puts into the hands of irresponsible individuals and agencies a wicked tool. It gives rise to a new and vicious expression of Ku-Kluxism, in which an innocent person may be beaten by unknown assailants, who are cloaked in anonymity and at times immunity, and whose whips are cleverly constructed lists of so-called subversive organizations and whose floggings appear all too often to be sadistic in spirit rather than patriotic in purpose." [37]

Reams upon reams of newsprint have told about the numerous employees who have lost their jobs because of invoking the constitutional guarantee against compulsory self-incrimination. But it is rarely pointed out that this guarantee is only one of five provisions in the Fifth Amendment; and that actually it is not so important as the one which says that no person shall "be deprived of life, liberty or property without due process of law." The Fourteenth Amendment embodied this same principle and made it mandatory for the States. What the Congressional committees constantly do is precisely to neglect or negate "due process of law."

This brings out the fact that the protections of established legal procedure are central in the whole American system of justice. Five Articles, IV-VIII, in the Bill of Rights concern themselves exclusively with procedure. As Justice Frankfurter, speaking for the majority in a Supreme Court decision, phrased the matter: "The history of liberty has largely been the history of observance of procedural safeguards." [38]

Fundamental to due process in the United States has been the principle that a man is to be considered innocent until proved guilty. But the Congressional committees of investigation have thrown this concept into reverse and proceeded on the assumption that a man, once accused, is guilty until proved innocent. Since it is almost impossible for an accused witness convincingly to disprove vague, wild charges hurled at him by talkative ex-Communists turned well-paid professional informers—especially since the committee rules deny him the right to cross-examine his accusers —he usually comes out on the short end. And the result is guilt by accusation, guilt by hearsay, guilt by association, and guilt by newspaper headline.

Walter Lippmann pointed out in the *New York Herald Tribune* how difficult it was for the average witness before the McCarthy Committee, for example, to refute accusations made at a hearing and then published by the press: "The unsupported denial of an accused man will not balance a charge by a United States Senator operating with the whole apparatus of a Senatorial committee and of a staff and of a whole reservoir of paid and voluntary informers. . . . The heart of the evil is that an investigation by McCarthy is persecution and it is not a judicial inquiry intended to develop the whole truth and to do justice. . . . The news editors cannot substitute themselves for good Congressional committees, and out of their own resources provide the balancing facts which are not provided by these committees." [39]

In the committee procedures and findings the doctrine of guilt by association—*vicarious* guilt—has been more and more supplanting the old juridical concept that guilt is always personal. If it can be shown that a person belongs or belonged to an organization listed as "subversive" by the U.S. Attorney General, or even to one that is unpopular, then that individual is likely to be smeared as a Communist or fellow-traveler and lose his job or at least his standing in the community. Because of pressures from Congressional committees, men have been fired for subscribing to a liberal publication like *The Nation* or *New Republic,* or for signing a public petition protesting the violation of civil liberties, or for having friends or relatives who are deemed radical.

Professor Henry Steele Commager has called this doctrine of guilt by association wrong in logic, wrong legally, wrong practically and wrong morally. He writes: "If a cause is worthy of

support, it does not cease to merit support because men we dis-
approve support it; if all the subversives in the land asserted that
two and two make four, two and two would still make four. . . .

"There is a persuasive reason why conservatives and liberals
alike should subscribe to this principle, and that is a practical one.
For if bad support could damage a good cause, then all that
would be needed to tarnish the Declaration of Independence or
to destroy the Constitution would be the endorsement of these
documents by the Communist Party; all that would be needed to
ruin the Republican Party or the American Legion or the American Bar Association would be approval of their policies and objectives by the *Daily Worker*. It is a common device—perhaps
trick is the better word—of members of Congressional committees
to confront witnesses whom they wish to embarrass with the fact
that they have been favorably quoted in the *Daily Worker*. But
it is well to remember that Herbert Hoover and the late Senator
Taft have been cited both frequently and favorably in *Pravda*.
The doctrine that a good cause can be damaged by disreputable
support is one that cuts both ways." [40]

The concept of guilt by association is wrong morally, Professor
Commager concludes, "because it assumes a far greater power in
evil than in virtue. It is based therefore on a desperate view of
mankind. It rests on what may be called the rotten-apple theory
of society—the theory that one wicked man corrupts all virtuous
men, and that one mistaken idea subverts all sound ideas. This
business of contamination, be it noted, works only one way. Apparently one Communist or one subversive can contaminate an
entire organization, but a thousand Republicans or Legionnaires
are without perceptible influence! Why is there no doctrine of
innocence by association?" [41]

While this weapon of guilt by association has been wielded
mainly against liberals and radicals, it can also boomerang against
the conservatives. Thus in the 1954 campaign of Clifford P. Case,
Republican candidate for the U.S. Senate from New Jersey, his
political enemies suddenly tried to discredit him by charging
that his sister, Adelaide Case, had been active in "Communist-

front" organizations. The charge was based on testimony by Bella V. Dodd, an ex-Communist informer. It turned out, however, that Miss Dodd had been referring to a different Adelaide Case who had taught at Teachers College, Columbia, and at the Episcopal Theological School in Boston. Since Professor Case had died in 1948 before Miss Dodd made her revelations, it was difficult to disprove them.

A political tempest resulted from the guilt-by-association accusation against Mr. Case, and he had to spend a great deal of time endeavoring to refute it. Although he took a strong anti-McCarthy position in his campaign, he did not mention the fact that the Eisenhower Administration itself had long been using the doctrine of guilt by association as a bludgeon in the witch-hunt. Mr. Case was elected to the Senate in November 1954 with a very slim margin over his Democratic opponent.

In April 1955 another leading Republican, Edward J. Corsi, lost his job as special assistant to Secretary of State Dulles on refugee and immigration problems after Democratic Representative Francis E. Walter had repeatedly attacked him for alleged "Communist-front" associations in past years. Mr. Corsi denied the charges, and said that when he discussed the matter with Secretary Dulles, the latter "talked as if there was no use bucking Walter's opposition, that it would interfere with a lot of other things; he had to do business with Congress." [42] Corsi had served as U.S. Commissioner of Immigration under both President Hoover and President Franklin D. Roosevelt, and was New York State Industrial Commissioner under Governor Dewey.

One of the worst aspects of reliance on guilt by association is that this doctrine, as frequently put into practice by Congressional committees, violates, at least in spirit, the provision in the United States Constitution forbidding *ex post facto* laws. [43] An *ex post facto* law is one that imposes punishment for an act that was not illegal when committed. The investigating committees make guilt retroactive in this sense by bringing about the punishment of persons because ten or fifteen years before being questioned they joined in good faith an organization which is later declared "subversive."

The Congressional investigating committees also negate due process by disregarding, at least indirectly, the constitutional ban on bills of attainder.[44] The U.S. Supreme Court has defined a bill of attainder as "a legislative Act which inflicts punishment without a judicial trial." [45] In a recent case the Court held: "When our Constitution and Bill of Rights were written, our ancestors had ample reason to know that legislative trials and punishments were too dangerous to liberty to exist in the nation of free men they envisioned. And so they proscribed bills of attainder. . . . Were this case to be not justiciable, *Congressional action,* aimed at three named individuals, *which stigmatized their reputations and seriously impaired their chance to earn a living,* could never be challenged in any court. Our Constitution did not contemplate such a result." [46] [Italics mine—C.L.]

Another constitutional provision violated by the Congressional committees is that which establishes the Federal Government as one of limited powers. This is embodied in the Tenth Amendment: "The powers not delegated to the United States by the Constitution, nor prohibited by it to the States are reserved to the States respectively, or to the people." Both the Jenner and Velde committees were guilty of pushing aside the Tenth Amendment by their investigations of teachers in public schools and colleges, in such cities as Boston, New York and Philadelphia. Public schools and municipal educational institutions in general have always been regarded in America as a distinctively local responsibility. The Federal authorities have no more business interfering with local education than with local police or fire departments.

The Congressional committees purport to be exposing and counteracting far-reaching Communist plots for overthrowing the Government. But in fact they are engaged in a ruthless campaign against all ideas and associations that do not conform to right-wing orthodoxy. Mr. George F. Kennan, former Ambassador to Soviet Russia, analyzed this situation in an address at Notre Dame University in 1953. He talked of forces in our society which "march, in one way or another, under the banner of an alarmed and exercised anti-communism. . . . One has the impression that if uncountered, these people would eventually narrow the area of political and cultural respectability to a point where it included only themselves, the excited accusers, and excluded everything and everybody not embraced in *the profession of denunciation*." [47] [Italics mine—C.L.]

The Federal Bureau of Investigation possesses long dossiers on almost all those who are called before the Congressional witch-hunting committees. But since these persons—the bulk of them radicals, liberals or dissenters of some sort—have not violated any law and are guilty at most of some ideological indiscretion, the committees attempt to encompass their ruin through extra-legal, and often illegal, methods of inquiry. Moreover, it is plain that the FBI, improperly, has provided Congressional committees with confidential data from its files in order to give them leads for the questioning of victims.

Professor Robert K. Carr, of Dartmouth College, in his authoritative book *The House Committee on Un-American Activities, 1945-50*, writes that many of the hearings made public "information already known to the FBI." He asserts that: "Often the leading witness in such committee hearings was an undercover FBI agent who had infiltrated the Communist movement. . . . It is quite apparent that these hearings were designed to serve the purpose of publicizing information in FBI files." [48]

Representative J. Parnell Thomas stated in 1948 when he was Chairman of the Un-American Activities Committee: "The closest relationship exists between this committee and the FBI. I cannot say as much as between this committee and the Attorney General's office, but the closest relationship exists between this committee and the FBI. I think there is a very good understanding between us. It is something, however, that we cannot talk too much about." [49] Senator Karl Mundt of South Dakota, a ranking Republican member of the McCarthy Committee, was franker: "The FBI may compile much evidence on Communist infiltration, but not enough to justify indictments. Often in such cases,

the FBI will tip off a Congressional committee." [50] Senator
Everett Dirksen, Republican of Illinois, another McCarthy Committee member, stated in a radio broadcast that it was easier to
tell whether a witness is lying or covering up "when you have
an FBI report at your elbow."

Senator J. W. Fulbright of Arkansas, one of the most reliable
Democratic leaders, brought all this to a head in March 1954
when he publicly protested the repeated "leaks" from FBI files
to such individuals as Senator McCarthy and his Committee
counsel, Mr. Cohn. It would be bad enough, Senator Fulbright
noted, if unauthorized persons were getting accurate, proven facts
from the FBI, but instead they were using "every kind of gossip,
hearsay and undocumented materials of all kinds." [51]

The questions that the inquisitorial committees of Congress ask
are rarely of the sort that might reveal facts useful for legislation,
but are designed to hold the witness up to detraction and abuse,
or worse, to ensnare him in a perjury indictment. As Bishop Oxnam said about his hearing in 1953 before the Un-American
Activities Committee, the atmosphere throughout was one of "en-
trapment." In attempting to lay the basis for perjury prosecutions,
Congressional committees again usurp the Judicial function by
taking over the duties of district attorneys and grand juries.

At a hearing on U.S. foreign relations in 1950 Senator McCarthy
was very frank about his newly assumed role of public prosecutor
and asserted: "We find where Communists are concerned they are
too clever. They work underground too much. It is hard to get
them for their criminal activities in connection with espionage,
but a way has been found. We are getting them for perjury and
putting some of the worst of them away. For that reason I hope
every witness who comes here is put under oath and his testimony is gone over with a fine-tooth comb, and if we cannot convict some of them for their disloyal activities perhaps we can
convict them for perjury." [52]

Another alarming feature of the Congressional Inquisition is
the extent to which one-man subcommittees have toured the na-

tion and carried on inquiries.* This practice concentrates too much power in the hands of one Senator or one Representative who might be restrained to some degree were other members of the committee present. Senator Joseph McCarthy provided the most flagrant example of this trend toward personal dictatorship.

In truth, members of Congress who belong to the main investigating committees have become more and more diverted from their primary function of proposing and passing on legislation conducive to the welfare of the American people. They are hellbent on tracking down the Communists, sharing in the headlines that the great Red-hunt evokes, and trying to advance their own political fortunes by posing as champions in the fake cause of saving America from "subversion." Of course in the process they waste a large proportion of the funds which Congress appropriates—a record $8,000,000 in 1953-1954—for investigation.

Such appropriations, however, are only a small part of the national cost involved in the Congressional inquisitions. In addition, the many individuals and organizations summoned for or threatened with investigation must expend large sums in getting ready for hearings, in hiring lawyers and perhaps finally defending themselves in the courts. President Henry P. Van Dusen of Union Theological Seminary dwelt upon this theme in a letter to *The New York Times:* "To take a single instance. The Cox committee's † investigation of foundations spent less than the $75,000 appropriated for the purpose. But the expenses of several foundations in preparing the required answers to the committee's 120-item questionnaire ran into five and even six figures. It has been estimated that the total cost to the 1,500 foundations questioned may have been something in the area of ten million dollars of philanthropic funds 'diverted from the purposes of the founders' to satisfy Congressional curiosity." [53]

* The House of Representatives in 1955 eliminated one-man committee hearings. See pp. 79-80.

† This refers to the House of Representatives Select Committee to Investigate Tax-Exempt Foundations and Comparable Organizations. See Chapter 9.

President Van Dusen also called attention to the lamentable
effects of "the orgy" of Congressional probes on public opinion in
foreign countries: "The American people need to realize that in
the eyes of the world the current procedures are rapidly making
this aspect of their Government something of an international
laughing-stock, not to say scandal." [54]

Nothing could have been more unfortunate for America's reputation abroad than the European trip made in the spring of 1953
by two members of the McCarthy Committee's staff, Roy M. Cohn
and G. David Schine. The Senator sent these young men, both in
their twenties, to investigate "subversive" influences in U. S. Government institutions in Europe. These two irresponsible snoopers
aroused tremendous resentment wherever they went on their
ill-will tour. Opposition to them was so pronounced in England
where the press described them as "aggressive, brash, ignorant,
evasive and puerile," that they remained only five hours in London and called off their scheduled loyalty investigation of British
subjects employed by the American Government in Great Britain.

All in all McCarthy's antic emissaries did serious damage, especially in bringing additional pressure on the overseas libraries of
the State Department to ban suspect books and journals. This was
part of the Senator's general "book-burning" campaign and resulted in the literal burning of a few volumes by panicky State
Department officials. Many titles and several magazines, such as
The Nation and the *New Republic*, were removed from the library
shelves.

McCarthy's numerous investigations into books and authors
were patent violations of the First Amendment clause guaranteeing freedom of the press. He also made a direct attempt to undermine this freedom when, in 1953, he called before his Committee
three well-known newspaper executives: Cedric Belfrage, Editor
of the *National Guardian*, James Aronson, Executive Editor of the
same newsweekly; and James Wechsler, Editor of the *New York
Post*. In grilling these men, the Senator was obviously taking revenge on them for their anti-McCarthy attitude and trying to
intimidate them into changing the policies of their newspapers.

McCarthy went after Belfrage and Aronson because, in addition, they had worked in the SHAEF (Supreme Headquarters Allied Expeditionary Force) press project in Occupied Germany. Both of them invoked the Fifth Amendment in refusing to answer the Senator's questions. Two days after the hearings the Department of Justice arrested Mr. Belfrage for the purpose of deporting him back to England, whence he had immigrated to the United States in 1936. The trumped-up charge against Belfrage was that he had been a member of the Communist Party in 1937.

Later General Joseph M. Swing, U.S. Commissioner for Immigration and Naturalization, admitting frankly that the Government was prosecuting Belfrage for his ideas, asserted that his "political beliefs are allied to a world-wide conspiracy to destroy the free world and make him, in our opinion, a threat to the national security." [55] After fighting the case for upwards of two years and spending more than four months in jail in the process, Belfrage finally lost out and was deported to England in August 1955. He then assumed the title of Editor-in-Exile of the *National Guardian* and has been writing regularly for it since he arrived in London.

There has been a good deal of talk to the effect that the methods of investigation followed by the Senate Committee on Internal Security have been essentially fair to witnesses. But the record of this Committee under the chairmanship of the late Senator Patrick McCarran of Nevada and subsequently of Senator William E. Jenner of Indiana was not reassuring on this point.

During the summer of 1951 the Internal Security Committee spent most of its time trying to portray the American Institute of Pacific Relations and its supporters as Communists and as responsible for the alleged betrayal of American foreign policy in the Far East. In its tawdry endeavors the Committee attempted to give the false impression that I was a Far Eastern expert and a prime mover in the affairs of the Institute, whereas I had been a member for only a few years and a very inactive one at that. In order to make the picture totally misleading, the Committee did not even mention that my father, Thomas W. Lamont, Chairman of the Board of J. P. Morgan & Co., who had had a considerable knowledge of the Far East, actively participated in the work and financing of the Institute of Pacific Relations for more than twenty years. It was obviously the Committee's intention to conceal the fact that leading bankers, conservatives and Republicans, such as my father, had been among the chief backers of the Institute.

At a hearing on August 22, 1951, the Committee counsel made a further effort to discredit this excellent organization by pretending that I was intimately associated with it. He craftily brought forth a brief memorandum headed "C. L. from E.C.C." and suggested that it had been written to Corliss Lamont from Edward C. Carter, former Secretary General of the Institute. Nobody was given an opportunity to refute this idea and to show that the memo was from Mr. Carter to Clayton Lane, at one time an officer of the Institute. I must confess that this little frame-up alarmed me, since I could not help wondering whether some day I might be accused of a real crime because my initials happened to be the same as someone else's.

The Internal Security Committee's "investigation" of the Institute of Pacific Relations was a prime example of the point that current Congressional committees are not seeking full factual data that would give an impartial picture of an organization's activities. What they aim to do, for crude political purposes and through deliberate misrepresentation, is to make the organization in question seem to fit into some preconceived pattern of subversive, conspiratorial or Communist activity.

It was this same Committee, under Senator McCarran's chairmanship, that in 1952 grilled Professor Owen Lattimore of Johns Hopkins University for a record twelve days of hearings. Lattimore was already a controversial figure, whom Senator McCarthy had called a "top Russian espionage agent in the United States." When McCarthy's charges blew up from sheer absurdity, his Democratic counterpart—Pat McCarran—took up the vengeful harassment of Professor Lattimore.

Since Lattimore answered fully and freely hundreds of questions, many of them most trivial which the McCarran Committee asked about speeches made, meetings attended, trips taken and engagements, associations, conversations and even thoughts he had had over the previous twenty-five years, it is not in the least surprising that occasionally he fell into minor inaccuracies and inconsistencies. Let the reader ask himself how precise he could be if a Congressional committee suddenly inquired of him the date and place of a luncheon with Mr. X some ten years ago. Yet this was just the type of question which was put to Lattimore and which was instrumental in involving him in a new and more trying ordeal.

For the McCarran Committee insisted that in several of his answers Professor Lattimore had wilfully lied; and it was able, through political deals and pressures of the most unscrupulous variety, to get him indicted late in 1952 for perjury on seven counts.* The fifth count was that Lattimore had testified he had luncheon with the late Constantine Oumansky, Soviet Ambassador to the United States, subsequent to June 22, 1941, the date of the Nazi invasion of Soviet Russia, and then, when confronted with evidence that he had made a mistake, placed the meeting as before that date. But what could have been more natural than for Lattimore to fall into such a slip of memory, or more outrageous than for a Congressional committee to refuse a witness the right to correct his testimony under such circumstances?

During 1952 and 1953 the Internal Security Committee made a long investigation of allegedly subversive Americans on the staff of the United Nations. This inquiry violated the United States Constitution because it dealt with the political beliefs and associations of the individuals subpoenaed. Moreover, since the Committee represented the Legislative branch of the American Government and brought heavy pressures to bear on U.N. employees, it also violated the United Nations Charter. This provides that "Each Member of the United Nations undertakes to respect the exclusively international character of the responsibilities of

*The Department of Justice dropped the Lattimore indictment in 1955. For a fuller discussion of this case see Chapter 7.

the Secretary-General and the staff and not to seek to influence them in the discharge of their responsibilities." [56]

Since Secretary-General Trygve Lie yielded to the pressures of the Internal Security Committee to dismiss U.N. employees who pleaded the Fifth Amendment in not answering questions, he too violated the United Nations Charter where it states: "In the performance of their duties the Secretary-General and the staff shall not seek or receive instructions from any government or from any other authority external to the Organization." [57] The special Administrative Tribunal of the United Nations later declared illegal the dismissal of eleven out of twenty-one of the American employees who had lost their jobs. It ordered four of these reinstated; but out of deference to the U.S. Government, Mr. Lie's successor as Secretary-General, Dag Hammarskjold, refused to carry out the directive.

The Tribunal then ruled that all eleven discharged illegally should receive substantial payments, totaling $179,420, from the United Nations in lieu of reinstatement. The U.S. Government, however, opposed this award of indemnities and appealed the issue to the International Court of Justice. In July 1954 that court affirmed the ruling of the Administrative Tribunal; and in December the American Government finally bowed to this decision.

The U.N. investigations conducted by the Internal Security Committee went on month after month, creating demoralization and havoc on the United Nations staff. The situation became more and more tense; and as a direct consequence the U.N.'s General Counsel, Abraham H. Feller, committed suicide on November 13, 1952, by jumping out of his twelfth-story apartment window in New York City. Secretary-General Lie immediately issued a public statement about Mr. Feller and asserted: "He had worked tirelessly day and night under my direction to uphold due process of law and justice in the investigations against indiscriminate smears and exaggerated charges. This placed him under a prolonged and serious strain. The terrible tragedy of his death today is the result." [58]

In 1954 Senator Eastland of Mississippi, who was facing strong opposition for re-election that year, staged a particularly shabby investigation in New Orleans as a one-man subcommittee of the Internal Security Committee. The Eastland inquiry was into alleged Communist plotting behind the Southern Conference Educational Fund and resulted in some unexpected fireworks. The Fund is an outgrowth of the old Southern Conference for Human Welfare and is one of the few liberal organizations functioning in the South. Senator Eastland's little inquisition relied chiefly on two ex-Communist informers, John Butler and Paul Crouch.

Witnesses called and duly tarred with the Red brush included quiet, scholarly James Dombrowski, Executive Director of the Fund; Aubrey Williams, its President and Editor of *Southern Farm and Home;* Mrs. Virginia Durr, a Director, and wife of Clifford Durr, former FCC member; and Myles Horton, a Director, and head of the Highlander Folk School. Mr. Horton was forcibly ejected from the hearings when he declined to answer certain questions and while he was trying to get into the record a statement by President Eisenhower in favor of civil rights.

When informer Crouch accused Mrs. Durr of having full knowledge of a Communist spy ring, it was too much for her husband. He whipped around the railing in front of the witness benches and rushed at Crouch, shouting, "I'll kill you, you dirty dog, for lying about my wife." [59] United States marshals restrained Mr. Durr who afterwards collapsed outside the courtroom. He had been suffering from a heart condition and was taken to the hospital.

Mention of the notorious Paul Crouch leads to the observation that the Internal Security Committee, as well as the House Un-American Activities Committee and the Senate Subcommittee on Investigations, have all relied in their investigations on a motley crew of professional informers, cringing ex-Communists and confessed ex-spies all receiving from $25 to $50 a day for their slanderous testimony. Again and again in the Congressional inquiries since World War II there have appeared the same troupe of traveling performers whose continued pay depends upon their being able constantly to present new and sensational evidence.

In 1951 the McCarthy Committee went to the lengths of hiring a spy to facilitate its disreputable work. In that year an American citizen, Charles E. Davis, was convicted by a Swiss court of political espionage after confessing that, while in the employ of Senator McCarthy, he had tried to frame John Carter Vincent, American envoy to Switzerland, as a secret Red. He falsely signed the name of a top Swiss Communist to a faked telegram to Vincent, hoping to trick the latter into an indiscreet reply. Davis told the details of his sordid story in a signed series in *The Daily Compass* entitled "I Was a Spy for McCarthy." [60]

Of course the Congressional inquisitors are vociferous in proclaiming themselves as outstanding patriots saving the Republic from terrible dangers. But what they have done to wreck America's free institutions and Government services points to just the opposite. Senator McCarthy, as we have already shown, did his best to bring into disrepute the United States Army. He was more successful in regard to the State Department and its Foreign Service. Early in 1954 *The New York Times* printed in this connection a letter signed by five prominent American diplomats, including Norman Armour, ex-Ambassador to four different countries, and Joseph C. Grew, ex-Ambassador to Japan and former Under Secretary of State. The communication asserted:

"Recently the Foreign Service has been subjected to a series of attacks from outside sources which have questioned the loyalty and the moral standards of its members. With rare exceptions the justification for these attacks has been so flimsy as to have no standing in a court of law or in the mind of any individual capable of differentiating repeated accusation from even a reasonable presumption of guilt. Nevertheless these attacks have had sinister results.

"The conclusion has become inescapable, for instance, that a Foreign Service officer who reports on persons and events to the very best of his ability and who makes recommendations which at the time he conscientiously believes to be in the interest of the United States may subsequently find his loyalty and integrity

challenged and may even be forced out of the service and discredited forever as a private citizen after many years of distinguished service. A premium therefore has been put upon reporting and upon recommendations which are ambiguously stated
or so cautiously set forth as to be deceiving. . . .

"Fear is playing an important part in American life at the present time. As a result the self-confidence, the confidence in others,
the sense of fair play and the instinct to protect the rights of the
non-conformist are—temporarily, it is to be hoped—in abeyance.
But it would be tragic if this fear, expressing itself in an exaggerated emphasis on security, should lead us to cripple the Foreign Service, our first line of national defense, at the very time
when its effectiveness is essential to filling the place which history
has assigned to us." [61]

McCarthy's raids on the State Department's Voice of America
were also ruinous to the efficiency and morale of that staff. One
of his prime victims here was Mr. Reed Harris, of the Class of
1931 at Columbia College, whose crime it had been to be a
campus dissenter more than twenty-five years before and to have
written a book shortly after his graduation entitled *King Football*,
which was critical of college sports. Harris had become a firm
anti-Communist liberal, but was forced to resign from the Voice
of America after McCarthy questioned him and publicized his
past. As a teacher at Columbia I had known Reed Harris as an
intellectually alert young student, and had defended his freedom of opinion when, as the crusading editor of the *Columbia
Daily Spectator*, his outspoken editorials got him into trouble with
the college administration.

In April 1953 *The New York Times* made a special study of
morale among United States employees in Europe and reported:
"The morale of Americans has been disintegrating at an acceler-
ated pace during the last three months under the impact of
Congressional investigations in Washington. Resignations and
dismissals of colleagues from Government service in foreign posts
without apparent cause has had a shattering effect on the morale
of Americans in Germany. They believe they are sitting targets,

and are no longer in a position to defend themselves against anonymous denunciations or hearsay aspersions on their private lives or political views." [62]

The brutal going-over that McCarthy gave the Voice of America staff resulted in another gruesome episode attributable to the current American inquisition. In February 1953 the McCarthy Committee heard bizarre testimony that two expensive Voice of America radio transmitters had been planned for unfavorable sites in the State of Washington because the signals from such locations could be more easily jammed by Soviet transmitters. A radio engineer, Raymond Kaplan, had borne much of the responsibility for the selection of these sites. Disturbed lest McCarthy blame him for decisions he had made in good faith, Kaplan brought about his own death by hurling himself in front of a truck in Cambridge, Massachusetts.

In a suicide note to his wife and son, Kaplan stated: "I have not done anything in my job which I did not think was in the best interests of the country or of which I am ashamed of. And the interest of my country is to fight communism hard. . . . You may hear many things about me in the press which may be stirred up. Believe me, the bad things will not be true because how could they be if in my heart I did what I thought best? . . . Since most of the information passed through me, I guess I am the patsy for any mistakes made. . . .

"This is not an easy thing to do but I think it is the only way. You see once the dogs are set on you, everything you have done since the beginning of time is suspect. It will not be good to be continuously harried and harassed for everything that I do in a job. I have never done anything that I consider wrong but I can't take the pressure on my shoulders any more. . . . I am afraid you too through absolutely no fault of your own will be continuously hounded for the rest of your lives. This way you may have a chance to live in some future happiness." [63] A few days later Senator McCarthy publicly admitted that his Committee had found nothing to indicate any wrong-doing on the part of Mr. Kaplan.

The McCarthy Committee bears heavy responsibility for another death which occurred during its investigation of Army personnel at Fort Monmouth, N. J., in the fall of 1953. When Senator McCarthy subpoenaed Mrs. S to appear before the Committee in October, she was already seven months pregnant. The Senator and his aides questioned Mrs. S at length, threatened her with contempt and perjury actions, and at one point suggested capital punishment. She testified for a second time early in November. Her husband was also called before the Committee, refused to answer improper questions, and was told he would be cited for contempt.

Mrs. S's counsel repeatedly urged the Committee to take into consideration his client's advanced state of pregnancy. But McCarthy had no mercy and insisted that Mrs. S testify for a third time on November 24 at a public session. Informed of this news on November 20, Mrs. S was rushed to the hospital two days later and gave birth to a dead baby. Her lawyer stated: "There is no doubt in her mind nor in the mind of her counsel that the strain of the executive session and the anticipation of the public session were the cause of this tragedy." [64]

Another of McCarthy's 1953 investigations resulted in alarming threats against friends of mine, the T's, living in a suburban community near New York City. After publicity broke in the local press about Mrs. T taking the Fifth Amendment before the McCarthy Committee, anonymous phone calls and letters started coming in to Mr. and Mrs. T, threatening them and their children with violence. One of their neighbors stated openly that he was going to beat up Mrs. T. The situation became so ominous that Mr. and Mrs. T hired a guard for their home. They turned the scurrilous letters over to the Federal Bureau of Investigation, which reported there was really nothing to be done about them.

Dr. Irving Peress and his family underwent similar experiences in 1954 after Senator McCarthy's bitter attacks on Peress as a "Fifth Amendment Communist." Dr. Peress received many unsigned letters full of abuse and anti-Semitic remarks. One of the letter-writers announced that he would kill Peress within ten days; others lamented that Hitler had not done away with more Jews. Then one night hoodlums threw rocks through the windows of the bedrooms where Dr. Peress's two daughters, aged six and eight, were sleeping. The missiles shattered the glass and scattered it over the girls' beds. "This is the terror that stems from McCarthyism," said Dr. Peress.

Concerning the general sowing of suspicion for which Congressional committees bear so much responsibility, the Most Reverend Bernard J. Sheil, a bishop of the Roman Catholic Church, had this to say in a speech at Chicago in 1954, denouncing Senator McCarthy: "An America which has lost faith in the integrity of the Government, the Army, the schools, the churches, the labor unions, press, and most of all an America whose citizens have lost faith in each other—such an America would not need to bother about being anti-Communist; it would have nothing to lose. Such an America would have nothing to recommend it to freedom-loving men." [65]

Senator McCarthy's vicious assault on the State Department, and later the Department of the Army, brought his Committee's investigations full circle, and convincingly demonstrated once more that the democratic rights guaranteed under the American Constitution are indivisible. For McCarthy's callous violation of the civil liberties of Communists or alleged Communists, of so-called fellow-travelers, of trade unionists and of progressives, finally led—as his inquisition gathered momentum—to the hounding of anti-Communist liberals, State Department officials and Army personnel with long records of heroism. He started by violating the constitutional doctrine of the separation of powers through holding *de facto* trials of witnesses and thus usurping the Judicial function; and ended up by trespassing on the Executive function through interfering with established Army procedures and trying to order around military officers as if he were the Commander-in-Chief.

It is perfectly clear that Grand Inquisitor McCarthy undertook to ruin anyone—no matter what his views, affiliations or party—who stood in the way of his ambition to become supreme political boss of the country, operating through intimidation and rabble-rousing. This is why he did not hesitate to tangle with the highest officials of the Republican Administration and to imply, by making speeches entitled "Twenty Years of Treason" about the Democratic Administrations from 1932 through 1952, that most Democrats are traitors. In May 1954 McCarthy included in this slur the first year of the Eisenhower Administration by referring to "the evidence of treason that has been growing over the past twenty, twenty-one years."

McCarthy and his fellow-inquisitors in Congress have answered every criticism by shouting loudly that they are exposing Communists and communism. Bishop Sheil made a highly relevant comment on this in his Chicago address when he spoke out against "the phony anti-communism that mocks our way of life, flouts our traditions and democratic procedures and sense of fair play. . . . It has been said that patriotism is the scoundrel's last refuge. In this day and age anti-communism is the scoundrel's first defense. As I remember, one of the noisiest anti-Communists of recent history was a man named Adolf Hitler." [66]

Viewing the general character of Congressional investigations in recent years, I think that Abe Fortas, an able Washington attorney, has put the matter succinctly: "There are no standards of judgment, no rules, no traditions of procedure or judicial demeanor, no statute of limitations, no appeals, no boundaries of relevance, and no finality. In short, anything goes; and everything frequently does—and often on television." [67]

Trying to summarize in some detail the unconstitutional actions, anti-democratic practices and other evils perpetrated or brought about by Congressional committees, I find that they can be conveniently outlined under twenty-five points:

1. These Congressional committees violate the First Amendment, particularly its provisions on freedom of speech and freedom of the press, by inquiring into ideas, beliefs and associations.

2. They violate the Fourth Amendment by attempting to carry through "unreasonable searches and seizures."

3. They violate the most important provision of the Fifth Amendment by denying "due process of law" to the witnesses whom they summon.

4. They violate the intent of the Fifth Amendment provision against self-incrimination by attributing guilt to those who invoke it and by bringing about their punishment.

5. They violate the spirit of the Sixth Amendment by not permitting witnesses to cross-examine their accusers and to have witnesses in their own defense.

6. They violate the Tenth Amendment, which limits the power of the Federal authorities, by interfering with local self-government.

7. They violate, in effect, that section of the Constitution which forbids Congress to pass bills of attainder.

8. They violate, in effect, the accompanying provision in the Constitution that bans *ex post facto* laws.

9. They disregard the tripartite separation of powers in the Federal system of government by usurping the functions of the Judiciary. Thus they transform themselves into legislative "courts" that hold "trials" of individuals and organizations; and act as district attorneys and grand juries that initiate criminal prosecutions.

10. They attempt to trap witnesses into slips of memory or careless answers that will pave the way for perjury indictments.

11. They violate the separation of powers, again, by invading the prerogatives of the Executive, trespassing upon the functions of various Government Departments responsible to the President of the United States.

12. Their members repeatedly violate their solemn oath to support the American Constitution by trampling it underfoot, especially the Bill of Rights, in the ways I have described.

13. These committees violate the legally binding rules of Congress by asking questions beyond the limited scope of investigations and not pertinent to legislation.

14. They abuse Congressional powers by permitting their chairmen or other members to operate as irresponsible one-man com-

mittees touring the country, summoning witnesses and staging hearings at will.*

15. They continually use, protect and encourage professional informers whose sworn testimony is of dubious honesty and value.

16. They seriously injure the reputations and careers of witnesses and others through public allegations and innuendoes based on unproved and unevaluated charges, and gravely impair the morale of government employees through the same unscrupulous procedures.

17. They repudiate the long-established juridical concept that guilt is always personal and substitute for it the new and unacceptable doctrine of guilt by association.

18. They violate the time-honored legal doctrine that a man is to be considered innocent until he is proved guilty.

19. They employ "third degree" methods in that they attempt to make individuals confess to or renounce unpopular beliefs and associations through threats and the infliction of mental suffering.

20. They arrogate unto themselves the setting up of qualifications for teaching, preaching, writing, acting and other cultural pursuits, employing the standard of ideological conformity instead of professional competency.

21. They waste the money of tax-payers to the tune of millions annually in worse than useless inquiries, piling up pyramids of piffle in an unending flood of reports and forcing individuals and organizations to expend vast sums in self-defense.

22. They divert the attention of Senators and Representatives from their proper business of considering and enacting legislation that will benefit America.

23. They facilitate the rise in influence and power of dishonest demagogues who exploit the investigative functions of Congress to further their own personal political aggrandizement and to increase their own incomes from lecturing and writing opportunities that notoriety brings them.

* The House of Representatives in 1955 eliminated one-man committee hearings. See pp. 79-80.

24. They keep the country in an uproar, constantly expanding the circle of repression, conditioning public opinion to accept greater and greater invasions of freedom and deflecting the attention of the people from the vital national and international problems which confront the United States.

25. Finally, these Congressional committees make American professions of democracy seem a mockery in foreign lands and steadily weaken American influence abroad.

Despite all this havoc wrought by Congressional committees, despite their power and the fears they create, they can be stopped by counter-pressures. The best example of what can be done in this regard by an aroused public opinion is what happened to Representative Velde's proposal in the spring of 1953 for his House Committee on Un-American Activities to launch a nation-wide investigation of Communists in the churches. He claimed that "hardened and well trained Communists have been planted in the clergy. If I find a Communist, whether he be in overalls or in sanctified cloth, I will see that he is investigated." [68]

Throughout the country public reaction to Velde's proposal was overwhelmingly hostile. Individual clergymen, local congregations and large church organizations hit back hard, all taking the position that such an inquiry was totally unnecessary and would cast a serious reflection on American religion. Prominent newspapers and radio commentators also opposed the investigation. In July, J. B. Matthews, head of the McCarthy Committee's staff, tried to come to Velde's rescue by publishing an article in the *American Mercury*, in which he alleged that the Communist Party had been able to enlist "the support of at least 7,000 Protestant clergymen"; and that "the largest single group supporting the Communist apparatus in the United States today is composed of Protestant clergymen." [69]

But this only made matters worse, leading to a great wave of public indignation and to a special statement by President Eisenhower. In reply to three outstanding clergymen—representing the Catholic, Jewish and Protestant faiths—who had telegraphed him protesting the Matthews libel, he said in part: "I want you to know that I fully share the convictions you state. The issues here are clear. Generalized and irresponsible attacks that sweepingly condemn the whole of any group of citizens are alien to America. Such attacks betray contempt for the principles of freedom and decency; and when these attacks, whatever their professed purpose be, condemn such a vast portion of the churches or clergy as to create doubt in the loyalty of all, the damage to our nation is multiplied." [70]

In exactly one hour and six minutes after the White House had released the President's message, Senator McCarthy accepted "very reluctantly" Mr. Matthews's resignation from the Committee's staff.*

After all this Representative Velde cooled off and called only two or three ministers before the Un-American Activities Committee. He also heard melodramatic testimony about "Communist infiltration of religious organizations" from several professional informers, such as Herbert Philbrick, nine years an FBI spy within the Communist Party, and Benjamin Gitlow, a disillusioned ex-Communist who left the Party in 1929. These hearings went on for some six months and the record of them totaled 270 pages.

Yet Mr. Velde had been so shaken by the nation-wide opposition to his investigation of religion that the Committee's 1953 Report stated: "The House Committee on Un-American Activities has conducted no investigation of subversive infiltration of the clergy or religion and no such investigation is contemplated." [71] This was in flat contradiction to the earlier hearings and to the contents of the Report itself, which devoted several pages to the alleged infiltration of religion.

Another step forward, however faltering, that public opinion has forced was the adoption by the House of Representatives in 1955 of a special code for fair investigative procedures.† The

* Cf. p. 39.
† A decidedly more adequate Code of Investigative Procedure was recommended to Congress by the American Bar Association, Aug. 17, 1955.

House resolution, ruling out one-man committee hearings, provides that the minimum quorum shall be at least two committee members; that witnesses shall be supplied with the rules of procedure and may submit brief and pertinent sworn statements for inclusion in the record; that they be permitted to have their own counsel present and to obtain transcripts of their testimony if they pay for them; that testimony taken in executive session shall not be made public without consent of the committee; and that any person, if the committee decides that evidence tends to defame, degrade or incriminate him, may appear voluntarily as a witness and, with committee consent, have other witnesses subpoenaed on his behalf.

The trouble with this code embodying minor procedural reforms is that it does not come to grips in the slightest with the most important investigative evils of all: those of Congressional committees violating the Bill of Rights by inquiring into ideas, beliefs and associations; usurping the powers of the Judiciary and Executive; arrogating to themselves the prerogative of "legislative omnipotence"; and doing through investigation what the Constitution forbids Congress to do through legislation.

There is one other method of bringing about basic reforms in Congressional investigations. That is through combating committee excesses in the courts of the United States, by reliance primarily on the First Amendment and the tripartite separation of powers. This is what I myself was seeking to do when I refused to answer the questions of the McCarthy Committee; and I recommend the same procedure to other witnesses who are called before Congressional committees which trample upon the Bill of Rights. Whatever reforms are finally instituted, they must of course extend impartially to all individuals and organizations, whatever their political orientation or economic viewpoint, that are summoned to Congressional hearings.

Supporting the position of constitutional non-cooperation with the House and Senate inquisitors, we have the historic letter written in 1953 by one of the great minds of this age—the late Albert Einstein. In this document Dr. Einstein, with the example of the Nazis in Germany fresh in his mind, said: "The reactionary politicians have managed to instill suspicion of all intellectual efforts into the public by dangling before their eyes a danger from without. . . . What ought the minority of intellectuals to do against this evil? Frankly, I can see only the revolutionary way of non-cooperation in the sense of Gandhi's. Every intellectual who is called before one of the committees ought to refuse to testify, i.e., he must be prepared for jail and economic ruin, in short, for the sacrifice of his personal welfare in the interest of the cultural welfare of his country."

This refusal to testify, Dr. Einstein went on to say, should not be based on the Fifth Amendment, "but on the assertion that it is shameful for a blameless citizen to submit to such an inquisition and that this kind of inquisition violates the Constitution. If enough people are ready to take this grave step they will be successful. If not, then the intellectuals of this country deserve nothing better than the slavery which is intended for them." [72]

Americans of whatever origin, political party and walk of life can do no better than to heed Albert Einstein's words, conceived in courage and matured in wisdom.

5

SUPPRESSION THROUGH LAW

While prating hypocritically about preserving America's freedom, Congress has legislated us steadily in the direction of fascism. We must remember that Hitler's accession to power in Germany in 1933 was achieved legally. In 1954 the Eisenhower Administration and Congress made an all-time record by pushing through no less than eight anti-subversive laws that violate the Constitution and the Bill of Rights, including one outlawing the Communist Party. The measures in question enacted much of Senator McCarthy's program; they are McCarthyism sweetened by the appearance of legality.

These and earlier Acts have gone a long way towards repealing the Bill of Rights through unconstitutional Congressional fiat. They amount to repressive amendments to the Constitution illegally voted by Congress. I shall now discuss eight of the worst laws of this nature.

The Smith Act passed by Congress in 1940 was the first Federal peacetime sedition law enacted since 1798 and has provided substantial precedent for other suppressive legislation. This statute was smuggled through Congress as a small part of a lengthy bill entitled the Alien Registration Act of 1940; and few Americans realized at the time that a concealed "anti-citizen" section was being written into what was ostensibly an anti-alien measure.

Section 2 of the Smith Act makes it a crime, with penalties running up to $10,000 in fines and ten years in prison, for any person "to knowingly or wilfully advocate, abet, advise or teach the duty, necessity, desirability or propriety of overthrowing or destroying any government in the United States by force or violence"; or "to organize or help to organize any society, group or assembly of persons who teach, advocate or encourage the overthrow or destruction of any government in the United States by force or violence; or to be or become a member of, or affiliate with, any such society, group or persons, knowing the purpose thereof."

Section 3 then states that "it shall be unlawful for any person to attempt to commit, or to conspire to commit, any of the acts prohibited by the provisions of this title." Here the Smith Act brings into play the juridical concept of *conspiracy*, a doctrine easily and often perverted by tyrannical governments to make a crime out of otherwise legal acts performed in concert by two or more individuals.

This law of ill fame is unconstitutional because it violates the First Amendment by penalizing mere advocacy of political ideas. It runs counter to the great American tradition of free speech, which has always held that opinion and advocacy, even of revolution, are permissible in our democracy and that only overt illegal acts or direct incitements to such are punishable.

In 1941 the Administration of Franklin D. Roosevelt, in one of its few actions violative of the Bill of Rights, indicted twenty-nine members of the Socialist Workers Party (Trotskyites) in Minneapolis under Section 3 of the Smith Act on the grounds that they were unlawfully conspiring to advocate violent revolution. The defendants were found guilty and carried their appeal up to the United States Supreme Court, which inexplicably refused to review the case. In January 1944 the convicted Trotskyites all went to prison for terms up to sixteen months. The American Communist Party made one of its biggest mistakes when it supported this prosecution of its bitter enemies under a bad law which was later to be used against the Communists themselves.

For in the summer of 1948 the Truman Administration, as a political move to prepare for the fall elections and offset Repub-

lican accusations of "softness towards communism," indicted
twelve top leaders of the Communist Party under the Smith Act.
The indictment charged that they had violated Section 3 by "conspiring" to put into effect the ideological and organizational
"crimes" forbidden by Section 2.

The trial of William Z. Foster, Chairman of the Party, was
severed from that of the others because of his serious heart condition.* The eleven remaining defendants went to trial in March
1949, at the Federal Court House in New York City, with Judge
Harold R. Medina presiding. They were found guilty after a prolonged and turbulent trial. Judge Medina sentenced ten of them
to five years in jail and one of them to three. All of the defendants
also received heavy fines. The case was finally appealed to the
United States Supreme Court, which in June 1951 affirmed the
verdict of guilty, 6-2.

Justices Hugo L. Black and William O. Douglas both wrote
forceful dissents in the Smith Act case. I can do no better in
clarifying the main issues at stake than to quote extensively from
Justice Black's opinion. He stated in part:

"At the outset I want to emphasize what the crime involved in
this case is, and what it is not. These petitioners were not charged
with an attempt to overthrow the Government. They were not
charged with overt acts of any kind designed to overthrow the
Government. They were not even charged with saying anything
or writing anything designed to overthrow the Government. The
charge was that they agreed to assemble and to talk and publish
certain ideas at a later date: The indictment is that they con-
spired to organize the Communist Party and to use speech or
newspapers and other publications in the future to teach and
advocate the forcible overthrow of the Government. No matter
how it is worded, this is a virulent form of prior censorship of
speech and press, which I believe the First Amendment forbids.
I would hold Section 3 of the Smith Act authorizing this prior restraint unconstitutional on its face and as applied. . . .

* On account of his continuing illness Mr. Foster has still not been
brought to trial.

"So long as this Court exercises the power of judicial review of legislation, I cannot agree that the First Amendment permits us to sustain laws suppressing freedom of speech and press on the basis of Congress' or our own notions of mere 'reasonableness. Such a doctrine waters down the First Amendment so that it amounts to little more than an admonition to Congress. The Amendment as so construed is not likely to protect any but those 'safe' or orthodox views which rarely need protection. . . .

"Public opinion being what it now is, few will protest the conviction of these Communist petitioners. There is hope, however, that in calmer times, when present pressures, passions and fears subside, this or some later Court will restore the First Amendment liberties to the high preferred place where they belong in a free society." [73]

Regarding the conspiracy aspects of the trial, Justice Douglas had this to say in his dissent: "Not a single seditious act is charged in the indictment. To make a lawful speech unlawful because two men conceive it is to raise the law of conspiracy to appalling proportions. That course is to make a radical break with the past and to violate one of the cardinal principles of our constitutional scheme." [74]

The majority of the Supreme Court declared the Smith Act constitutional on the basis of an exaggerated and unacceptable extension of the well-known "clear and present danger" rule. As laid down by Justice Oliver Wendell Holmes in 1919 in the Schenck case, "The question in every case is whether the words used are used in such circumstances and are of such a nature as to create a clear and present danger that they will bring about the substantive evils that Congress has a right to prevent. It is a question of proximity and degree." [75]

In 1927 Justice Louis D. Brandeis, in his concurring opinion in the Whitney case, attempted to clarify the matter: "To courageous, self-reliant men, with confidence in the power of free and fearless reasoning applied through the processes of popular government, no danger flowing from speech can be deemed clear and present, unless the incidence of the evil apprehended is so imminent that it may befall before there is opportunity for full discussion." [76] In 1941 in the Bridges case, the Supreme Court further held "that the substantive evil must be extremely serious and the degree of imminence extremely high before utterances can be punished." [77]

Professor Alexander Meiklejohn, in his little book, *Free Speech and Its Relation to Self-Government,* brilliantly argues that despite the great contributions of Justice Holmes to a liberal jurisprudence, his origination of the "clear and present danger" test was a mistake. I think Professor Meiklejohn is right and that in any event the Supreme Court's application of the Holmes doctrine to the Smith Act is wrong. For here in its 1951 decision it transformed the original idea of a clear and imminent danger into that of a clear and probable one at some indefinite future time that might be a hundred years hence.

What the Supreme Court did in this case was to scrap the First Amendment to the Constitution as a poor security risk which it is too hazardous for America to retain during a period of crisis. Thus the Court shelved as out of date the basic principle established in 1866 by an earlier Supreme Court in the famous Milligan case: "The Constitution of the United States is a law for rulers and people, equally in war and in peace, and covers with the shield of its protection all classes of men, at all times, and under all circumstances. No doctrine involving more pernicious consequences was ever invented by the wit of man than that any of its provisions can be suspended during any of the great exigencies of government." [78]

The Smith Act decision has in effect outlawed the teaching or advocacy by any group or organization of the very doctrine embodied in our Declaration of Independence. This revered document states that when the American people have suffered under some system of government a long train of abuses, usurpations and other evils, "it is their right, it is their duty, to throw off such government, and to provide new guards for their future security." We surrender this nation's birthright and denigrate its origin when we deny to citizens, however misguided, the liberty to say that violent revolution is justified.

No doubt all but a handful of Americans would agree with me that there exists in the United States the necessary political machinery for peaceful and democratic change in either a radical or conservative direction. But we could be wrong; and as democrats we cannot legitimately outlaw either legally or morally those who challenge our position on this issue. In the field of politics there are no impregnable absolutes. As professional or amateur observers of the political scene, we surely would not wish to claim that America has attained such a high state of democratic development that from now till the end of time no advocacy of revolution, or an actual revolution, could be warranted.

To quote Justice Jackson once more: "We cannot ignore the fact that our own government originated in revolution and is legitimate only if overthrow by force may sometimes be justified. That circumstances sometimes justify it is not Communist doctrine but an old American belief." [79]

Implicit in the method of science and democracy is the rejection of a dogmatic attitude and the encouragement of constant questioning—questioning even of the most basic assumptions. Hence persons and groups in a truly democratic community have the legal and moral right to argue, if they so choose, that the nation should substitute for intelligence the dictates of some revealed, authoritarian religion or for democracy some form of authoritarian, political dictatorship. They have a right to attempt to win over, if they can, a majority of the electorate to one or the other of these anti-democratic theses. As Justice Holmes put it in his dissenting opinion in the Gitlow case in 1925: "If, in the long run, the beliefs expressed in proletarian dictatorship are destined to be accepted by the dominant forces of the community, the only meaning of free speech is that they should be given their chance and have their way." [80]

So far as violent revolution is concerned, we can state that there is a "clear and present danger" of it only when a conspiracy is under way and actual preparations are being made for carrying it into effect. But in such circumstances the United States Government can move at once on the basis of Section 6 of the Criminal Code which forbids conspiracies to overthrow the government and conspiracies to resist or obstruct the execution of *any* Federal law. The Communist leaders have been prosecuted, however, not for a conspiracy to commit a crime of conduct, but for an alleged conspiracy to commit an alleged crime of *opinion*.

This is seen all the more clearly when we realize that the Government prosecution relied primarily on the defendants' belief in and discussion of the principles enunciated in the following four books: *Foundations of Leninism,* by Joseph Stalin; *The Communist Manifesto,* by Karl Marx and Frederick Engels; *History of the Communist Party of the Soviet Union (B);* and *State and Revolution,* by Vladimir I. Lenin. It may be said that any American found reading or discussing these volumes stands in danger under the Smith Act.

In its Smith Act decision the Supreme Court, in the majority opinion delivered by the late Chief Justice Vinson, admitted that it was sanctioning an invasion of free speech in order to avoid the peril envisaged. Justice Felix Frankfurter in his concurring remarks asserted: "The Smith Act and this conviction under it no doubt restrict the exercise of free speech and assembly. . . . Suppressing advocates of overthrow inevitably will also silence critics who do not advocate overthrow but fear that their criticism may be so construed. . . . It is a sobering fact that in sustaining the convictions before us we can hardly escape restriction on the interchange of ideas." [81]

Actually, in my opinion, there is no conclusive evidence that the indicted Communist leaders did plan to advocate the forceful overthrow of the American Government. In 1943 the Supreme Court itself took the position that one reasonable interpretation of Communist doctrine was that the Party was not plotting violent revolution. This was in the Schneiderman case argued on appeal by the late Wendell Willkie. Referring to the basic Communist documents, the Court stated: "A tenable conclusion from the foregoing is that the Party in 1927 desired to achieve its purpose by peaceful and democratic means, and as a theoretical matter justified the use of force and violence only as a method of preventing an attempted forcible counter-overthrow once the Party had obtained control in a peaceful manner, or as a method of last resort to enforce the majority will if at some indefinite future time, because of peculiar circumstances, constitutional or peaceful channels were no longer open." [82]

The Constitution of the Communist Party of the United States does not support the thesis that this organization is plotting violence of any kind. In fact, the Constitution in effect in 1948, when the first group of Communist leaders were indicted and as later amended, backs democratic majority rule in America and provides that any member of the Party who advocates force, violence or terrorism shall be immediately expelled. The U.S. Government's theory that this is "Aesopian" language concealing the real purposes of the Communist Party I find distinctly far-fetched.

The American Communists, as the Schneiderman decision indicates, do hold that a ruling class, when its accustomed prerogatives are gravely threatened by the vote of the majority, is likely to initiate violence to thwart the democratic process or overthrow the democratic state. The Communists assert that if this happens, then they and the rest of the people are justified in resorting to counter-violence in order to protect their interests. This Communist *prediction* of probable ruling-class violence and suggestion of appropriate defense measures to offset it are often misinterpreted as a reckless call to revolution at the earliest possible date.

In any case Communist tactics vary according to the different conditions prevailing in different countries. As Karl Marx himself declared in a speech at Amsterdam in 1872: "We know that special regard must be paid to the institutions, customs and traditions of various lands; and we do not deny that there are certain countries, such as the United States and England, in which the workers may hope to secure their ends by peaceful means." [83]

The American people can no more afford to accept as final the ruling of the Supreme Court on the Smith Act than they accepted as final the Court's Dred Scott decision of 1857 broadening the scope of slavery in the United States. What the noted historian Burton J. Hendrick said about that decision in his book, *Bulwark of the Republic: A Biography of the Constitution,* is suprisingly relevant to the current Communist case: "The main incentive actuating the judges' minds was political. It is a startling conclusion, but it rests upon definite evidence. The majority judges clearly abandoned, for the moment, the unbiased interpretation of the Constitution and sought to step into a new arena and solve the great political question of the time." [84]

Americans would also do well to keep firmly in mind the warning given by Professor Zechariah Chafee, Jr., in his classic, *Free Speech in the United States:* "The truth is that the precise language of a sedition law is like the inscription on a sword. What matters is the existence of the weapon. Once the sword is placed in the hands of the people in power, then, whatever it says, they will be able to reach and slash at almost any unpopular person who is speaking or writing anything that they consider objectionable criticism of their policies." [85]

After the U.S. Supreme Court decision had given the go-ahead signal, the U.S. Department of Justice, from 1951 through 1955, indicted and arrested on conspiracy charges 119 more Communist officials, of whom eighty-six have been tried and convicted and three acquitted. The Supreme Court refused to hear the appeals of six defendants convicted in Baltimore and of thirteen second-string Communist leaders convicted in New York City; but in 1955 it consented to review the convictions of fourteen Communists found guilty in Los Angeles. Mr. A. L. Wirin, skilled Counsel for the Southern California Branch of the ACLU, will argue the constitutional issues in this case before the Court.

In New York City Federal Judge Edward J. Dimock granted a new trial to two Communists, George Blake Charney and Alexander Trachtenberg, after the professional informer, Harvey Matusow, had confessed in a sworn affidavit and in his book,

False Witness, that he had testified falsely against these men at their original trial.

In 1954 the Department of Justice, which in previous prosecutions of Communists had chosen to press the anti-conspiracy provision of the Smith Act, started to use the clause (Section 2) in this statute making mere membership in certain organizations a crime. Thus it has indicted four Communists on the charge that as members of the Communist Party they knowingly belonged to an organization advocating the overthrow of the U.S. Government by force and violence, and that they themselves intended to bring about such overthrow.

The first Communists to be tried under this new type of indictment were Claude M. Lightfoot, executive secretary of the Illinois Communist Party, and Junius I. Scales, Chairman of the Party in North and South Carolina. They were both found guilty in 1955 and received stiff sentences. The weakest link in the Government's claim that membership in the Communist Party is in itself criminal is that the Internal Security Act specifically states that "neither the holding of office nor membership in any Communist organization by any person" shall constitute *per se* a violation of the Act "or of any other criminal statute." If the U.S. Supreme Court upholds the Lightfoot and Scales convictions, the way will be open for the Department of Justice to proceed in the same manner against thousands of rank-and-file Communists throughout the country.

In 1948 when the Department of Justice brought to trial the eleven first-string Communists, it indicted them under both the conspiracy and membership provisions of the Smith Act. The defendants, however, obtained a severance of these indictments, and the Government prosecutors never pressed the one based on membership in the Communist Party. But when five of these originally convicted Communists came out of jail in March of 1955, the Department of Justice immediately had them re-arrested under the old membership clause indictment. It is difficult to see how this new prosecution can succeed in the face of the Fifth Amendment guarantee against any person being "twice put in jeopardy" for the same offense.

The Internal Security Act of 1950 (McCarran Act) is an extension of the earlier Mundt-Nixon bill and was passed during the height of the tension over the Korean War. On account of its wider scope, it is an even graver menace to civil liberties than the Smith law and is surely one of the worst pieces of legislation affecting the Bill of Rights ever enacted in America.

The stated aim of this Act is: "To protect the United States against certain un-American and subversive activities by requiring registration of Communist organizations, and for other purposes." The major portion of the measure is concerned with "Subversive Activities Control" and the duties of the "Subversive Activities Control Board." The very existence of a Federal agency called the Subversive Activities Control Board (SACB) shows how far the United States has departed from the original civil liberties principles of its founders.

Congress voted the Internal Security Act over the veto of President Truman, who condemned it as "an omnibus bill" that "would put the Government of the United States in the thought-control business"; and "would give Government officials vast powers to harass all of our citizens in the exercise of their right of free speech." Mr. Truman denied that the bill would fulfill its aim of hurting the Communists; instead, he said, it "would strike blows at our own liberties and at our position in the forefront of those working for liberty in the world. . . . It would help the Communist propagandists throughout the world who are trying to undermine freedom by discrediting as hypocrisy the efforts of the United States on behalf of freedom."

The Internal Security Act sets up a Subversive Activities Control Board composed of five members to be appointed by the President of the United States, with the advice and consent of the Senate. The main function of this Board is to decide what organizations are "Communist-action" or "Communist-front" groups under the definitions laid down by the Act. When an organization is adjudged by the Control Board to come within one of these categories, it must register with the U.S. Attorney General, file with him the names of its officers and annually send him its complete financial reports, including lists of all contributors. It is a crime for any member of such an organization to apply for or receive a United States passport. Communist-action organizations, such as the Communist Party, must hand over to the Attorney General the names of all members.

Both Communist-action and Communist-front groups must stamp all publications that they send through the mails, together with their envelopes or wrappers: "Disseminated by _____ a Communist organization," with the name of the organization appearing in lieu of the blank. If any such group puts on a radio or television broadcast, it must be announced at the beginning: "The following program is sponsored by _____ a Communist organization," with the name of the organization being stated in place of the blank. These requirements manifestly contradict a unanimous U.S. Supreme Court ruling, of almost twenty years standing, that any constitutional restriction on freedom of opinion must be based on *what* is said, not on who says it.

One of the main criteria for determining whether a group is a Communist-front organization is "the extent to which the positions taken or advanced by it from time to time on matters of policy do not deviate from those of any Communist-action organization, Communist foreign government or the world Communist movement." [86]

President Truman's comment on this section of the Act was: "This provision could easily be used to classify as a Communist-front organization any organization which is advocating a single policy or objective which is also being urged by the Communist Party. In fact this may be the intended result, since the bill defines 'organization' to include 'a group of persons permanently or temporarily associated together for joint action on any subject or subjects.' Thus, an organization which advocates low-cost housing for sincere humanitarian reasons might be classified as a Communist-front organization because the Communists regularly exploit slum conditions as one of their fifth-column techniques. . . . The bill would open a Pandora's box of opportunities for official condemnation of organizations and individuals for perfectly honest opinions which happen to be stated also by Communists."

Mr. Truman showed how these various provisions would violate the First Amendment by abridging and discouraging freedom of speech when he pointed out: "Obviously, if this law were on the statute books, the part of prudence would be to avoid saying anything that might be construed by someone as not deviating sufficiently from the Communist propaganda line. And since no one could be sure in advance what views were safe to express, the inevitable tendency would be to express no views on controversial subjects."

Senator McCarthy utilized the same assumptions that are embodied in the Internal Security Act when he attacked the Watkins Senate Committee which had called for his censure. This, he declared, revealed the Committee's Communist aims. "The real strength of the Communist Party," the Senator said, "is measured by the extent to which Communist objectives have been embraced by loyal Americans. . . . I would have the American people recognize, and contemplate in dread, the fact that the Communist Party—a relatively small group of deadly conspirators—has now extended its tentacles to that most respected of American bodies, the United States Senate; that it has made a committee of the Senate its unwitting handmaiden." [87]

It is perfectly clear that neither the Communist Party nor any so-called Communist-front organization will choose to remain in existence if the Subversive Activities Control Board decides that it comes under the provisions of the Internal Security Act and if the courts uphold such a decision. No self-respecting body of any sort could in conscience cooperate with the United States Government in subverting the Bill of Rights by agreeing to categorize all materials mailed by it as "disseminated by a Communist organization." Nor would any group be safe in continuing to function when once officially classified as a Communist-action or Communist-front organization.

In fact, Section 4(a) of the Internal Security Act itself constitutes a grave threat to all individuals and organizations in America reputed to be or admitting that they are in some sense Communist. It reads as follows: "It shall be unlawful for any person knowingly to combine, conspire, or agree with any other person to perform any act *which would substantially contribute to the establishment within the United States of a totalitarian dictatorship* as defined in paragraph (15) of section 3 of this title, the direction and control of which is to be vested in, or exercised by or under the domination or control of, any foreign government, foreign organization, or foreign individual: Provided, however, That this subsection shall not apply to the proposal of a constitutional amendment." [Italics mine—C.L.] Anyone who violates this provision is subject to a fine of not more than $10,000, or imprisonment for not more than ten years, or both.

Here is another broad conspiracy statute of the sort so liable to abuse by governmental authorities. And the vagueness of the clause which I have italicized makes the whole provision particularly dangerous to individuals working on behalf of economic, social or political reform.

One of the worst features of the Internal Security Act is that which makes provision for "emergency detention," that is, concentration camps, in case of the invasion of U.S. territory, a declaration of war by Congress or an insurrection in aid of a foreign enemy. In such an event the President is authorized to proclaim an "Internal Security Emergency." Whenever such an emergency is declared, the Attorney General is authorized immediately to arrest and detain "each person as to whom there is reasonable ground to believe that such person probably will engage in, or probably will conspire with others to engage in, acts of espionage or of sabotage." [88]

The use of the word *probably* in the provision just quoted demonstrates how loosely this part of the Act could be used. The section as a whole means that tens of thousands of Americans may be thrown into detention camps merely on suspicion. They would be imprisoned first and only later have an opportunity to prove their innocence. Such a statute is unprecedented in American law. It follows the lead of Congressional investigating committees in nullifying the doctrine that a man is innocent until proved guilty and assumes that he is guilty until proved innocent.

A large part of the Internal Security Act is concerned with setting up new, unjust and arbitrary standards for controlling immigration to the United States and the treatment of aliens within this country. In opposing the deportation provisions, President Truman exposed the anti-democratic spirit of this portion of the Act: "Section 22 is so contrary to our national interests that it would actually put the Government into the business of thought control by requiring the deportation of any alien who distributes or publishes, or who is affiliated with an organization which distributes or publishes, any written matter advocating (or merely expressing belief in) the economic and governmental doctrines of any form of totalitarianism. This provision does not require an evil intent or purpose on the part of the alien."

I shall not pursue further the Internal Security Act's provisions regarding immigrants and aliens, since the McCarran-Walter Immigration Act of 1952 codified most of these enactments, and I shall discuss them under that heading.*

Although the Internal Security Act concentrates on how to identify "subversive" individuals, organizations and activities, it nowhere even attempts to define this vague catch-all word "subversive." In a speech made in April 1940 to the Annual Conference of United States Attorneys, Justice Jackson, then U.S. Attorney General, cautioned his listeners about the prosecution of "cases which deal with so-called 'subversive activities.' They are dangerous to civil liberty because the prosecutor has no definite standards to determine what constitutes a 'subversive activity,' such as we have for murder or larceny.

"Activities which seem benevolent and helpful to wage-earners, persons on relief, or those who are disadvantaged in the struggle for existence may be regarded as 'subversive' by those whose property interests might be burdened or affected thereby. Those who are in office are apt to regard as 'subversive' the activities of

* See pp. 110-118.

any of those who would bring about a change of administration. Some of our soundest constitutional doctrines were once punished as subversive. We must not forget that it was not so long ago that both the term 'Republican' and the term 'Democrat' were epithets with sinister meaning to denote persons of radical tendencies that were 'subversive' of the order of things then dominant."

More recently Judge Learned Hand has criticized the increasingly common resort to the term "subversive" and "other question-begging words. Their imprecision comforts us by enabling us to suppress arguments that disturb our complacency and yet to continue to congratulate ourselves on keeping the faith as we have received it from the Founding Fathers. . . . The precipitate of our experience is far from absolute verity, and our exasperated resentment at all dissent is a sure index of our doubts. Take, for instance, our constant recourse to the word, 'subversive,' as a touchstone of impermissible deviation from accepted canons. All discussion, all debate, all dissidence, tends to question and in consequence to upset existing convictions: that is precisely its purpose and its justification. He is, indeed, a 'subversive" who disputes those precepts and seeks to persuade me to substitute his own." [89]

In 1952 the new Subversive Activities Control Board started hearings, on the petition of the U.S. Attorney General, to determine whether the American Communist Party is a Communist-action organization as defined by the Internal Security Act and must therefore register under the Act. In April 1953 the Board gave an affirmative answer to this question and the Communist Party took the decision on appeal to the courts. In December 1954 the Federal Appeals Court in Washington, D.C. upheld the SACB 2 to 1 and declared the relevant provisions of the Act constitutional.

Judge E. Barrett Prettyman delivered the majority opinion and frankly stated: "We assume, without deciding, that *this statute will interfere with freedoms of speech and assembly.* . . . The problem is whether the restrictions imposed are valid in this situation. . . . The right to free expression ceases at the point where

it leads to harm to the Government." [90] [Italics mine—C.L.]
Judge Prettyman's new criterion—"harm to the Government"—
of what justifies violation of the Bill of Rights opens the door
wide for repression. A Republican administration, for instance,
might well decide that certain vigorous Democratic criticisms
were doing "harm to the Government."

The Communist Party appealed this decision to the U.S. Supreme Court and asserted in its brief, prepared by attorneys John
J. Abt and Joseph Forer, that the Internal Security Act is, in the
name of anti-communism, "an enabling act for a totalitarian
state." The Court heard argument on the case in November 1955
and accepted for consideration a friends-of-the-court brief signed
by 360 prominent Americans and urging that the Act be pronounced unconstitutional.

In 1953 Attorney General Brownell had petitioned the SACB
to require twelve organizations to register as "Communist fronts."
These were the American Committee for the Protection of the
Foreign Born, the Civil Rights Congress, the Jefferson School of
Social Science, the Labor Youth League, the National Council of
American-Soviet Friendship, Veterans of the Abraham Lincoln
Brigade, the American Slav Congress,* the Committee for a
Democratic Far Eastern Policy,* the United May Day Com-
mittee,* the Council on African Affairs,† the International Work-
ers Order † and the Joint Anti-Fascist Refugee Committee.† In
1955 the Attorney General asked the SACB to order the American
Peace Crusade, the California Labor School and the [State of]
Washington Pension Union to register as Communist-front organ-
izations.

The National Council of American-Soviet Friendship, of which
I had once been Chairman, went on trial before the SACB in May
of 1954. The hearings, concluded in October of the same year,
were typical of the strange and prejudiced procedures pursued

* This organization was no longer in existence when the Attorney
General filed his petition, and its case was dropped.

† This organization went out of existence after the Attorney General
filed his petition, and its case was dropped.

by the U.S. Government and its creature, the Subversive Activities Control Board. The Government put little emphasis on the National Council's actual program and indeed made repeated efforts to keep it out of the record. The Council wished, for instance, to have its publications entered into the record, but the Government objected that they were irrelevant. The presiding official, a venerable Republican obscurity, upheld practically all of the Government's objections to questions and over-ruled virtually all of the Council's.

In questioning witnesses the Government put its main emphasis on the alleged subversive opinions and associations of Council officers and ex-officers, depending on a large array—sixteen in number—of professional informers. These included Louis Budenz, the acknowledged chief of the racket, and Harvey Matusow, who later confessed that his testimony about the Council "was distorted to make it appear as though the defendants were guilty as charged." [91]

The Council witnesses included Dr. John Kingsbury, Chairman of the organization; the Reverend William Howard Melish, a former chairman; Professor Robert Morss Lovett, Emeritus, of the University of Chicago; Professor Arthur Upham Pope, former Chancellor of the Asia Institute, and Professor Ralph Barton Perry, Emeritus, of Harvard University. These witnesses testified to their conviction that the Council's activities on behalf of world peace and American-Soviet cooperation were in the best interests of the United States; that neither the Communist Party nor any outside group directed or dominated the work of the Council; and that policy and program were shaped and executed democratically by the decisions of the Board of Directors.

The Government's answer was mainly to charge, through Budenz, that most of the Council's witnesses, including Professors Lovett, Perry and Pope, had been members of the Communist Party and had belonged in addition to "front" organizations on the Attorney General's blacklist. The Department of Justice lawyers introduced scores of Communist publications to show "parallelism" between the policies of the National Council and the American Communist Party. A number of these policies had been supported by prominent conservatives and some by the United States Government itself.

The Government attorneys at one point tried to read a sinister Communist implication into an airplane trip which Professor Pope made to Soviet Russia shortly after World War II. The Council's lawyer, David Rein, then brought out through his questions that the plane for the flight had been provided by the U.S. War Department on the orders of President Truman. "Who else was on that plane?" asked Mr. Rein. But Dr. Pope was not permitted to answer, because a Government attorney objected to the question and Mr. Coddaire, the hearing master, sustained the objection. Hence Dr. Pope was not able to get into the record the fact that sixteen leading American scientists were also on the plane and that the purpose of the trip was to attend the 220th Anniversary of the Russian Academy of Sciences at Moscow.

In a similar crude attempt to weaken the Council's case Mr. Coddaire ordered stricken from the record Dr. Melish's testimony that he believed his work for the organization was in the best interests of the United States. The hearing master gave the Government attorney complete freedom to go into Dr. Melish's associations, speeches and personal opinions, although counsel for the defense objected to the irrelevance of many of the questions.

After he had left the witness stand at the close of his nine days of testimony Dr. Melish stated: "This has been an extraordinary experience. Activities that were carried on publicly and on the highest level, involving two presidents, a commander-in-chief, top departments of Government and some of the outstanding personalities of the nation, are now being treated as a kind of common criminal conspiracy at the police court level. . . . The arraignment of our Council is a political act. The Government appears determined to put out of business an organization of citizens who criticized foreign policy, petitioned for the change of such policy and appealed to public opinion. At stake is the right of the American people to scrutinize, criticize and, if need be, to change foreign policy." [92]

The Internal Security Act, with all of its workings, stands as a monumental example of the sort of vicious legislation which a Know-Nothing Congress has been voting into effect during the past decade. And since passing this measure in 1950, Congress has made it a great deal worse by adding as amendments certain sections of the Communist Control Act and the Welker Act for the registration of printing equipment.

The Communist Control (Brownell-Butler) Act of 1954 outlaws the Communist Party and is the worst of the measures passed by the 83rd Congress (1953-54). It deprives the Communist Party of "any of the rights, privileges and immunities attendant upon legal bodies," thus making it impossible for the Party to collect dues, have bank accounts, sue in the courts or run candidates for public office. The Act also makes it a crime, with possible penalties of five years in jail and a $10,000 fine, for any person to become or remain a member of the Communist Party.

The most novel feature of the Act is that which sets up the new classification of the "Communist-infiltrated organization," which is defined as a group the effective management of which is conducted by one or more individuals who are agents of the Communist movement or who are engaged in giving aid or support to it. All trade unions or employers found to be Communist-infiltrated will lose their rights under the National Labor Relations Act and so will be fatally crippled in their functioning. Of course it is the trade unions which will feel the chief impact of this provision. And, sure enough, in July 1955 Attorney General Brownell started a proceeding, the first under the Act, to have the International Union of Mine, Mill and Smelter Workers officially pronounced a Communist-infiltrated organization.

It is clear that the Communist Control Act is unconstitutional because it violates that section of the Constitution which forbids Congress to pass bills of attainder, that is, to enact legislation which inflicts punishment without regular judicial proceedings in the form of an indictment and trial. To achieve its purposes, this measure drastically amends the Internal Security Act and utilizes much of the machinery already set up under it. For example, it is the Subversive Activities Control Board established under the latter Act which is to determine whether or not an organization is Communist-infiltrated.

Many of the criteria for determinations written into the Communist Control Act are so vague as to threaten all liberals and dissenters, and are of most questionable constitutionality. Thus one of the criteria for judging a Communist-infiltrated organization is "To what extent, if any, the personnel and resources of such organization are, or within three years have been, used to further or promote the objectives of any such Communist organization, government or movement." Under such a loose definition, almost any trade union is liable to get into trouble.

Equally dangerous is the long list of criteria for judging "membership or participation in the Communist Party." In this connection the Act reads that "the jury, under instructions from the court, shall consider evidence, if presented, as to whether the accused person:

"(1) has been listed to his knowledge as a member in any book or any of the lists, records, correspondence, or any other document of the organization;

"(2) has made financial contribution to the organization in dues, assessments, loans, or in any other form;

"(3) has made himself subject to the discipline of the organization in any form whatsoever;

"(4) has executed orders, plans, or directives of any kind of the organization;

"(5) has acted as an agent, courier, messenger, correspondent, organizer, or in any other capacity in behalf of the organization;

"(6) has conferred with officers or other members of the organization in behalf of any plan or enterprise of the organization;

"(7) has been accepted to his knowledge as an officer or member of the organization or as one to be called upon for services by other officers or members of the organization;

"(8) has written, spoken, or in any other way communicated

by signal, semaphore, sign, or in any other form of communication, orders, directives or plans of the organization;

"(9) has prepared documents, pamphlets, leaflets, books, or any other type of publication in behalf of the objectives and purposes of the organization;

"(10) has mailed, shipped, circulated, distributed, delivered, or in any other way sent or delivered to others material or propaganda of any kind in behalf of the organization;

"(11) has advised, counseled, or in any other way imparted information, suggestions, recommendations to officers or members of the organization or to anyone else in behalf of the objectives of the organization;

"(12) has indicated by word, action, conduct, writing, or in any other way a willingness to carry out in any manner and to any degree the plans, designs, objectives, or purposes of the organization;

"(13) has in any other way participated in the activities, planning, actions, objectives, or purposes of the organization.

"(14) The enumeration of the above subjects of evidence on membership or participation in the Communist Party or any other organization as above defined, shall not limit the inquiry into and consideration of any other subject of evidence on membership and participation as herein stated." [93]

The Communist Control Act was passed in August 1954 during the last hectic days of the 83rd Congress. So many amendments had been tacked onto the bill that at the end, neither Senators nor Representatives knew precisely what they were voting for. There was not even a copy of the final measure available. In fact, after the Act had been passed by both Houses "the various bits of language were pieced together by a Senate clerk. He then sent the material to the Government Printing Office for the required engrossed copy to be made." [94]

To quote *The New York Times,* the Act "was promoted as a political coup by so-called Democratic 'liberals'" in the Senate. These Democratic Senators wished to pose, in an election year, as more anti-Communist than the Republicans, particularly because

McCarthy had been accusing the Democratic Party of treason. So, for the paltry purposes of partisan political advantage, there was enacted a bill which the anti-Communist *New York Post* describes as "a wretched repudiation of democratic principles" and "an outrageous affront to free society." The Act sets a precedent whereby conceivably the Republican Party might outlaw the Democratic Party because of its "treasonable" activities.

The Immunity Act of 1954 goes far in nullifying the Fifth Amendment which guarantees every American against compulsory self-incrimination. The pretext for this legislation was that so many witnesses before Congressional committees had invoked the Fifth Amendment.

This Immunity Act provides that a Federal judge may grant immunity from prosecution to a witness testifying on matters of national security or defense before a Congressional Committee, a grand jury or a Federal court. If a witness under these circumstances still refuses to answer questions, then he can be sent to jail for contempt. If he lies, he will face perjury charges. There is doubt, however, whether the grant of immunity will protect an individual against prosecution by a State or municipality; and it certainly will not protect him against extra-legal penalties, such as being dismissed from employment or being socially ostracized when it is revealed that he has "subversive" associations or opinions.

The Fifth Amendment has impeded the main inquisitorial committees of Congress because the types of questions they ask are calculated, not to elicit information on behalf of legislation, but instead to pry into the political beliefs, personal conduct and associational activities of the witness. The over-riding reason, then, for the passage of the compulsory testimony Act was to give these committees greater scope for violating the Bill of Rights, for usurping the powers of the Judiciary and for forcing witnesses to become informers on their friends, relatives and co-workers.

The minority report of the House Judiciary Committee firmly opposed the measure and asserted that it would "turn men of conscience into informers." "What legislative lack does the reported bill fill?" the signers of this dissenting statement asked. "It is not the function of Congress to expose private personal guilt. It is not the function of Congress to prepare cases for prosecution. It is not the function of Congress to relieve the Executive branch of the Government of its constitutional responsibility of law enforcement.

"When a committee of the Congress investigates, it does so to gather evidence for its own purposes, that of legislating wisely and adequately. The investigations of Pearl Harbor, Teapot Dome, the work of the Truman Defense Committee and the LaFollette Civil Liberties Committee did not suffer for lack of Congressional power to immunize witnesses. In the areas of treason, sabotage, espionage, sedition, the Communist conspiracy, etc., the Congress has not heretofore hesitated to legislate, though lacking the power of immunization, session after session in its history." [95]

Erwin K. Griswold, Dean of the Harvard Law School, has published a short book, *The Fifth Amendment Today*, which is in effect one continuous argument against the Immunity Act. Filling in some of the historical background, Dean Griswold writes: "I would like to venture the suggestion that the privilege against self-incrimination is one of the great landmarks in man's struggle to make himself civilized. . . . The establishment of the privilege is closely linked historically with the abolition of torture. . . . Where matters of a man's belief or opinions or political views are essential elements in the charge, it may be most difficult to get evidence from sources other than the suspected or accused person himself. Hence, the significance of the privilege over the years has perhaps been greatest in connection with resistance to prosecution for such offences as heresy or political crimes. In these areas the privilege against self-incrimination has been a protection for freedom of thought and a hindrance to any government which might wish to prosecute for thoughts and opinions alone." [96]

In 1955 Chief Justice Earl Warren, on behalf of the U.S. Supreme Court, delivered an opinion which provides cold comfort for the supporters of the Immunity Act: "The privilege against self-incrimination is a right that was hard-earned by our fore-fathers. . . . The privilege, this Court has stated, 'was generally regarded then, as now, as a privilege of great value, a protection to the innocent, though a shelter to the guilty, and a safeguard against heedless, unfounded or tyrannical prosecutions.' Co-equal-ly with our other constitutional guarantees, the Self-Incrimination Clause 'must be accorded liberal construction in favor of the right it was intended to secure.' . . .

"To apply the privilege narrowly or begrudgingly—to treat it as an historical relic, at most merely to be tolerated—is to ignore its development and purpose. . . . It is precisely at such times—when the privilege is under attack by those who wrongly con-ceive it as merely a shield for the guilty—that governmental bodies must be most scrupulous in protecting its exercise." [97]

During 1955 two persons started court tests of the constitu-tionality of the Immunity Act. These were William Ludwig Ull-mann and Edward J. Fitzgerald, both of whom held important Government posts during World War II and both of whom were sentenced to six months in jail when, offered immunity under the compulsory testimony Act, they refused to answer a number of questions before a Federal grand jury. The Ullmann appeal has already gone to the U.S. Supreme Court.

The Welker Act of 1954, passed by Congress as an amendment to the Internal Security Act, requires registration with the Govern-ment "of all printing presses and machines including but not limited to rotary presses, flatbed cylinder presses, platen presses, lithographs, offsets, photo-offsets, mimeograph machines, multi-graph machines, multilith machines, duplicating machines, ditto machines, linotype machines, intertype machines, monotype ma-chines, and all other types of printing presses, typesetting ma-chines or any mechanical devices used or intended to be used, or capable of being used to produce or publish printed matter or material, which are in the possession, custody, ownership, or con-trol of the Communist-action or Communist-front organization or its officers, members, affiliates, associates, group or groups in which the Communist-action or Communist-front organization, its officers or members have an interest."

This unprecedented bill was voted unanimously by a House and Senate that had evidently become terrified of the written word. The clause "have an interest" at the very end of the Act gives it an elastic scope that could conceivably bring under its provisions all important organizations in the country. For Communists might well "have an interest" in such groups.

The Expatriation Act of 1954, first proposed by President Eisenhower in his annual message to Congress of that year, deprives of citizenship any person, even though native-born, who is convicted of knowingly and actively participating in a conspiracy to overthrow the Government by force and violence. An individual so convicted loses the right to run for political office, to serve on a jury or to obtain a passport. This vindictive measure is directed primarily at Communists who, already sent to jail under the Smith Act, are liable to receive this additional punishment for having dangerous thoughts.

Congress voted the Labor-Management Relations (Taft-Hartley) Act in 1947 over President Truman's veto. This measure was sponsored jointly by the late Senator Robert A. Taft, Republican of Ohio, and Representative Fred A. Hartley, Jr., Republican of New Jersey. The law supersedes to a large extent the National Labor Relations (Wagner) Act of 1935 under which the democratic rights of trade unions were guaranteed and membership in them greatly expanded. The Taft-Hartley Act has had such a crippling effect on labor that all trade union organizations, including the conservative American Federation of Labor, have advocated its repeal.

From the civil liberties standpoint, the most dangerous provision in the Taft-Hartley Act is that requiring every union official to sign, as a condition of his union's access to the National Labor Relations Board, an affidavit swearing that "he is not a member

of the Communist Party or affiliated with such Party, and that he
does not believe in, and is not a member of or supports any organization that believes in or teaches, the overthrow of the
United States Government by force or by any illegal or unconstitutional methods." [98] The U.S. Supreme Court has upheld this
stipulation as constitutional.

Yet I must insist that the non-Communist oath sets up a political
criterion for labor leadership and thus interferes with free elections in the trade unions. The phrase "affiliated with" is so vague
that any liberal or progressive trade union leader runs the danger
of perjury charges if he signs the affidavit. And in fact the Department of Justice has pressed perjury indictments against union
officials even after they have resigned from the Communist Party
and then taken the non-Communist oath.

A typical case here is that of Hugh Bryson, former President of
the National Union of Marine Cooks and Stewards, who signed
the non-Communist affidavit in 1951 and was found guilty of
perjury in 1955 * on the grounds that when he signed the non-
Communist affidavit he was still "affiliated" with the Communist
Party. The jury had such trouble with the word "affiliated" that it
asked for a copy of *Webster's Dictionary;* but the presiding judge
refused the request. He told the jurymen that they could render
a verdict of guilty against Bryson if he had associated in meetings
with people who were Communists. The defense attorney pointed
out that this instruction was "a clear violation of the First Amendment, which permits any American to associate with anyone as
long as he is not engaged in committing a crime." [99] The conviction on the vague "affiliation" charge also violated the due process
clause of the Fifth Amendment and the Sixth Amendment requirement that the accused be informed of "the nature and cause of
the accusation."

Another Taft-Hartley provision that impinges on the rights of
trade unions is that which amends the Federal Corrupt Practices
Act of 1925 by making it unlawful for labor organizations, as well
as business corporations, to contribute, either in cash or in the

* Cf. the case of Clinton E. Jencks in Chapter 7.

form of publicity, to the campaigns of candidates for Federal office. Since wealthy businessmen can continue as individuals to support such campaigns financially, it is primarily the workers who are hit by this new clause. For the natural and most efficient way for them to make sizable joint donations to political campaigns is through the unions. The ruling out of assistance to candidates through publicity is patently a violation of freedom of the press.

Shortly after the law was passed, the late Philip Murray, as President of the Congress of Industrial Organizations (CIO), publicized in a union journal his support of a Maryland candidate for the House of Representatives. The Department of Justice promptly prosecuted Mr. Murray under the Taft-Hartley Act. In 1948 the U.S. Supreme Court unanimously reversed the action of the lower courts in convicting Murray and so freed labor unions from the Taft-Hartley ban against publishing their views on Federal political candidates in their own press. The decision, however, left in effect the prohibition against unions appropriating funds directly to Federal political campaigns.

In July 1955 the issue of union sponsorship of Federal candidates via television was raised when a grand jury in Detroit indicted the country's biggest union, the United Automobile Workers, CIO, for using its weekly television shows to endorse certain Democratic candidates for Congress in the 1954 election. The indictment charged the Union with spending a total of $5,985 of its funds in violation of the Corrupt Practices Act. This move against the UAW by the Republican Administration was undoubtedly another example of political reprisal and an attempt to offset the Union's influence in the approaching 1956 election campaign.

From the viewpoint of labor one of the worst features of the Taft-Hartley law is its restoration of the injunction to respectability as a strike-breaking weapon. In cases where a labor dispute involves an inter-state or nation-wide industry, or threatens the national health or safety, the President of the United States may direct the U.S. Attorney General to obtain an injunction from the courts enjoining the threatened strike or lock-out for eighty days. The Act also requires a "cooling off period" of sixty days before any strike for a change in a contract; and it forbids strikes by employees of the U.S. Government and of Government-owned corporations.

The closed shop, which makes union membership a prior condition of employment, is banned by the Taft-Hartley Act in cases where either a worker or an employer complains to the National Labor Relations Board. Actually, however, there have been comparatively few complaints and hence the closed shop is still common. The Act permits the union shop, which makes it obligatory for a worker, *after* he has taken on a new job, to join the union at his place of employment providing that it represents a majority of the employees.

Trade union militants have complained bitterly not only about the Taft-Hartley provisions regarding the closed shop, but also because the law gives the employer the right of free speech and anti-union propaganda as long as "there is no threat of reprisal or promise of benefit." It is perfectly clear that from an impartial civil liberties standpoint both pro-union propaganda on the part of workers and anti-union propaganda on the part of management should be permitted in a factory, plant or other place of employment as long as the literature or spoken word is not associated with coercion. If, for example, management on some occasion inserted in each pay envelope an anti-union leaflet, that would be ruled out as an implied threat.

Senator Patrick McCarran, who was Joseph McCarthy's opposite number in the Democratic Party, bore primary responsibility not only for the Internal Security Act, but also for the McCarran-Walter Immigration and Nationality Act which was passed over President Truman's veto in June 1952.

This Act, which grants ominous powers to State Department consular officials and to the Attorney General and his subordinates, in effect declares open season on aliens and foreign-born Americans. President Truman, in vetoing it, called it "harsh and repressive," "worse than the infamous Alien Act of 1798." Representatives of professional, educational and cultural groups, religious groups, labor organizations, and veterans, have called it "heartless," "vicious," "a club of oppression," a "hodgepodge of racial discrimination . . . [and] of sullen hostility to many of the peoples of the world."

Because of the public protests, and his own opposition to the provisions of the Act, President Truman created a seven-member Commission on Immigration and Naturalization to study and make recommendations for changes in policy. After hearings in eleven cities during October 1952, the Commission issued a report in January 1953. Their conclusions were a scathing indictment of the McCarran-Walter Act: "The immigration and nationality law embodies policies and principles that are unwise and injurious to the nation. . . . It applies discriminations against human beings on account of national origin, race, creed and color. . . . It contains unnecessary and unreasonable restrictions and penalties. . . . It is badly drafted, confusing and in some respects unworkable. It should be reconsidered and revised from beginning to end." [100]

In other words, the Congress, like the mountain, had labored for five years to codify the immigration laws, and had brought forth a morass.

The law itself runs to 120 pages of fine print. What does it do?

First, it hands the Immigration and Naturalization Service of the Justice Department literally police-state powers over 3,000,000 alien residents in the United States and 11,000,000 naturalized American citizens and their families. It empowers the Justice Department to arrest non-citizens without warrant, hold them without bail for indefinite periods of time, conduct hearings without regard for due process; deport aliens for acts committed years ago which may have been legal at the time of commission; and send them to jail for ten years if they fail to try to deport themselves.

If no country will accept the deportees, the immigration service can put them on "supervisory parole." This is a new species of "house arrest," which requires the deportee to report from time to time to the immigration authorities, submit to medical and psychiatric examinations, answer questions about his "habits, associations, and activities," and even about the books, newspapers and magazines he reads. Questions about associations are of course meant to preclude the alien's participating in any labor group or leftist political activity. Parolees who wilfully violate supervisory parole can be punished by a year in jail, or a $1,000 fine. These are the more extreme provisions.

On the workaday side, the law requires every non-citizen in the United States to be registered and fingerprinted, and, if he is over eighteen years of age, to carry his alien registration card with him "at all times." In addition, every alien during January of each year is required to "notify the U.S. Attorney General in writing of his current address." If he moves at any time, he must notify the Attorney General within ten days of his moving. Penalties for failure to do so are six months in jail, or a fine of $1,000.

Deportation proceedings can be brought on flimsy, vague and repressive grounds, including "subversive" political beliefs. This applies, of course, mainly to anarchists and Communists, even though the Communist affiliation may have been terminated years before. Thus, for some of the grounds there is no statute of limitations; and the alien lives under a perpetual sword of Damocles. At any moment the blade may drop, punishing him by deportation for acts which were not so punishable when committed, or at the time when he entered the United States.

To many minds, the grounds for deportation of a non-citizen should be limited to those cases in which the alien obtained entry to this country by wilful and material fraud. In Section 241 of the McCarran-Walter Act, however, grounds for deportation run on for eighteen subsections and several sub-subsections. They include becoming a public charge within five years after entry (whether for physical or mental illness, or for economic distress); being convicted (within five years after entry) of any crime involving moral turpitude or—to strike a fine balance—of *two* crimes of moral turpitude *at any time after entry*. They include being engaged, or having engaged, or having "a purpose to engage" in any of those activities which in the opinion of the Attorney General are "prejudicial to the public interest" or a menace to the welfare, safety, or security of the United States. How a U.S. official determines whether an alien "has a purpose to engage" in something is left to the imagination of the Justice Department.

The law also provides for the deportation of any non-citizen who "is or at any time has been, after entry," a member of, or affiliated with, the Communist Party, or any other organization required to register under the Internal Security Act. In the latter case, if the alien can prove he did not know the subversive character of the organization (that is, if he is willing to acknowledge that he was a "dupe"), he may escape deportation.

If non-citizens live under the constant threat of deportation proceedings, the law also provides new and sinister threats for naturalized American citizens, who can lose their citizenship on several new grounds. Whereas previously the law provided that naturalization could be revoked only if the alien had illegally or fraudulently procured citizenship, the McCarran-Walter Act introduces broad language so that "concealment of a material fact" in the naturalization process is sufficient to open up cancellation proceedings at any time. What constitutes a "material fact" is not defined, but is left to the discretion of the immigration authorities.

Moreover, the law literally creates second-class citizenship for naturalized Americans by decreeing that they shall lose their citizenship if, within ten years of naturalization they refuse to testify before a Congressional committee, or if, within five years, they belong to an organization which the Attorney General says is a Communist front.

As with many other police-state provisions of the McCarran-Walter Act, denaturalization proceedings can be instituted by the Justice Department at any time. There is no statute of limitations.

These deportation and denaturalization provisions harass, intimidate, oppress, and even get rid of the alien once he is here. In addition, the same political restrictions, plus even more sweeping grounds for exclusion, militate against more and more foreigners who wish to come here either permanently or temporarily.

Among the more noxious restrictions to immigration is the national origins quota system, inherited from a 1924 law which went into effect in 1929. Through the "national origins" device, sponsors of the McCarran-Walter Act perpetuate racial discrimination, while professing to have abolished it simply because they established token quotas for Asiatic and African countries which previously had no quotas whatever.

Thus, although nominally no one is excluded because of race, according to the national origins formula, the number of admissible immigrants for a given nationality is based on the proportion contributed by that nationality to the total United States population in 1920. Since the population at that time was predominantly Anglo-Saxon, the continuance of this formula operates to exclude Asiatics, Africans, Indians, and southeast Europeans. As Senator Herbert Lehman said, the national origins system "is based on the same discredited racial theories from which Adolf Hitler developed the infamous Nuremberg laws. This system is based on the hypothesis that persons of Anglo-Saxon birth are superior to other nationalities and therefore better qualified to be admitted into the United States, and to become American citizens." [101]

Under the quota law an annual total of less than 155,000 immigrants may be admitted here. Out of this number, northern and western Europe is given the largest bite, amounting to 80 percent of all quotas. Of these, Great Britain gets the highest number, or 65,361, while Germany is next, with 25,814. Greece, on the other hand, is allowed only 308; and Italy, whose population is greater than that of England, has an annual total of 5,645. This "Nordic-superiority" arrangement effectively excludes "inferior" southern and eastern Europeans.

To deal with similarly "inferior" Asiatics, the law has another gimmick; it establishes (Section 202(b)) a vast Asia-Pacific triangle, the independent countries or territories of which are handed negligible quotas of 100 each. This triangle includes, among other areas, China, India, Burma, Indonesia, Korea and

Japan. A contrast of quota treatment is illuminating. Northwest Europe, which accounts for only 10 percent of the world's population, receives 80 percent of all immigration quotas, while just two countries in the Asia-Pacific triangle, China and India, which together have about 40 percent of the world's inhabitants, are restricted to minimum quotas of 100 each.

In addition to this direct discrimination against persons born inside the Asia-Pacific triangle, the law reaches out further to discriminate against persons born elsewhere, if they are unlucky enough to trace back half their ancestry to the triangle. This means, for example, that a native of England, whose father was English, but whose mother was Indian by ancestry, cannot enter the United States under the liberal British quota of 65,361, but would have to wait for years to come in under the Indian quota of 100.

As Senator Hubert H. Humphrey, Jr. said, "The code of racial prejudice twists like a cowpath." [102] The cowpath takes another turn to deal with Negroes in the Western Hemisphere. Section 202(c) of the law provides that colonial people, who heretofore were chargeable without restriction to the quotas of their mother countries, are now limited to using only 100 of the governing country's quota numbers in a year. This slaps West Indians, whose use of British, French, and Netherlands quotas has now been drastically reduced.

To the xenophobes who have forgotten Franklin Roosevelt's reminder that "We are all descendants of immigrants," and who fear the country may become flooded with immigrants, it can be pointed out that since 1924, 56 percent of the annual quotas has always gone unused. The reason for this, as one authority says, is that "the peoples of northern and western Europe are not keen to leave their own countries and migrate to the United States." [103] While British and Irish quotas go a-begging, Italians, Greeks, Chinese and Indians find the doors closed against them. Yet from 1925 to 1952, a total of nearly two and a half million quota numbers was unused.

While the racial exclusion provisions of the McCarran-Walter

Act operate lethally, but quietly, the results of Section 214 have brought spotlight publicity. This Section operates to keep out temporary visitors by insisting on the same rigid clearances for them as for immigrants seeking to remain here permanently. Students, teachers, artists, writers, scientists, and tourists wanting visas for even the briefest sojourn in the United States are subjected to painful and humiliating cross-examinations by consular officials with virtually autocratic power to admit or exclude them without divulging the reasons. In some instances, travelers whose planes have been grounded at U.S. airports have been treated with the suspicion and hostility usually reserved for criminals, while many distinguished foreigners have never been permitted to arrive. This is in sharp contrast to the treatment accorded American visitors abroad, who are permitted to enter West European countries and roam around at will, without even a visa.

Congressman Walter, who co-sponsored this law, is fond of dismissing attacks on it by a pat and supercilious reply: the critic just "hasn't read the law." He has used this stick to beat everybody from President Eisenhower on down. On one occasion Walter dismissed critics as "professional Jews." Later he retreated to the position that lawyers are the only ones entitled to express opinions about his brainchild. This means, of course, lawyers who are *pro,* and not *contra,* since many distinguished lawyers have expressed wholesale denunciations of this law.

For example, Jacob K. Javits, then a member of the House of Representatives, now Attorney General for the State of New York, told the President's Commission in 1952 that some of the provisions were such as "to make a lawyer blush for this law." He referred to the denaturalization of people who are once naturalized, and to the indefinitely retroactive character of some of the grounds for deportation and denaturalization. He added: "When this point was raised in Congress, the advocates of the law stated on the record that it was a package. Now, I happen to think it was a very bad package." [104]

Jack Wasserman, legislative representative of the Association of Immigration and Nationality Lawyers, told the President's

Commission that the law was "unfair, unwise, unworkable, unjust, unreasonable, un-American, and unconstitutional"; and on behalf of the Association, he recommended its repeal.[105]

The key word in his statement is "repeal." For despite the fact that this statute embodies numerous violations of the Bill of Rights, the remedy for it is apparently not judicial. For over half a century it has been held by the Supreme Court that Congress has unlimited authority to legislate regarding the admission or exclusion of immigrants. It can exclude or deport them according to any criteria whatsoever, including for opinions or beliefs. This power is not restricted by the Bill of Rights. Judicial review of a deportation case is generally limited to deciding whether the procedures laid down by Congress were followed. A review of the merits is not held to be a function of the courts.

Behind all this is the notion that aliens are here on sufferance. The Supreme Court decided substantially this in 1893; and as recently as 1952, reaffirmed that aliens are allowed to enter this country or to remain here purely by the permission and tolerance of Congress, acting as a sovereign body.

Thus, in a deportation proceeding the alien may be arrested without warrant and held indefinitely without bail; and he remains outside the protection of the Fourth, Fifth, and Sixth Amendments. He may be deported and his family broken up, which is surely a "cruel and unusual punishment"; but the Eighth Amendment offers no relief. Deportation is "not punishment," but is a civil proceeding, unrestricted by the Bill of Rights. Several Supreme Court Justices, including most recently Douglas, Black, Rutledge and Murphy, have dissented from this proposition; but the mischief remains, because the prevailing view remains, as Justice Frankfurter has said, that ". . . the place to resist unwise or cruel legislation touching aliens is the Congress, not this Court." [106]

By mid-March 1955 over forty bills had been introduced in Congress for the repeal or revision of the McCarran-Walter Act. Many of these bills correct the discriminatory racist features, and open the gates for full use of the annual quota through a pooling

arrangement. They do away with vaguenesses in language and
establish a statute of limitations. But they do little towards removing the frantic "security" provisions.* To leave these un-
touched is to alleviate the symptoms without curing the disease,
and may even serve to take the spotlight off some of the sinister
aspects of the immigration and naturalization law. These aspects
have been well summarized by Laurent B. Frantz, in an article
in *The Nation:*

"The professed aim of our anti-alien legislation is to rid the
country of 'undesirable' residents. . . . About 60 percent of all
political deportation cases are brought against persons whom the
immigration service must know . . . that it has no substantial
prospects of deporting. It follows, then, that the real motive for
the deportation proceedings is not the ostensible one of ridding
the country of 'undesirables.' It seems rather to be to subject the
non-citizen to the utmost possible harassment *as a lesson to others,
citizens included, to stay away from 'imprudent' activities and
associations.* . . . Plainly the purpose of the new law is intimidation, and its enactment shows clearly that repressive measures
against non-citizens, if not effectively combated, are ultimately
extended to everyone." [107] [Italics mine—C.L.]

In the struggle for freedom it is essential to fight against unconstitutional and repressive laws of the type I have been discussing,
to seek their repeal and to carry cases testing their constitutionality up to the Supreme Court of the United States. Yet when all is
said and done in this sphere of endeavor, we must agree with
Justice Frankfurter when he reminds us that "Civil liberties draw
at best only limited strength from legal guarantees. Preoccupation by our people with the constitutionality, instead of with the
wisdom, of legislation or of executive action, is preoccupation
with a false value. . . . Focusing attention on constitutionality
tends to make constitutionality synonymous with wisdom. When
legislation touches freedom of thought and freedom of speech,

* Even the President's Commission made ultra-conservative recommendations as to security. See *Whom We Shall Welcome*, pp. 265-266.

such a tendency is a formidable enemy of the free spirit. Much that should be rejected as illiberal, because repressive and envenoming, may well be not unconstitutional." [108]

Furthermore, a defendant may carry his case, on the basis of a significant constitutional question, to the U.S. Supreme Court only to win on some rather unimportant technical point. For example, in 1955 that Court decided that Dr. John P. Peters of the Yale Medical School had been illegally dismissed from the Government service because the Loyalty Review Board had exceeded its authority in re-opening his case after he had twice been cleared. Dr. Peters, however, had not even raised this issue in his appeal, but had relied on the claim that at the loyalty hearings he had a constitutional right to confront and cross-examine his accusers. The Supreme Court did not rule on this point.

Explaining the decision, Chief Justice Warren declared: "From a very early date this Court has declined to anticipate a question of constitutional law in advance of the necessity of deciding it." [109] As Justice Frankfurter put it during the argument before the Supreme Court on the Peters appeal, the Court "reaches constitutional issues last, not first."

Yet it seems likely that in the near future the Supreme Court will take another case involving the question of anonymous informers and may give a clearcut decision on that issue. For in the fall of 1955 a Federal Court of Appeals in San Francisco struck at U.S. Coast Guard screening procedures and stated it was a violation of due process to deprive an individual of his livelihood and reputation on the basis of undisclosed evidence impossible for him to refute. The Court severely criticized the Government's "system of secret informers, whisperers and talebearers," and said: "It is not amiss to bear in mind whether or not we must look forward to a day when substantially everyone will have to contemplate the possibility that his neighbors are being encouraged to make reports to the FBI about what he says, what he reads and what meetings he attends." [110] Presumably the Government will appeal this opinion to the Supreme Court.

In any event there can be no doubt that the wheels of justice grind slowly in the United States. A case usually takes at least two years to get to the U.S. Supreme Court, and often four or five. Meanwhile, the individuals or organizations involved must suffer legal harassment, large defense costs and public disrepute. So it is that repressive statutes, illegal Government actions or unconstitutional Congressional inquiries can cause immeasurable harm to civil liberties and the spirit of freedom before the Supreme Court passes upon them.

Various citizens' committees have been set up to bring pressure on Congress for the repeal of some of the evil legislation I have discussed in this chapter. This, too, is a slow process. Perhaps a more hopeful procedure is to persuade the Government simply to put these anti-freedom laws on the shelf and ignore them.

Finally, I must point out, bad laws are the consequence of a sickness in the body politic. The American people have elected the Senators and Representatives responsible for the current rash of lawless legislation. The fundamental cure for such measures lies in a great awakening among the people to the full meaning of liberty. When this occurs, true representatives of democracy will be voted into the seats of legislative power.

6

THE LOYALTY-SECURITY PROGRAM

In 1884 the newly created U.S. Civil Service Commission adopted its first rule governing the hiring of Federal employees. This regulation, which continued in force until 1939, provided that "No question in any form of application or in any examination shall be so framed as to elicit information concerning the political or religious opinions or affiliations of any applicant, nor shall any inquiry be made concerning such opinions or affiliations, and all disclosures thereof shall be discountenanced."

This rule, which did no more than implement the Bill of Rights, held good for more than half a century while America weathered an armed conflict with Spain, the First World War, the most catastrophic depression in the history of the country, the rise of a native Socialist movement far stronger than any before or since, and the birth of international communism.

The rule was changed on August 2, 1939. It was changed not because anyone saw in it a loophole for the nation's enemies, but purely as an act of appeasement of an insignificant but clamorous section of the far Right. The House Committee on Un-American Activities, under the chairmanship of Representative Martin Dies, had been working for little more than a year. The Committee had made headway against the CIO, the WPA and the National Labor Relations Board, and was in fact nibbling at the roots of the New Deal.

Before Congress was the Hatch Act, designed to prevent politi-

cal influence over civil servants by their superiors. To satisfy the
Dies Committee the New Dealers threw in a bone: they incor-
porated into the Act a section having no relevance to the law's
purposes, but providing that no Federal employee shall "have
membership in any political party or organization which advocates the overthrow of our constitutional form of government in
the United States." [111]

Each year or so Congressional liberals tossed more small bones
of appeasement to the witch-hunters, such as a rider to the 1940
Emergency Relief Appropriation Act forbidding payment to anyone who "advocates, or is a member of an organization that advocates, the overthrow of the Government of the United States by
force and violence." In the following year every appropriation act
included that clause.

With each new concession the area affected grew larger and
larger, the limits more and more vaguely defined. Advocacy of
overthrow—even if it were conversational, theoretical or academic
—became the test. Where once Civil Service Rule No. I strictly
forbade the questioning of political opinions, these now became
important qualifications for job-holders. An applicant had to prove
himself not only of sound mind and body but of sound opinions
as well. By and large the definitions of what was sound came
from the Dies Committee lexicon.

In 1941 the FBI was put onto the job of detecting opinions, of
stalking a man's views through his public speeches, his writings,
his conversation, other people's conversation about him, and
finally, conversation which had nothing to do with him but in
which the principals involved might be closely associated with
him. In this same year Congress voted a modest appropriation of
$100,000 to the FBI for such purposes. The FBI used much of
this money to establish dossiers on individuals. Since the criteria
measuring a Federal employee's loyalty were vague, all facts,
hearsay and rumor about him were deemed relevant.

Although the concept of "Communist front" was already current in those days, U.S. Attorney General Francis Biddle in 1941
expressly cautioned all Federal agencies that membership in

"fronts" was not enough to condemn a man. But as the dossiers grew and loyalty testing became more of a preoccupation, the cautions were quickly forgotten so that in time those who preached caution found themselves under suspicion. In 1943 President Franklin D. Roosevelt made one of his major blunders when he directed the Department of Justice to draw up a list of subversive organizations for the confidential guidance of the heads of Government departments. In general, however, the Second World War, in which Soviet Communists were allied with America, slowed the spread of loyalty probing into left-wing and liberal associations.

The death of President Roosevelt and with him the New Deal, the accession of President Truman and with him the Cold War, restored a climate favorable to loyalty probers. Moreover, it offered them a wider choice of targets, for history was being rewritten and no one in the whole New Deal was above suspicion, from the highest officials down.

In the 1946 election campaign the Republicans made much of "subversives-in-government"; and in March of 1947 President Truman, in order to dodge the Republican charge of "Communist coddling," issued an unprecedented Executive Order (No. 9835), the basic principles of which he himself did not believe in. This Order established new loyalty procedures to cover the more than 2,000,000 Federal employees ° and all those seeking employment with the Government; and it set up a Loyalty Review Board to rule on doubtful cases.

Worst of all, the Truman directive stated that one of the main criteria for determining the disloyalty of an individual was: "Membership in, affiliation with or sympathetic association with any foreign or domestic organization, association, movement, group or combination of persons, designated by the Attorney General as totalitarian, fascist, Communist or subversive, or as having

° As of 1955, the U.S. loyalty-security program affected about 10,-000,000 persons: approximately 2,300,000 Government employees, approximately 3,500,000 military personnel and approximately 4,200,000 civilians in jobs relevant to national security.

adopted a policy of advocating or approving the commission of acts of force or violence to deny other persons their rights under the Constitution of the United States, or as seeking to alter the form of the Government of the United States by unconstitutional means."

Although such evidence was supposed to be only one element in the Loyalty Review Board's final decision about any employee, in practice an individual's connection with an organization on the Attorney General's list has almost invariably resulted in his discharge from the Government service. Thus the blacklist has brought into effect on a wide scale the doctrine of guilt by association. Government employees, no matter what their personal merits, have been judged disloyal simply on the grounds that they belonged to one of the proscribed organizations either at the time their cases were under consideration or many years previously. Here again guilt was made retroactive and persons were punished in 1948, for instance, for doing something in 1938 which at that time was entirely legal and consistent with loyalty in the eyes of the U.S. Government.

Professor Henry Steele Commager has ably summed up the situation: "The most pernicious form which the current drive for loyalty assumes is the attack on association and the doctrine of guilt by association. Here, too, can be seen most clearly the all but inevitable progression of the spirit of oppression from suspicion to censorship and from censorship to punishment. Thus the Federal loyalty program originally made membership in 'subversive' organizations merely one factor to be considered in any evaluation of loyalty. New York's Feinberg Law made such membership a *prima facie* cause of dismissal; and Maryland's Ober Law, now widely copied by other States, made such membership a felony punishable by five years imprisonment. . . .

"Though the Federal loyalty program theoretically disqualifies for a great number of reasons, actually association has come to be the major and almost the exclusive reason for arriving at a 'reasonable doubt' about loyalty. . . . It is the effort of Loyalty Boards to arrive at evaluation of loyalty through such intangible things as association with organizations, persons, books and ideas, that gives an Alice-in-Wonderland quality to much of the Federal program." [112]

In 1951 President Truman made the situation measurably worse through a new Executive Order calling for the discharge of a Government employee if there was "reasonable doubt" as to his loyalty. This replaced the previous—and slightly more concrete— standard of "reasonable grounds" for believing an employee disloyal. In 1953 President Eisenhower set up even more drastic standards of loyalty. Under his Administration the Loyalty Review Board gave way to boards within each Government Department or agency; these boards can dismiss an employee without hearing or charges, without confronting the accused with his accuser, without trial or proof. The dismissed individual almost always leaves under a cloud, sometimes tagged as disloyal, sometimes given no explanation at all.

The Eisenhower Administration increasingly injected political considerations into the loyalty-security program. In order to bolster the G.O.P. charge that the Federal Government under Truman was heavily infested by Communists, Republican officials promoted a "numbers game" that would enable them to report the highest possible total of "subversives" separated from Government employment. In an ill-concealed return to the spoils system, such officials also harassed and drove out innocent employees so that they could be replaced by safe, conservative Republicans. The civil service standards developed laboriously over decades were thrown overboard in the name of security.

President Eisenhower's Executive Order of 1953 led to the reopening of the case of Dr. J. Robert Oppenheimer, who had received security clearance in 1947 for serving on the United States Atomic Energy Commission and who had taken a leading part in the creation of the first U.S. atomic bombs. The special three-man Personnel Security Board of the AEC decided in May 1954 that although Dr. Oppenheimer was a loyal American citizen, he was a security risk and therefore ineligible for further work with the AEC. In the Government program a man may be adjudged loyal, yet be dismissed as a security risk because he is considered irresponsible or indiscreet.

In reaching these conclusions about Oppenheimer the Board relied heavily on the theory of guilt by association. It emphasized the fact that Dr. Oppenheimer had had radical friends, that he had belonged to several organizations cited as Communist fronts by the House Committee on Un-American Activities, that he had once subscribed to a left-wing newspaper in California and that his wife had been a member of the Communist Party before he married her. The Security Board also noted in its report that Oppenheimer's brother and sister-in-law had been associated with organizations on the U.S. Attorney General's subversive list. Dr. Albert Einstein's comment on the Oppenheimer case was: "The systematic attempt to destroy mutual trust and confidence constitutes the severest possible blow against society." [113]

Another scandalous case of a scientist harassed beyond all reason was that of Dr. Edward U. Condon, formerly head of the U.S. Bureau of Standards and a former President of the American Association for the Advancement of Science. In December 1954 Dr. Condon resigned as Director of Research and Development at the Corning Glass Works to devote his energies to private scientific research at his home in California. The reason? Dr. Condon was tired of being "cleared." A physicist who had played a major role in the initial development of the atomic bomb, Dr. Condon had been cleared successively by the Manhattan Project, the Atomic Energy Commission, the Department of Commerce and the Eastern Industrial Personnel Security Board.

After Secretary of the Navy Charles Thomas suspended his last clearance in October 1954, Dr. Condon decided that he had had enough of the Government run-around. He explained in his statement of resignation that his long-drawn-out clearance difficulties had begun to affect the efficiency of his work and to impair his health. "I now am unwilling," he said, "to continue a potentially indefinite series of reviews and re-reviews." [114] He also felt that his uncleared status would impair his usefulness to the Corning Company.

The inane workings of the loyalty-security program were again revealed in the case of Wolf I. Ladejinsky, General MacArthur's expert on land reform in Japan, who after being cleared three times, was suddenly dismissed as a security risk by the Department of Agriculture in December 1954. The main points against Mr. Ladejinsky were that he was Russian-born, had two sisters in Soviet Russia whom he had visited there in 1939, and had done considerable anti-Communist writing over the past twenty years. The incredible argument offered by Department of Agriculture officials was that Ladejinsky's anti-Communist writings might be a cover-up for secret Communist sympathies on his part!

In this typical Washington merry-go-round, another Government agency, the Foreign Operations Administration, then cleared Ladejinsky and hired him. And in July 1955 the Department of Agriculture decided that, after all, it had wronged Ladejinsky and canceled the records declaring him a security risk.

Sometimes even a man who is cleared by a U.S. Loyalty Board is barred from a job in the Government because of the publicity resulting from unproved allegations against him. This is what happened to Dr. Philip C. Jessup, Professor of International Law and Diplomacy at Columbia University, whom the Senate Foreign Relations Committee in 1951 refused, 3 to 2, to approve as a member of the United States delegation to the U.N. General Assembly. Two of the Senators voting against Dr. Jessup acknowledged that they were convinced of his ability and loyalty, but that they voted against him because they felt the charges of disloyalty by Senator McCarthy and others had undermined public confidence in him. The reasoning here proceeded on the premise that if an unscrupulous politician stirs up a great clamor by falsely accusing a person, the victim thereby becomes so suspect and controversial as to make him unfit for a Government job.

It was no surprise that in 1953 Scott McLeod, head of the State Department's security system, revealed that he would neither hire a Socialist for a policy-making job nor retain one in such a post. He even boasted to the American Legion that he was getting rid of Socialists. Norman Thomas, veteran Socialist Party leader, protested against McLeod's position and against other Federal discriminations against Socialists.

Yet Mr. Thomas for many years has been one of the most vociferous of those politicians who try to excite the public to white heat over the alleged Communist menace. In spite of his genuine services to civil liberties, he bears much responsibility for the general witch-hunt both within and without the Federal Government; and so has helped to create the atmosphere in which the purge engulfs Socialists and liberals as well as Communists. I repeat that civil liberties are indivisible.

The pretext for the loyalty-security program is that the Communist movement at home and abroad so threatens the national security of the United States that it is better to sacrifice a few of our liberties and democratic traditions than to open a chink of our armor to the enemy. But in fact the Government purges that have taken place since World War II have weakened America. This can be seen best in the field of science insofar as it serves the U.S. Government.

The endless search for subversives has resulted in segregating the various branches of science, in compartmentalizing and isolating each line of research, in setting up repeated roadblocks to communication. The Washington witch-hunters so dread the possibility that a Government-employed scientist may pass on information to some unauthorized person that they "must either extend security clearance to all who may meet a scientist, or, alternatively, must prevent our 'cleared' scientists from having contact with the 'uncleared' world which surrounds them." [115]

The Government has tended to choose the second alternative and to build inaccessible towers for the scientists, isolating them from their colleagues both in America and in foreign countries. We have approached the point described by Major General William J. Donovan, formerly Director of the Office of Strategic Services, when he said with some irritation: "You can have an organization that is so secure it does nothing."

Our security program has brought the military mind into the laboratories. It has succeeded, not so much in making war scien-

tific as in making science military. It has set up army censors over
the facts of science with the power to classify and declassify.
But an army censor will always find it safer to mark a development top secret than to declassify it. No Congressional prober will
haul him over the coals for being overcautious, but he may face
charges of criminal negligence for releasing information someone
else may consider "top secret."

Therefore, the findings of scientists as reported to their colleagues must have whole sections blacked out. Each scientist must
work in such isolation that he is handicapped in training others.
The compartmentalization of scientific research for security
reasons prevents one scientist from profiting from another's research, including his mistakes. Science has been advanced in in-
numerable ways through by-products having little relevance for
the project in hand—often signifying a failure in that particular
field—but leading to great advances in other fields.

The standards and procedures set up by the Government in regard to loyalty are not only puerile and absurd; they have already
done incalculable harm to the Government services, including national defense, by excluding many useful talents and scaring away
even more. Investigation and dismissal are ever-present possibilities, with Congressional committees constantly on the lookout
for promising new victims. A Government employee may consider
himself lucky if he goes out with only his reputation destroyed;
many have passed quickly from what they thought was the security of Government service to embarrassment, ignominy or the
dead-end of the blacklist. Some have landed in prison.

The Government's attitude has had a disturbing impact beyond
official circles, causing concern in universities and private insti-
tutes carrying on scientific work. These educational and other
institutions widely rely on U.S. Government grants, which may be
refused for loyalty-security reasons. The net effect of the Government program has been to make science less attractive as a profession to young men and women choosing a career.

The "new loyalty" in the United States today, as Professor
Commager has said, "is, above all, conformity. It is the uncritical

and unquestioning acceptance of America as it is—the political institutions, the social relationships, the economic practices. It rejects inquiry into the race question or socialized medicine, or public housing, or into the wisdom or validity of our foreign policy. It regards as particularly heinous any challenge to what is called 'the system of private enterprise,' identifying that system with Americanism. It abandons evolution, repudiates the once popular concept of progress, and regards America as a finished product, perfect and complete." [116]

The established criteria of the Atomic Energy Commission for determining security clearance list eighteen different types of derogatory information which indicate that an individual is a security risk. Of course, membership in any organization on the Attorney General's blacklist automatically bars a person from employment by the AEC. Also likely to be excluded is anyone who maintains, in the words of the official AEC directive, a "close continuing association with individuals (friends, relatives or other associates) who have subversive interests and associations. . . ." A close continuing association may be deemed to exist if: "(1) Subject lives at the same premises with such individual; (2) Subject visits such individual frequently; (3) Subject communicates frequently with such individual by any means." [117]

The criterion of guilt by kinship has not been limited to the AEC, but has spread to other branches of the Government and particularly to the Armed Forces. In the present purification process the entire family, including in-laws, of a draftee or cadet is screened; and it is no longer a truism that a boy's best friend is his mother, at least so far as the U.S. Government is concerned. In 1955 an epidemic of cases came to light in which soldiers had been rated disloyal, not for any misdeeds of their own, but because of their mothers' alleged radical affiliations.

One Merchant Marine Academy honors graduate was denied a commission in the Naval Reserve because his mother had formerly been a member of the Communist Party. (He was subsequently cleared and commissioned.) A Naval psychologist who received clearance to retain his officer's commission was never-

theless dismissed from his paid Navy civilian job because of his
family's reported views; and the Air Force planned a dishonorable
discharge of one young reservist whose father was supposedly a
Communist.

Army authorities accusingly informed one draftee that he had
"a mother-in-law who was reported to have been 'lying low as a
Communist for a long time' and was supposed to become active
in the peace movement again." [118] On further investigation it
turned out that the lady had been in her grave since the soldier
was eight years old. Another laurel wreath for absurdity goes to
the Coast Guard, which withheld ensign stripes from an officer
candidate because his mother once belonged to organizations on
the Attorney General's list. Finally, however, the Coast Guard
granted the commission, saying reassuringly in its official statement that the young officer's "relationship to his mother has not
been close, especially during his scholastic and more mature
years." [119]

Even more reprehensible than the denial of commissions on
such grounds, however, was the Army practice of giving undesirable security risk discharges to draftees whose alleged pre-induction activities or associations were suspect. An inductee with the
"wrong" family ties, or with a history including any suspect affiliation, might receive an undesirable discharge not only during his
two-year term of active military service, but also at any time during his subsequent six-year period in the reserve. According to a
study financed with the aid of the Fund for the Republic, some of
the grounds for undesirable discharges were capricious and arbitrary in the extreme, while the degree of official concern for
blights on future careers was at best unpredictable. In 1955 a
number of soldiers brought court tests challenging the Army's
authority to award discharges on the basis of anything other than
performance during the two-year service period.

Meanwhile, during 1955 public criticism of these Army policies
mounted; and by late October, adverse press reports and private
protests had reached such a pitch that Army Secretary Wilber M.
Brucker announced that a thorough revision of loyalty-security

procedures would be made. A month later the Department of
Defense moved into action and issued a directive that the Army,
the Navy and the Air Force were henceforth to conduct security
investigations of draft registrants before they entered the service,
and that no further undesirable discharges were to be given for
pre-induction civilian activities or associations.

In his notable book, *Security, Loyalty and Science*, Professor
Walter Gellhorn of the Columbia University Law School quotes
the chairman of a Government loyalty board as saying to him:
"Of course, the fact that a person believes in racial equality
doesn't *prove* that he's a Communist, but it certainly makes you
look twice, doesn't it? You can't get away from the fact that racial
equality is part of the Communist line." [120]

No wonder, then, that a loyalty board probing into the views of
a scientist asked his supervisor this question: "Have you had conversations with him that would lead you to believe he is rather
advanced in his thinking on racial matters?—discrimination, non-
segregation of races, greater rights for Negroes, and so forth?" [121]

A Federal employee became suspect because, in the quaint language of officialdom, an informant, "reported to have been ac-
quainted with the employee for a period of approximately three
years, from 1944 to 1947, reportedly advised that while informant
did not have any concrete or specific pertinent information reflecting adversely on the employee's loyalty, informant is of the
opinion that employee's convictions concerning equal rights for
all races and classes extend slightly beyond the normal feelings of
the average individual, and for this reason informant would be
reluctant to vouch for the employee's loyalty." [122]

The questions put by loyalty boards indicate that we have
strayed far from the standard of allegiance to the American Constitution and have come to the conclusion that "excessive" loyalty
to the Constitution is itself a symptom of "disloyalty." It is a curious commentary on the atmosphere prevalent in the capital of
this country that a firm belief in civil liberties and racial equality
should be ascribed to communism rather than to Americanism.

Our passion for conformity can only lead to sterility. The creative scientist—the only kind who can be efficient in war and productive in peace—has a natural bent for unorthodoxy. If he is more than a technician, he is sure to let his exploring mind roam out of the laboratory into the world about him. No professor can adequately teach the most recondite subject matter if he dwells in that subject alone. Neither a university nor a laboratory can be used as an intellectual prison. And if the scientist and the professor may come and go and live not as a specialized sort of animal but as human beings, they will have thoughts, very likely political ones, very likely critical ones, very likely non-conformist ones.

The establishment of any political overseer in a laboratory is dangerous, even if that overseer were intelligent and devoted to the highest democratic ideals. But in fact we have established as our requirement for Federal employment a conformity not to democracy, but to the changing tactics and policies of the Administration that happens to be in power. Hence an individual has to check with the party in office before he can be certain what brand of loyalty is necessary in order to hold a job.

One of the more unfortunate aspects of the U.S. loyalty program has been its extension to Americans who work for the United Nations. Not only the Senate Internal Security Committee, going far outside of its jurisdiction, but also the U.S. State Department, has put constant pressure on the Secretary-General of the U.N. to dismiss suspect American employees. In October 1954, Ambassador Henry Cabot Lodge, Jr., permanent United States representative to the U.N., bitterly attacked Dr. Luther Evans, Director of the United Nations Educational, Scientific and Cultural Organization (UNESCO), for failing to dismiss immediately—without due process—seven Americans who had received adverse U.S. loyalty reports.

These Americans were employed in the Paris headquarters of UNESCO and refused to testify at U.S. loyalty board hearings on the grounds that this was improper for employees of an international agency. Dr. Evans, however, was merely waiting to dismiss the seven "legally." Mr. Lodge's castigation of him was in obvious

violation of the U.N. Charter, under which member states pledge
themselves not to interfere with the exclusively international
character of the U.N. staff. After Dr. Evans had discharged or
terminated the contracts of the seven individuals, the International
Labor Organization's Administrative Tribunal at Geneva
handed down, in 1955, a strong opinion upholding the position of
the employees and ordering UNESCO either to reinstate them or
pay them substantial damages.

Nobody has more cogently analyzed the United States loyalty
program than Clifford J. Durr, for seven years, 1941-1948, an able
and conscientious member of the Federal Communications Commission
(FCC). Referring to President Truman's original Executive
Order of 1947, Mr. Durr stated: "I am convinced that the
evils of the Order far outweigh any possible good that can come
from it. It has within it such potentialities of injustice, oppression
and cruelty that its administration will inevitably result in the
alienation rather than the promotion of the loyalty of Government
employees. . . .

"Loyalty is a condition of the mind and emotions and, in my
opinion, is too subtle a matter to be measured by any such standards
as those laid down in the Order, or any which are likely to
be laid down under it. I do not believe that men should be officially
empowered to sit in judgment on the minds and emotions,
or even the associations, of other men and to judge them by tests
short of overt acts or expressions tantamount to overt acts. . . .
Men are to be known not by the fruits which they have borne,
but by prognostications as to the fruits they may bear. They are
to be tried, moreover, not by judges dedicated to impartiality but
by men 'personally responsible for an effective program to assure
that disloyal officers or civilian employees are not to be retained
in employment.' The judges acquit at their personal peril for they,
themselves, may be brought to account for their acquittals. They
are assigned the role of judges, but are accountable as prosecutors. . . .

"I am convinced that the end result of the Executive Order will
be to endanger national security rather than to safeguard it. . . .

It impairs the morale, and therefore, the efficiency of Government employees by exposing their reputations and jobs to continuous attack by nameless accusers. It discourages, and in many instances bars the entry into Government service of men of ability, integrity, experience and imagination, because of their inability to answer unspecific charges of unidentified informers or their unwillingness to subject their reputation to the hazards which are now made a part of Government service. It deprives the heads of Government agencies and departments of effective control over their own personnel and places in the hands of the Federal Bureau of Investigation a dictatorial power over Government employment practices.

"Even though the principles of the Executive Order are not officially extended beyond government, the example of government will inevitably be followed outside of government. The brand of 'disloyalty' will not fade into invisibility once the employee has passed into private life. Moreover, private branding irons are already being made after the Government's pattern and more will be made. Can anyone be sure that he will never feel their burn? We are on the way to creating a new class of outcasts from society—a caste of economic and social 'untouchables.'" [123]

The warnings given by Mr. Durr and others that the loyalty-security program would lead to the impairment of morale received striking documentation from an expert source in 1955 when a report was made to a group of mental health specialists who were meeting in Washington that "the effects of the security program are now, or soon will be, of sufficient scope to constitute a mental hygiene problem of national proportions." A reporting psychiatrist, Mrs. Charlotte A. Kaufman, based her conclusions on a study of thirty disturbed Government employees. She urged her associates "to realize how easily a man who believes himself innocent of all wrong may feel the increasing terror and helplessness in face of an unknown and overwhelming force." [124]

Some critics of the U.S. loyalty-security program have suggested that since excesses and injustices exist, all that is needed is a revision in procedures, improved machinery for the investigation of Government employees and for their right of appeal. In the Government's program, however, as in Congressional inquiries, it is impossible to set up fair and democratic procedures for what is essentially thought control; for unconstitutionally examining a man's ideas and associations; for determining from his present opinions whether he might at some future time prove unreliable; for a guessing game based on the principle of *guilt by anticipation*. In other words, since the *ends* of the loyalty security system are violative of civil liberties, the *means* used are inevitably infected by the same evil.

In 1955 Congress created by law a special twelve-man bipartisan commission to investigate the whole loyalty-security program of the Government. Its members, including Senators, Congressmen and representatives of the general public, were appointed in November. What recommendations they will make to rectify prevailing practices remains to be seen.

In my judgment the only intelligent course is to return to our nation's first principles that a man shall be judged not by his ideas, but by his actions; not by his associations, but by his own personal behavior. Such a program would seek loyalty by carrying out in practice the principles to which America has traditionally been loyal. And it would require the restoration of the Civil Service Commission's Rule No. I which prohibits any inquiry into political or religious opinions or affiliations and says that "all disclosures thereof shall be discountenanced."

The list of proscribed organizations drawn up by the U.S. Attorney General for the Government's loyalty program has played such havoc in the field of civil liberties that we need to discuss the matter separately. President Truman's original directive neither laid down nor suggested any standards by which the Attorney General was to determine what groups were totalitarian, fascist, Communist or subversive. All of these four terms are slippery ones, and particularly the word "subversive." Furthermore, in compiling and making public his first blacklist of more than

100 organizations in the fall of 1947, Attorney General Tom C. Clark, now a Justice of the Supreme Court, did not give any of the groups involved a chance to be heard and present their side of the case. Nor was any opportunity provided for judicial review. There was no improvement in method when Clark's successor, Attorney General J. Howard McGrath enlarged the list to almost 200.

These arbitrary procedures patently violate due process of law and amount to an unconstitutional bill of attainder through which the Attorney General usurps the functions of the Judiciary and inflicts punishment without a judicial trial. As a consequence of the blacklisting and the resulting injury to their reputations, the organizations concerned have lost numerous members, officers and sponsors; lost general support, lost attendance at meetings; lost contributions; and have been denied meeting places, radio time and television time. A number of the groups suffered special financial losses because the Attorney General's action led to the U.S. Treasury withdrawing the tax exemption which had enabled contributors to deduct the amount of their gifts from their income taxes. Many contributors thereafter greatly decreased the size of their donations or cut them off altogether.

Through the Attorney General's list, the Federal Government for the first time in the history of this country has promulgated an official standard of what is orthodox and what is unorthodox. This standard has been set up primarily in terms of the ideas and educational or propaganda materials which organizations disseminate. Accordingly, the list is actually a blacklist of *ideas*. And it impinges directly on the First Amendment and sets at naught the U.S. Supreme Court's statement in 1943: "If there is any fixed star in our constitutional constellation it is that no official, high or petty, can prescribe what shall be orthodox in politics, nationalism, religion or other matters of opinion, or force citizens to confess by word or act their faith therein." [125]

In 1952 Congress pushed the use of the Government's blacklist to a new and fantastic extreme when it added to the Federal Housing Act the Gwinn Amendment, which requires from all tenants in residential units constructed under the Act a sworn

statement that they do not belong to any organization designated
as subversive by the Attorney General. Any tenant who makes a
false allegation in this connection is liable to criminal prosecution
for perjury, with possible penalties running up to five years in
jail and a $10,000 fine. In 1954 and 1955 courts in various juris-
dictions declared this madcap law unenforceable or unconstitutional. And in November 1955 the U.S. Supreme Court declined
to review a Wisconsin Supreme Court decision that this statute
violated both the Federal and Wisconsin Constitutions.

Meanwhile, from 1953 through 1955, Herbert Brownell, Jr., Attorney General in the Eisenhower Administration, made numerous
additions to the official roster of alleged subversive organizations
and brought the total up to 279. He included in his blacklist a
number of groups whose sole purpose was to defend civil liberties,
such as Californians for the Bill of Rights, the Massachusetts Committee for the Bill of Rights and the National Committee to Win
Amnesty for Smith Act Victims.*

Mr. Brownell announced that he would grant the newly listed
organizations hearings at which they might protest their designation as subversive. But by publicly branding them first he was
tipping the scales against them and rendering an adverse verdict
in advance. He actually devoted part of a speech at the American
Bar Association to telling in some detail why he was going to put
the National Lawyers Guild on his list as "a Communist dominated and controlled organization." He claimed that the Guild
had "followed the Party line . . . excepting only those issues so
notorious that their espousal would too clearly demonstrate the
Communist control." [126] This curious reasoning is based on the
premise that if an organization is anti-Communist on important

---

*In 1951 the House Committee on Un-American Activities issued its
own blacklist under the title of *Guide to Subversive Organizations and
Publications*. This *Guide* contains no less than 829 designations based
on the Attorney General's list, and on numerous reports of the House
Committee itself and of various State committees investigating un-
American activities. It has had a wide circulation among private vigilante groups.

issues, that only goes to prove that it is essentially Communist! The Guild in point of fact had opposed the aggression of the North Korean Communists against South Korea in 1950 and the Communist trial of Rudolph Slansky and others in Czechoslovakia in 1953. Later the Guild contested Attorney General Brownell's designation in the courts.

I myself was at one time chairman of no less than three organizations on the initial blacklist of the Attorney General. These were the American Friends of the Soviet Union, which went out of existence in 1939; the American Council on Soviet Relations, 1939-1942; and the National Council of American-Soviet Friendship,* founded in 1943 and still actively functioning. All three of these groups had the purpose of furthering understanding between the United States and the Soviet Union, and of distributing information that would be helpful to this aim.

I remain proud of having been head of these organizations and of having made some contribution through them towards American-Soviet cooperation, which is so essential for world peace. It is absurd and unjust for the Attorney General or anyone else to accuse these three associations of subversion or of attempting to overthrow the American Government by violence. None of them took a position on American domestic issues or concerning social-economic systems, such as capitalism, socialism and communism.

Until the deterioration of relations between the United States and Soviet Russia after the end of the Second World War, the National Council of American-Soviet Friendship was, as I pointed out in Chapter 2, in good repute in Government circles. President Roosevelt sent the organization greetings in 1944, and President Truman and General Eisenhower, in 1945. Speakers at National Council mass meetings during or just after the Second World War included Dean Acheson, then Under Secretary of State; Edward R. Stettinius, Jr., Secretary of State; Donald M. Nelson, Chairman of the War Production Board; and the Earl of Halifax, British Ambassador to the United States.

---

* I was Chairman of the National Council from 1943 to 1946 and a member of its Board of Directors from 1943 to 1950.

In June of 1948 the National Council of American-Soviet Friendship brought suit against the U.S. Attorney General and the Loyalty Review Board to have the Council's name stricken from the list of allegedly subversive organizations and to have the designation pronounced unconstitutional and illegal. I and several other officers of the National Council joined in the suit as individuals in order to give it additional strength. We claimed that we had been damaged personally in our professional work by the Attorney General's proscription of the organization.

The lower Federal District Court in Washington, D.C. dismissed the National Council's complaint on the grounds that no justiciable issue was involved; and the U.S. Court of Appeals affirmed this decision. However, in April 1951 the National Council won a limited victory when the U.S. Supreme Court reversed the decision by declaring 5 to 3 that the organization did have a real case that must be argued and answered. Joined with the Council in this decision were the Joint Anti-Fascist Refugee Committee and the International Workers Order.

The Supreme Court stated that the Attorney General and the Loyalty Review Board had made "unauthorized publications of admittedly unfounded designations of the complaining organizations as 'Communist.' Their effect is to cripple the functioning and damage the reputation of those organizations in their respective communities and in the nation. The complaints, on that basis, sufficiently charge that such acts violate each complaining organization's common-law right to be free from defamation. . . . Whether the complaining organizations are in fact communistic or whether the Attorney General possesses information from which he could reasonably find them to be so must await determination by the District Court upon remand." [127]

This decision meant that the Attorney General had to show that it was reasonable for him to put the National Council of American-Soviet Friendship and the other two organizations on his subversive list. The implication was also that these groups should not remain upon the list unless and until the Attorney General proved his case. But the various Federal agencies continued year after year to treat the three organizations as if their original listing were legal and to dismiss employees who were or had been members of one or more of the groups.

After the case of the National Council went back to the original District Court, another legal tangle resulted. This was still unsettled when President Eisenhower, in 1953, issued a new Executive Order that purported to establish due process in the listing of subversive organizations and thus meet the objections made by the Supreme Court in its 1951 decision. The new procedure provides for a hearing, but first requires an organization to fill out a complex and voluminous questionnaire about its activities and all of the persons supposedly associated with it. This monstrous questionnaire, carrying the threat of perjury action for answers contrary to the "testimony" of professional informers, can hardly be considered an improvement from the viewpoint of due process.

In any event, in 1955 a U.S. District Court decided that the National Council's suit no longer had any legal validity because Eisenhower's Executive Order had superseded Truman's Executive Order, under which the U.S. Attorney General had originally listed the Council. Thus, after eight years of litigation, the Council's battle to have its name removed from the Attorney General's subversive list came to nothing. What this demonstrates is that law-abiding citizens and organizations in America may strive long and in vain to secure remedy against illegal actions on the part of the powerful United States Government.

7

POLICE STATE IN THE MAKING

It is a sinister paradox that the United States Department of Justice, the function of which is to enforce the law, has so often taken the lead in flouting the law. This is particularly true of the Department's Federal Bureau of Investigation and its unauthorized tapping of telephone conversations. In recent trials judges have repeatedly thrown out evidence brought forward by Government attorneys when the defendant showed that it was secured by means of illegal wire-tapping. Yet everyone knows that the FBI continues to carry on this contemptible form of eavesdropping and spying. In 1954 Attorney General Brownell pressed Congress to make the lawless behavior of his Department legal by passing a bill to authorize wire-tapping. The measure did not go through.

In opposition to this bill, James Lawrence Fly, a former chairman of the FCC, stated that wire-tapping is destructive of personal liberty and "necessarily invades the most private relations of the many innocent in the hope of finding one guilty person. In the tapping of one private phone, the dragnet would involve the privacy of all persons using the phone, all persons called and all calling in to anyone. . . . As a matter of physical necessity the wire-tapper reaches all the confidential relations protected by our democratic system, e.g., husband and wife, parent and child, minister and parishioner, lawyer and client, doctor and patient." [128]

FBI snooping in general has gone to extreme and outrageous lengths and frequently has had the effect of intimidation. A favorite device of the FBI is to send agents around to question the elevator man or other employees in an apartment house about the "subversive" views and associations of someone residing in the building. J. Edgar Hoover's men, who usually travel in pairs, often call on unsuspecting persons suspected of having the wrong friends, relatives or associations and scare them half to death. The average American does not know that he is under no legal obligation to answer the questions of FBI agents.

During the past few years FBI agents have questioned many of my friends about my beliefs and activities and have apparently been making a desperate effort to obtain information that could be used against me. Typical questions asked of such friends have been: "Does Mr. Lamont own a grand piano?" "Why does he live on Riverside Drive instead of Park Avenue?" "Is he influenced by women?" "Did you attend a dinner given in his honor by the Emergency Civil Liberties Committee?" and of course, "Is Mr. Lamont a member of the Communist Party?"

In questioning individuals, the FBI puts great stress on securing information about other people and expanding its lists of suspects. All of the information—and misinformation—it gathers by asking questions, tapping telephone wires, installing microphones and spying in other ways, the FBI records in its extensive dossiers. It maintains in its files the incredible total of more than 130,000,000 fingerprint cards, and has a staff of more than 1,000 persons working in the file section alone.

The Department of Justice created the Bureau of Investigation in 1908; in 1935 it was renamed the Federal Bureau of Investigation. In 1924 the Bureau was reorganized and its functions curtailed when Harlan F. Stone, later Chief Justice of the Supreme Court, became U.S. Attorney General. Several weeks after he took office, Mr. Stone stated: "There is always the possibility that a secret police may become a menace to free government and free institutions because it carries with it the possibility of abuses of power which are not always quickly apprehended or understood. . . . The Bureau of Investigation is not concerned with the political or other opinions of individuals. It is concerned only with their conduct, and then only with such conduct as is forbidden by the laws of the United States. When a police system passes beyond these limits, it is dangerous to the proper administration of justice and to human liberty which it should be our first concern to cherish." [129]

Discussing the methods by which the totalitarian state is established, the late Justice Jackson issued another warning. "All that is necessary," he wrote, "is to have a national police competent to investigate all manner of offenses and then, in the parlance of the street, it will have enough on enough people, even if it does not elect to prosecute them, so that it will find no opposition to its policies. Even those who are supposed to supervise it are likely to fear it. I believe that the safeguard of our liberty lies in limiting any national policing or investigative organization, first of all, to a small number of strictly Federal offenses, and secondly to nonpolitical ones." [130]

Unfortunately the Federal Bureau of Investigation, instead of devoting itself to the formidable job of combating the crime that is rife throughout the country, has concentrated more and more on investigating precisely what Justices Stone and Jackson ruled out, namely, the political opinions of individuals. It has become, in effect, a *political police* and has already set up an embryo police state.

In the building of a police state professional informers have always played an indispensable part. So in America today, working hand in hand with the FBI and testifying as witnesses both in regular trials and Congressional investigations, is an array of paid informers—more than eighty in number—whose dubious testimony has ruined the reputation of many a man, and sent some to jail.

These informers, whose earlier careers were unsavory to say the least, have been elevated by the Government into heroes and heroines whose every word is taken as sacred; and whose miraculously stimulated memory of events far in the past is considered sufficient to condemn teachers, writers, actors, clergymen, government employees, trade unionists and others who have long records of honorable and distinguished service. Moreover, these raconteurs from the underworld of politics have complete immunity from suits for libel or slander while telling their lurid tales at trials or hearings.

In February 1954 a group of nineteen leading churchmen in New York and New England, including five bishops, wrote to the Senate Judiciary Committee urging that its Subcommittee on Civil Rights * investigate the present role of informers in the United States. Their letter said: "The informer is a public accuser. When functioning under Government protection or privilege the informer accuses with immunity. Up to now, informers who have been profuse in accusations against fellow citizens have not been cited for or charged with perjury in a court of law.

"Yet we have strong reason to believe that some informers who have traduced large numbers of citizens have not spoken the truth. Sworn admissions by some of them, conflicting statements at different times, and the testimony of ministers of the Christian Church and others as to the untruthfulness of these various professional witnesses should be the subject matter of investigation by the Subcommittee on Civil Rights." [131]

No action was ever taken on the clergymen's petition for the reason that it was carefully sidetracked in the Judiciary Committee and never even presented to the special Subcommittee. Yet events soon demonstrated that no petition to a Congressional committee had ever more fully warranted attention and action.

In May 1954 Joseph and Stewart Alsop analyzed in their column, "Matter of Fact," in the *New York Herald Tribune* the contradictory testimony of one of the chief informers, Paul Crouch. They disclosed that Attorney General Brownell was investigating Crouch for possible perjury.

Mr. Crouch issued a statement defending himself in which he said: "If my reputation could be destroyed and my credibility demolished through the current frame-up plot, thirty-one Communist leaders convicted or on trial in Smith Act proceedings would get new trials, twenty immigration proceedings would be re-opened, the registration order against the Communist Party

* In 1955 the name of this Subcommittee was changed to Subcommittee on Constitutional Rights.

would be reversed and sent back, with the cost to the Government of many millons of dollars." [132] Crouch also hit back at Brownell's investigation by writing J. Edgar Hoover and demanding that he check on the loyalty of the Attorney General's office aides.

This revealing controversy finally came to an end in November 1955 when Paul Crouch died of lung cancer in San Francisco.

Another discredited informer is Manning Johnson, a Negro who testified in 1954 before the International Organizations Employees Loyalty Board that Dr. Ralph J. Bunche, then Director of the U.N. Department of Trusteeship, had been a member of the Communist Party in the 1930's. Dr. Bunche flatly denied this accusation. The Loyalty Board then cleared Dr. Bunche of all charges against him; and its chairman sent a transcript of the hearings to the U.S. Justice Department, with the request that Johnson be investigated for perjury.

The Justice Department, however, did not move, perhaps because Mr. Johnson was such a loyal informer and ardent patriot. For it was Johnson who was on the stand during the following colloquy before the Subversive Activities Control Board:

"Q. In other words, you will tell a lie under oath in a court of law rather than run counter to your instructions from the FBI. Is that right?

"A. If the interests of my Government are at stake. In the face of enemies, at home and abroad, if maintaining secrecy of the techniques of methods of operation of the FBI who have responsibility for the protection of our people, I say I will do it a thousand times." [133]

Still another character repeatedly used as a witness by the U.S. Government is one Maurice Malkin, foreign-born ex-Communist, who by his own admission is guilty of espionage. A brief filed in a deportation case in 1954 attacked Malkin's credulity as a witness and reviewed interesting highlights in his career. He served two years in Sing Sing (1929-1930) for a particularly brutal, felonious assault; and (said the brief) "is revealed as a character who has devoted his life to deception, violence and crime. He deceived a U.S. District Court to get his citizenship. . . . He attempted to deceive a court and jury in his trial for assault. . . . He deceived the New York election officials at least twenty-six times [by voting illegally after his release from Sing Sing]; [and] he attempted to deceive the Dies Committee about his part in the assault." [134]

The most notorious informer case of all, however, is that of Harvey Matusow. In April 1954 Matusow sought out Bishop Oxnam and poured out his heart to him, saying that he had had a moving religious experience and was a completely changed man. Matusow then confessed: "I have lied again and again in my statements to these committees and in my reports, and I want to go to each individual about whom I have falsified to ask his forgiveness." [135] When the Bishop asked him why he had been so willing to perjure himself, Matusow replied that "one fabrication led to another" and "there was a certain thrill in these revelations." [136]

Rumors about Matusow became rife as he went about telling individuals how conscience-stricken he was over the harm he had done innocent people by his lies. In October 1954 Albert E. Kahn, partner in the small New York publishing firm of Cameron & Kahn, reached Matusow on the long distance telephone in New Mexico and discussed with him the possibility of a book of confessions. Matusow agreed to the project and set to work to dictate his story to a stenographer. The result was *False Witness*, which appeared in March 1955 after a nation-wide fanfare of free advance publicity as accusations and counter-accusations were hurled about in the press and over the air.

In his book Matusow told in detail how he joined the Communist Party in 1947, became an FBI informer in 1950, was expelled from the Party in 1951 and continued to earn his living as an informer for three years more. He cited instance after instance in which he gave untrue testimony which was instrumental in persons being smeared in the newspapers, losing their jobs or going to jail as the result of Government prosecutions. His final estimate of the total number of victims he traduced during his career as a professional perjurer was 244.

Of course a man who for a long time has been in the habit of lying for profit does not necessarily tell the full truth when he

suddenly embarks on his confessions. But *False Witness* reproduces many original documents—letters, telegrams, memos, notes
and newspaper clippings—which corroborate substantial portions
of Matusow's story. Furthermore, the book analyzes testimony
which Matusow gave before Congressional committees and at
Government trials; and all this testimony, as well as his close
association with Senator McCarthy, is a matter of public record.

In a sworn affidavit, as well as in *False Witness*, Matusow
stated that he had lied in testifying at the Texas trial of Clinton
E. Jencks, an official of the Mine, Mill and Smelter Workers, who
was convicted of perjury under the Taft-Hartley Act and given
a five-year jail term. The Government's prosecuting attorney,
Charles F. Herring had written Matusow on Department of
Justice stationery, saying: "I am sincerely grateful to you for your
fine cooperation in the case of United States v. Clinton E. Jencks.
As you know, your testimony was absolutely essential to a successful prosecution and you presented it in a fine, intelligent
manner." [137]

Early in 1955 Matusow went to El Paso to appear before Fed-
eral Judge R. E. Thomason and back up his affidavit in person.
In an extraordinary ruling the Judge, far from granting Mr.
Jencks a new trial, lashed out angrily at Matusow and summarily
sentenced him to three years in prison for contempt of court.
Matusow has appealed this conviction.

In announcing his decision, Judge Thomason stated: "You deliberately and maliciously and designedly schemed to obstruct
justice and cause the filing of an affidavit that obtained this hearing on a motion for a new trial. You attempted to obstruct justice
to put aside the conviction of Clinton Jencks to further your own
personal ends." [138] After this opinion all other Government witnesses could well fear that confessing to the truth through a
recantation would probably land them in the penitentiary.

In another affidavit implementing the story in his book, Matusow swore that he had testified falsely as a Government witness
against the thirteen second-string Communists convicted in New
York City under the Smith Act. In reference to five of the de-

fendants he admitted that he had dishonestly made it appear that they favored the overthrow of the U.S. Government by force and violence. In addition, he claimed that Roy M. Cohn, then Assistant U.S. Attorney and later Chief Counsel for the McCarthy Committee, knowingly "developed" with him untruthful testimony against defendant Alexander Trachtenberg, a book publisher. Mr. Cohn denied this.

In April 1955, on the basis of Matusow's recantations, Federal Judge Edward J. Dimock granted new trials to both Trachtenberg and another defendant, George Blake Charney. In his decision Judge Dimock punctured the Department of Justice charge that Matusow's publishers and others were involved in a "Communist conspiracy" to obstruct justice by bribing the informer to recant. The Judge called attention to the fact that Matusow had confessed to Bishop Oxnam long before anyone approached him about writing a book.

However, with its whole rickety informer system perilously exposed, the Justice Department ignored Judge Dimock's views and concentrated on saving the remnants. In a wild exhibition of *post hoc* reasoning, it desperately strove to support Brownell's theory of a Communist plot: Matusow had admitted to perjury; the Communists had solicited affidavits from him; therefore the Communists had suborned him to a perjurious recantation of his testimony. Other informers with uneasy consciences were following Matusow's example; the system of subsidized lying was crumbling.

A lesson must be taught, not only to the informer—who having once lied, must be silenced—but also to liberal critics of the informer system, who had inveighed against it in the press: the publishers who had published Matusow's confessions; the printers who printed the book; and finally, in the Justice Department's far-fetched dragnet, the editors, publisher, lawyers, and office staff of *The Nation,* the magazine which had first touched off the whole exposure by printing in its April 10, 1954 issue an article on the informer racket in general. All were summoned before a grand jury in New York City, as were almost all individuals whom

Matusow had sought out in order to tell his story. All were harried and harassed for a period of five months.

The grand jury began investigations on February 7, 1955. On July 13, it handed down four indictments. Matusow himself was charged with perjury for alleging that Roy Cohn had induced him to testify falsely at the trial of the thirteen second-string Communist leaders. Also indicted with Matusow were two New York attorneys, R. Lawrence Siegel, general counsel of *The Nation* for many years, and his associate, Miss Hadassah Shapiro. Both were charged with obstructing justice, conspiracy to obstruct justice, and perjury in connection with allegedly destroying records of meetings between Matusow and Siegel. Another indictment for obstructing justice was returned against Martin Solow, assistant to the publisher of *The Nation,* who was accused of destroying, *before* the grand jury called him, correspondence relating to Matusow.

The Department of Justice made one concession during the uproar over the Matusow affair. Attorney General Brownell announced that the Department was abandoning the practice of retaining full-time "consultants" on communism at guaranteed salaries. He said, however, that "expert witnesses" would still be used and paid for testimony in specific cases.

Meanwhile, two Federal Communications Commission witnesses, Mrs. Marie Natvig and Lowell Watson, had publicly confessed that they had been lying. They had testified in 1954 before the FCC that Edward O. Lamb, broadcaster and publisher, who was seeking to have the license renewed for his television station at Erie, Pennsylvania, was guilty of dangerous Communist associations. Mr. Watson accused FCC lawyers and investigators of "coaching" and "brain-washing" him into lying, while Mrs. Natvig stated that FCC attorney Walter R. Powell, Jr., had "coerced" her into "manufactured" testimony against Mr. Lamb.

The embarrassed Department of Justice promptly took action in regard to Mrs. Natvig's confession. But instead of launching an investigation to find out whether her original testimony was true or untrue, the Department obtained her indictment and conviction for perjury on the basis of what she had said about the FCC lawyer, Mr. Powell. She received a jail sentence of from eight months to two years. Mr. Lamb, after two years of effort, has not yet secured his television license.

In May 1955 another FBI informer, David Brown, surprise witness before the Subversive Activities Control Board for the Civil Rights Congress, admitted that he had continually lied in his reports to the FBI about the Congress. He frankly stated that he had restorted to fabrications so that he could go on drawing pay, ranging from $25 a week to $250 a month, as an informer.

Brown related how, as an FBI agent, he had contrived to become an officer of the Congress in Los Angeles. He confessed that "he had made so many reports to the FBI that were without foundation that he could not recall having made one that had a foundation in fact"; [139] and that he had frequently submitted fictitious lists of individuals who had attended Communist meetings. He said he had "betrayed the working people generally; all of the American people, including my friends, my co-workers, my family —everybody who ever trusted me and had confidence in me." [140]

Some months earlier Brown had temporarily cracked up because of his emotional disturbance over the "dirty business," as he described it, in which he was engaged. He told the SACB of his sudden "disappearance" from Los Angeles, "of having mailed an envelope containing a favorite, conspicuous necktie, identification cards and other personal effects to indicate that he had been kidnapped and perhaps killed, and of an abortive suicide attempt in which he slashed himself sixteen times with a razor." [141]

These critical developments among the Government's stable of paid, professional informers have raised serious doubts as to the reliability of the main anti-Communist witnesses in trials, grand jury hearings and Congressional investigations. Many of these informers have made a mint of money by publishing books of confessions, writing newspaper articles and appearing on radio or television. And in general their distortions and exaggerations have played a leading role in instilling in the American mind its pathological fear of communism.

During the past decade the Government, with the help of its subsidized informers, has more and more resorted to the historic police-state device of utilizing spurious perjury actions as a political weapon against dissenters, radicals and "trouble-makers." A prime example of this was the 1950 perjury conviction of Harry Bridges, Australian-born leader of the International Longshoremen's and Warehousemen's Union, for denying that he had been a member of the Communist Party at the time of his naturalization in 1945. The Government pressed this prosecution not only in order to put Bridges away in jail for five years, but also in order to denaturalize and deport him. The U.S. Supreme Court threw out the case in 1953, ruling that the prosecution had been in violation of the Statute of Limitations.

Government harassment of Bridges began more than twenty years ago, in 1934, with an effort to deport him after he had led a successful strike of longshoremen on the Pacific Coast. Subsequently, throughout lengthy judicial and quasi-judicial proceedings, the Department of Justice scoured the country for witnesses against this trade union leader. Among those with top billing in the extravaganza have been habitual liars, at least one murderer, a thief, habitual drunkards, and others apparently trading information in return for immunity from prosecution.

In 1955 the Government undertook its fifth attempt to "get" Bridges, this time instituting denaturalization proceedings against him under the McCarran-Walter Act, the denaturalization provisions of which are not qualified by any statute of limitations. As the staid *New York Times* headlined the proceedings in an irreverent moment, the "Old Bridges disc is playing again." But the Government's rehash of stale charges was not convincing; for in July a Federal judge in San Francisco ruled in favor of Bridges. The Government decided not to appeal, and Bridges's naturalization as an American citizen finally stood unchallenged.

I also consider a frame-up the 1947 conviction of Carl Marzani for allegedly making false statements to a Government official in denying membership in the Communist Party. Marzani is a Williams College graduate who rendered exemplary service during World War II in the Office of Strategic Services and the State Department. During his vacation in 1946 he produced for the United Electrical Workers a motion picture critical of American business monopolies and President Truman's foreign policy. In November of the same year he resigned from the State Department in order to set up a film business for the service of trade unions. His resignation was officially accepted and with regret.

Then came the pay-off with Marzani's sudden indictment in January 1947. In order to influence the jury against him, the prosecution introduced evidence that Marzani had been dismissed from the State Department instead of having resigned. When Marzani subpoenaed the official record, it was discovered that State Department authorities had falsified it by crossing out a typed statement, "Resignation, November 15, 1946" and substituting in ink, "Removal, December 20." But the Department had neglected to cross out the original Budget Control stamp on the document verifying the resignation and reading, "Approved, Nov. 20, 1946." Marzani narrowly lost his appeal to the U.S. Supreme Court by the split vote of 4 to 4.* He then went to jail for more than two years.

As to the perjury trial of Alger Hiss, a high State Department official whose liberal policies had aroused the animosity of the reactionaries, I do not think that anyone who has impartially studied the record could believe that Hiss was guilty beyond all reasonable doubt.

One of the most contemptible perjury indictments engineered by the Department of Justice was that of Professor Owen Lattimore,† a Far Eastern expert and head of the Walter Hines Page School of International Relations at Johns Hopkins. Here was a man who as a scholar and teacher had devoted himself for a full quarter-century to the pursuit of the truth and had established an international reputation in his field. It was ironic that an individual who had made a profession of truth-seeking should be

---

* A tie vote in the U.S. Supreme Court means that the lower court's decision is not over-ruled and therefore becomes binding.

† Cf. Chapter 4.

prosecuted for the crime of not telling the truth. Lattimore's ordeal came about because Congressional reactionaries wished to discredit his version of the truth and to make him a scapegoat for the failures of American foreign policy in the Far East.

The first and key count against Professor Lattimore in his 1952 perjury indictment was that he had testified falsely when he said he had "never been a sympathizer or any other kind of a promoter of communism or Communist interests." [142] In 1953 Judge Luther W. Youngdahl of the U.S. District Court in Washington, D.C., dismissed this count because of its inherent vagueness and because it violated both the First Amendment guaranteeing freedom of speech and the Sixth Amendment giving a defendant in a criminal case the right "to be informed of the nature and cause of the accusation" against him. A United States Court of Appeals upheld Judge Youngdahl's ruling.

Fearful of appealing this decision to the Supreme Court, the Department of Justice took another tack in its vendetta against Professor Lattimore and in 1954 pushed through a new perjury indictment against him. This two-count indictment alleged that he had lied in stating before the Internal Security Committee that he had never been a follower of the Communist line or a promoter of Communist interests. The Department evidently hoped that the courts would not dismiss the slippery new count that merely rephrased the old count.

I can do no better than to quote Lattimore's own statement concerning this second indictment. "The definition in the indictment of a follower of the Communist line includes anyone who expresses any opinion knowing that that opinion also is shared by Communist Russia. Under this indictment, no writer on foreign affairs could be safe from prosecution unless during the past twenty years he had always opposed everything that Russia advocated. Under this indictment, the entire Democratic and Republic Administrations could be accused of perjury if they said they had never knowingly followed the Communist line—so could Presidents Roosevelt, Truman and Eisenhower, all of whom have been accused of following the Communist line. Inevitably this country cannot always take a position in exact opposition to the position taken by Russia." [143]

Shortly after the new indictment Leo A. Rover, the U.S. Attorney in charge of the Lattimore prosecution, filed an affidavit demanding that Judge Youngdahl disqualify himself as the presiding jurist in the trial because he had a "fixed personal bias and prejudice" in favor of Professor Lattimore. Judge Youngdahl dismissed Mr. Rover's affidavit as "scandalous," stating: "At bottom, the affidavit is based upon the virulent notion that a United States judge who honors and adheres to the sacred constitutional presumption that a man is innocent until his guilt is established by due process of law has 'a bent of mind' that disables him from conducting the fair and impartial trial to which both the accused and the Government are entitled. The affidavit is therefore so patently and grossly insufficient that I cannot escape from the conclusion that the purpose of the affidavit is to discredit, in the public mind, the final action of our courts, or else to intimidate the courts themselves." [144]

In January 1955 Judge Youngdahl threw out the second indictment against Lattimore and asserted: "To require defendant to go to trial for perjury under charges so formless and obscure as those before the court would be unprecedented and would make a sham of the Sixth Amendment and the Federal rule requiring specificity of charges." [145] This decision, too, was affirmed by the Appeals Court, on June 14, 1955.

Two weeks later Attorney General Brownell announced that the Government would not appeal to the Supreme Court and would drop all the perjury charges against Lattimore. The case came to a final end the next day when Judge Youngdahl granted U.S. Attorney Rover's motion to quash the indictment.

Professor Lattimore's long agony was over. In September Johns Hopkins University, which had given Lattimore a leave of absence with salary while he was under indictment, called him back to teach. But during a period of two-and-a-half years, Lattimore suffered incalculable injury to his reputation, formidable legal expenses, constant nervous strain and the interruption of his normal career.

Another revealing occurrence in the perjury racket was the Justice Department's withdrawal in 1954 of a perjury indictment against Val Lorwin, a former State Department official charged with falsely denying that he had been a member of the Communist Party, and that he had held a Party meeting at his home. Mr. Lorwin had been on Senator McCarthy's original list of "eighty-one Communists" in the State Department. The Eisenhower Administration obtained Lorwin's indictment in December 1953 in order to appease McCarthy and to demonstrate that the Government was able to clean house on its own.

Six months later Attorney General Brownell quashed the case because it was discovered that the U.S. Attorney in charge of the prosecution, William Gallagher, had deliberately misrepresented Mr. Lorwin before the grand jury which handed down the indictment. Mr. Gallagher had falsely told the grand jury that there were two FBI informants ready to identify Lorwin as a member of the Communist Party; and that there was no use in the grand jury's questioning Lorwin himself because he was sure to plead the Fifth Amendment.

When Senator William Langer, at that time Chairman of the Senate Judiciary Committee, asked Mr. Brownell why his aide had secured the fraudulent indictment, Brownell replied: "Mr. Gallagher indicated that he felt it was better to indict Mr. Lorwin on slight evidence rather than appear before a Senate committee to explain why he had not obtained an indictment." [146]

The Attorney General finally dropped Gallagher from the Department of Justice. But this action could hardly make up for all the damaging publicity Mr. Lorwin had received; nor did it erase the suspicion that perhaps there were other attorneys working for the Department who might frame a suspect "subversive" in order to advance their careers or out of fear of Congressional inquisitors.

The integrity of the Department of Justice—not to mention the American judiciary—is also at issue in the case of Julius and Ethel Rosenberg, electrocuted in 1953 for the crime of conspiring to commit espionage by transmitting atomic secrets to the Soviet Union. Casting doubts on the fairness of the conviction was the Government's dependence at the trial on the professional informer and ex-spy, Elizabeth Bentley, and on witnesses testifying under threat of prosecution or promise of immunity. Moreover, the inflammatory publicity against the Rosenbergs in the press, much of it stirred up by the prosecution itself, made an impartial verdict by the jury all but impossible.

The same flaws are inherent in the conviction of Morton Sobell, who was found guilty of being a co-conspirator of the Rosenbergs and sentenced to thirty years in jail. In addition, Sobell's legal defense suffered incalculable harm because the Government forced him to stand trial with the Rosenbergs. At the least, in my judgment, the Rosenberg-Sobell convictions did not measure up to the minimum standards of American justice; at the worst, the convictions were the result of a malignant political prosecution reminiscent of the Sacco-Vanzetti case in the nineteen-twenties.

In addition to its crew of disreputable public informers, some of whom I have mentioned, the U.S. Government makes constant use of a much larger group of secret, anonymous informers whose names are not revealed because, according to the Federal Bureau of Investigation, such revelations would cripple the Bureau's undercover work. These faceless informers provide information on suspects to different departments of the Federal Government, to Loyalty Boards and to Congressional investigating committees. Since their identity is always concealed, an accused person never has a chance to confront them and subject them to cross-examination.

In the well-known case of Dorothy Bailey, the U.S. Supreme Court split 4 to 4 and so affirmed the decision of a lower court that the Government was not obliged to produce or identify its informants in establishing a charge of disloyalty. Justice Douglas criticized the principle of the Bailey case as follows: "When the Government becomes the moving party and levels its great powers against the citizen, it should be held to the same standards of fair dealing as we prescribe for other legal contests. To let the Government adopt such lesser ones as suits the convenience of its officers is to start down the totalitarian path. . . . A disloyalty trial is the most crucial event in the life of a public servant. If condemned, he is branded for life as a person unworthy of trust or confidence. To make that condemnation without meticulous regard for the decencies of a fair trial is abhorrent to fundamental justice." [147]

The informer business has undoubtedly been stimulated by the appeals which various Government officials have made to the people of America to report information on "subversives" to the FBI. In 1950 J. Edgar Hoover went so far as to suggest that doctors violate their confidential relationship with patients, sworn to in the traditional Hippocratic oath, by becoming secret informers. In a guest editorial in the *Journal of the American Medical Association,* Hoover wrote: "Today the germs of an alien ideology, communism, are attempting to infect the blood stream of American life. . . . The physicians of America, like other citizens, can best help in the protection of the nation's internal security by reporting immediately to the FBI any information of this nature which might come into their possession." [148] In 1950 U.S. Attorney General J. Howard McGrath reported that the Communists "are everywhere" and urged all citizens to hand over to the FBI all information about them, however "insignificant or seemingly irrelevant." [149]

In May 1955 a group of private vigilantes composed of ex-FBI officials announced the establishment in Washington, D.C., of the Foundation for American Research as a library, open to the public, to make accessible free information on "subversive" individuals and organizations. The articles of incorporation stated that the library would function as a central depository to provide research material on "individuals, corporations, groups, associations or organizations whose activities are considered inimical to the best interests of the United States." [150]

There has been mounting evidence over the past few years that the U.S. Post Office has been cooperating with the Federal Bureau of Investigation in the opening and reading of mail addressed to suspects, and in listing the magazines and newspapers that are being sent to such persons. In 1952, at the behest of the chief counsel of a Senate Elections subcommittee investigating Senator McCarthy's finances, postal authorities put a so-called "mail cover" on first-class mail addressed to McCarthy and three of his associates. This meant that the Post Office reported the return addresses, postmarks and any similar information on the outside of the mail in question.

In 1955 a special Senate committee inquiring into this incident sent the U.S. Attorney General a report condemning the practice and urging appropriate action. The Attorney General decided there had been no violation of any law, and did nothing about the matter. It seems likely that the Department of Justice itself has been using the "mail cover" to track down alleged subversives. I believe that from the viewpoint of civil liberties the "mail cover" is impermissible, whether applied to Senator McCarthy or anyone else.

Turning to another important agency of the U.S. Government, we find that the Department of State has for many years been adopting police-state methods in denying passports to American citizens on political grounds. It has violated the fundamental right of hundreds of Americans to travel by canceling their passports by sudden decree, seizing their passports by force or guile, or refusing to issue new passports. The State Department has taken such actions for no other reason than that the victims have dissented from official Government policies or have belonged to an organization on the Attorney General's blacklist.

A curious paradox in this situation is that while our forefathers, chafing under the repressive atmosphere in seventeenth-century England, were permitted to leave the country in the *Mayflower* and other ships, persecuted Americans today who might wish to emigrate abroad permanently are not allowed to leave these shores because the U.S. Government will not grant them passports. They can go only to countries like Mexico or Canada where passports are not required for Americans. In fact, in Mexico there is already a sizable colony of self-exiled American progressives who have found it too difficult to earn a livelihood or enjoy ordinary freedom in their own homeland.

I myself am a victim of the State Department's arbitrary actions in regard to passports. In the spring of 1951 I made plans to visit Western Europe and the Soviet Union for pleasure and study, and went so far as to engage passage on the *Queen Mary*. On May 29 Mrs. Ruth B. Shipley, then Chief of the Passport Division, sent me a collect telegram curtly notifying me, "Your request extension passport disapproved." After I had protested this decision, Mrs. Shipley wrote me on July 3: "You are informed that your original request for the extension of your passport was carefully considered by various offices of the Department and it was concluded that your travel abroad at this time would be contrary to the best interests of the United States."

This was not, of course, a real explanation; and it became clear enough that the State Department had refused me a passport because I was a dissenter on issues of politics and international affairs. I discovered, too, that the Department had been swayed by the contents of a thick dossier concerning me and all my ideological crimes over the past twenty years. The Passport Division maintains extensive files on "subversives" and also borrows those of the FBI if they are needed.

In refusing passports to persons such as myself, the State Department has claimed that it is enforcing the provisions in the Internal Security Act of 1950 which deny passports to proved members of alleged "Communist-front" organizations. These provisions, however, do not legally come into effect until the Subversive Activities Control Board so designates certain organizations and until its decisions, if appealed, are finally upheld in the courts of the United States. Hence the State Department has been guilty of illegal pre-enforcement of an Act which may be held unconstitutional by the U.S. Supreme Court. Furthermore, in my own case the State Department afforded me no opportunity to show that I was not a member of any so-called Communist front.

On October 12, 1951, I sent an open letter of protest to President Truman in which I asserted: "The State Department's discrimination against me, obviously on political grounds, brings into effect the arbitrary and undemocratic procedures of restricting international travel which we in America have properly objected to when practiced by Soviet Russia and other nations. Indeed, Mr. President, you were presumably referring to these very practices in your own statement of July 7, 1951, when you wrote President Shvernik of the Soviet Union: 'We shall never be able to remove suspicion and fear as potential causes of war until communication is permitted to flow, free and open, across international boundaries.'

"From my extended correspondence with Government officials and from inquiries others have made on my behalf, it is evident that a primary reason for the State Department rejecting my passport application was that I have publicly expressed disagreement with certain aspects of United States foreign policy. In truth, I make no secret of the fact that I so dissent, and vigorously. But for the State Department to penalize me for exercising my right of dissent is to nullify the basic principles of our Constitution. The penalty is particularly heavy in the case of teachers, scholars and writers like myself, since travel abroad is of such importance for our regular work. . . .

"This is all the opposite of due process. Again, you yourself have given the answer in your Constitution Day address of September 18, 1951, where you say: 'Under our Constitution, it is not only the citizens who are made to conform to the principles of justice, but the Government itself. And the citizen has the right to enforce his rights against the Government. The rule of law is made supreme.'

"But the rule of law is evidently not yet supreme for the State Department, which has pushed further and further this repressive device of refusing or revoking passports. . . . I and these other Americans are now under a kind of House Arrest, for no ascertainable crime and with no satisfactory redress."

President Truman referred my protest to the Department of State, from which I received the following note dated November 6 and signed by Willis H. Young, Acting Chief of the Passport Division: "The Department has received by reference from the White House your letter of October 12, 1951, regarding the refusal of passport facilities to you. Your letter has been considered very carefully by the Department, but it does not feel warranted in reversing the decision set forth in previous communications to you."

I then wrote to Mr. Young, saying: "I hereby make a formal demand that I be advised of the specific reasons for the denial of my passport, including the alleged facts upon which you relied; that I be granted a hearing on the charges in question; and that I further be advised prior to that hearing as to the precise standards used by the Passport Division in granting or denying passports." The Passport Division never answered this final letter of mine. And I was left exactly where I had been six months before and with the feeling that I had been shouting loudly into a canyon from whose depths came no answer except echo.

In 1952 the State Department revoked without explanation the passport of Miss Anne Bauer, a free-lance writer. She promptly sued Secretary of State Dean Acheson and on July 9, 1952, won an important victory when a Federal Appeals Court decided that her constitutional guarantee of due process had been violated. The court ruled that the Passport Division could not refuse an applicant a passport without an explanation and hearing. It stated in part: "We hold that, like other curtailments of personal liberties for the public good, the regulation of passports must be administered, not arbitrarily or capriciously, but fairly applying the law equally without discrimination and with due process." [151]

As a result of this decision, Secretary Acheson issued new regulations for the creation of a special Board of Passport Appeals to which applicants who are denied passports may appeal their cases. But the autocrats of the State Department sabotaged the appointment of the Board and continued to thwart the Bauer ruling by simply failing to reach a final decision on controversial cases. After repeated failures to obtain the hearing which the court had decreed, Miss Bauer's fight ended when, romance intervening, she married a Frenchman and took out French citizenship.

The State Department created the Appeals Board in December 1952. While this step opened up possibilities of improvement in the passport situation, the Department did not alter its original position of denying Americans the right to travel on grounds of ideology or association. In fact, any applicant suspected of some sort of unorthodoxy by the Passport Division must fill out a long questionnaire under oath as to his political beliefs and organizational affiliations. The official regulation remains that he will not receive a passport if he has shown "consistent and prolonged adherence to the Communist Party line on a variety of issues and through shifts and changes in that line." [152]

In addition to those already mentioned, prominent persons who have had passports revoked or refused during the past few years are: Michael Blankfort, author; Dr. J. Henry Carpenter, Presbyterian minister; Jerome Davis, educator, sociologist and author; Dr. W. E. B. DuBois, veteran scholar and author; Clark Foreman, Director of the Emergency Civil Liberties Committee; Albert Kahn, author and publisher; Arthur Miller, playwright and author of the hit drama, *Death of a Salesman;* Otto Nathan, teacher and economist; Professor Linus C. Pauling, Nobel Prize winner in chemistry; Paul Robeson, singer; and Henry Willcox, businessman.

William L. Clark, former chief justice of the United States courts in Occupied Germany, had his diplomatic passport lifted because the U.S. Department of State did not like his views. When Judge Clark sued to get back his passport in order to return as a private citizen to Germany, the Department informed him he could have a passport only if he agreed in advance that he would say nothing abroad that was embarrassing to the Department. The U.S. Attorney in charge of the case generously said that Judge Clark would have "the right of free speech so long as it is not in conflict with the best interests of the United States in Germany." [153]

The *Chicago Tribune,* of all papers, gave the clear civil liberties answer to this statement: "This is a doctrine as pernicious as dangerous. It amounts to the assertion that the State Department can limit the constitutional right of utterance merely by decreeing that what a citizen says, or what he might say, does not serve some confused policy of its own. If the rights of citizens abroad can be limited in this way, it is difficult to see why the Government cannot assume the same power at home, forcing us all to root for its foreign policy, whether we like it or not." [154]

It was not until 1955, after Miss Frances G. Knight had succeeded Mrs. Shipley as Chief of the Passport Division, that the courts forced the State Department to take a more reasonable attitude on passports. In May of that year Federal Judge Henry Schweinhaut, claiming that the State Department had been evasive about the case of Dr. Otto Nathan, ordered Secretary of State Dulles to issue Nathan a passport on pain of contempt. It was the first order of its kind in the history of the United States. Dr. Nathan had applied for a passport in December 1952. He had become Albert Einstein's executor on the latter's death in April 1955.

A Federal Appeals Court granted the State Department a stay on the order, providing that it promptly gave Dr. Nathan a quasi-judicial hearing on his passport. But instead of holding the hearing and afterwards running the risk of another adverse court decision, the Department early in June suddenly let Nathan have his passport. A month later, when a Federal judge had ordered a hearing on Dr. Clark Foreman's application for a passport, the State Department took the same course and gave Foreman his passport without further ado. A few weeks after that former Judge Clark received his passport; and in September Jerome Davis, who had hired a lawyer and threatened to sue, got his passport for Japan.

Meantime, on June 24, a Federal Appeals Court in Washington, in deciding a passport action in favor of Max Schachtman, a Trotskyite, had declared: "The denial of a passport . . . causes a deprivation of liberty that a citizen otherwise would have. The right to travel, to go from place to place as the means of transportation permit, is a natural right subject to the rights of others and to reasonable regulation under law. A restraint imposed by the Government of the United States upon this liberty, therefore, must conform with the provision of the Fifth Amendment that 'No person shall be . . . deprived of . . . liberty . . . without due process of law.' " [155]

Mr. Schachtman's victory, however, did not obtain for him a passport, but only a new hearing. There is little evidence that the State Department has had a change of heart and will concede "the right to travel." Rather, its reluctance to litigate in the Nathan, Foreman and Davis cases indicates, as the astute I. F. Stone has said, that "it wants as test case the application of a man so close to the Communist Party line that it may use the Communist-phobia to establish its right to refuse passports for political reasons." [156]

In the fall of 1955 Federal Judge Youngdahl cut further into the discretionary powers exercised by the State Department in regard to passports. He ruled that the Department must not only give Leonard B. Boudin, New York attorney, a quasi-judicial hearing, but must also reveal the sources and content of the confidential information upon which the Passport Office had denied him a passport. The Judge, noting the irreparable damage caused by "the secret informer and the faceless talebearer," stated that the practice of keeping evidence hidden from scrutiny and review led to arbitrary and irresponsible government. He directed the State Department to enter its confidential information into the open record of the required hearing, so that Mr. Boudin would have a chance to refute it and to cross-examine the witnesses who had provided the derogatory testimony.

Despite the State Department's arbitrary refusal of passports to many persons, the overwhelming majority of American citizens wishing to travel have obtained passports without difficulty. Yet even their right to visit foreign countries has been sharply abridged. Beginning on May 1, 1952 U.S. passports, except in special cases, bore a stamp reading: "This passport is not valid for travel to Albania, Bulgaria, China, Czechoslovakia, Hungary, Poland, Rumania or the Union of Soviet Socialist Republics." In November 1955 the U.S. State Department lifted this restriction, except as it applied to Albania, Bulgaria and China.

The State Department has been as fatuous in denying visas for travel in America as in denying passports or banning travel in Communist countries. Distinguished scholars and scientists are frequently refused admission on the grounds that they once supported a suspect committee for peace or democracy; and sometimes persons officially engaged in United Nations business are barred from entering the United States. Even when their visas are approved, a number of potential visitors balk at the humiliating provision in the McCarran-Walter Act, which requires that all alien visitors be fingerprinted. Scientific associations have found it increasingly difficult to hold international conferences in America because so many foreign experts are unable to obtain visas. During the past few years seven such organizations have found it necessary to hold their international conferences abroad.

In the fall of 1952, two days after movie-director-actor Charles Chaplin and his wife Oona O'Neill Chaplin, daughter of the American dramatist, Eugene O'Neill, had left for a six months' trip to Europe, U.S. Attorney General McGranery brought shame on his country by ordering the Immigration Service to prevent Mr. Chaplin from re-entering the United States, pending a hearing on his beliefs and associations. Chaplin had lived in America for forty years, but had retained his British citizenship. Since World War II he had been under attack by super-patriots for his espousal of progressive causes. After learning of the Attorney General's order, Chaplin decided not to face the ordeal of trying to return to the United States, but to settle down abroad permanently. In this way America lost one of its most distinguished artists.

The recital I have given in this chapter of governmental actions that both violate the Constitution and smack of a police state lend weight to Professor Walter Gellhorn's telling observation: "If our freedoms are lost, it will be because our own timidity, our own lack of confidence in the solidity of American institutions and traditions, led to their repudiation by us rather than to their destruction by others." [157]

8

THE STATES ON THE TRAIL OF SUBVERSION

Since the end of the Second World War most of the State legislatures have followed the example of Congress in voting laws of a repressive character and of doubtful constitutionality. In fact, in the spreading epidemic of fear and unreason, the States have passed literally hundreds of such measures.

Each of the forty-eight States has, of course, its own Constitution guaranteeing the basic freedoms of its citizens, but these Constitutions have exercised little restraining influence on the enactment of anti-subversive legislation. The States are also supposedly limited by the Fourteenth Amendment, which was adopted in 1868 and declares in part: "No State shall make or enforce any law which shall abridge the privileges or immunities of citizens of the United States; nor shall any State deprive any person of life, liberty or property without due process of law; nor deny to any person within its jurisdiction the equal protection of the laws."

This provision specifically applies to the States the "due process" clause of the Fifth Amendment; and the U.S. Supreme Court has decided that under the Fourteenth Amendment the States must likewise abide by the guarantees of the First Amendment. These limitations on the States are of prime importance, but other provisions of the Bill of Rights ought also to be made applicable to them.

Typical of State statutes which disregard the fundamentals of

American civil liberties is New York's Feinberg Law, approved in 1949 by an overwhelming majority of the State legislature, and signed by the Republican Governor, Thomas E. Dewey. Although the New York State Supreme Court declared the law unconstitutional, the U.S. Supreme Court upheld the statute 6-3 in March 1952.

The purpose of the Feinberg Law is to "eliminate subversive persons from the public school system" and to reinforce earlier statutes of a similar nature. Thus it assigns to the Board of Regents of New York State the duty of rooting out all "subversives" (without defining the term), calls for detailed, annual progress reports and lays down the administrative procedures to be followed. These procedural requirements are:

"The Board of Regents shall, after inquiry, and after such notice and hearing as may be appropriate, make a listing of organizations which it finds to be subversive. . . . Such listings may be amended and revised from time to time. The Board, in making such inquiry, may utilize any similar listings or designations promulgated by any Federal agency or authority . . . and may request and receive from Federal agencies or authorities any supporting material or evidence that may be made available to it. The Board of Regents shall provide . . . that membership in any such organization included in such listing made by it shall constitute *prima facie* evidence of disqualification for appointment to or retention in any office or position in the public schools of the State."

In this paragraph the New York State legislature in effect incorporates in its directive to the Board of Regents the U.S. Attorney General's list of "subversive" organizations. And in making membership in such an organization "*prima facie* evidence of disqualification," it reverses ordinary civil service procedure and due process of law by putting on the defendant the burden of proving himself innocent.

The Feinberg Law's directive about "subversive" organizations is unconstitutional both because it establishes guilt by association and because it violates the proscription against bills of attainder.

As the decision of the New York Supreme Court stated: "It is a legislative finding of guilt of advocating the overthrow of the government by unlawful means without a judicial trial and without any of the forms and guards provided for the security of the individual by our traditional judicial forms." [158]

In his telling dissent from the U.S. Supreme Court ruling, Justice Douglas said: "I have not been able to accept the recent doctrine that a citizen who enters the public service can be forced to sacrifice his civil rights. I cannot for example find in our constitutional scheme the power of a State to place its employees in the category of second-class citizens by denying them freedom of thought and expression. . . . The present law proceeds on a principle repugnant to our society—guilt by association. A teacher is disqualified because of her membership in an organization found to be 'subversive.' The finding as to the 'subversive' character of the organization is made in a proceeding to which the teacher is not a party and in which it is not clear that she may even be heard." * [159]

As of 1955, forty-two States had enacted special laws designed to ensure the loyalty of all State officers and employees. Most of these statutes include the requirement of test oaths. A good example of this type of legislation is Maryland's Subversive Activities Act, passed in 1949, and commonly known as the Ober Act, from the name of the chairman of the special commission which drafted the law. This Act constitutes a far-reaching synthesis of applicable sections of the Smith Act, the Mundt-Nixon bill, which later evolved into the Internal Security Act, and the Federal loyalty program. The new statute was adopted unanimously by the State Senate, but the lower house mustered a majority of only 115 to 1 when a former schoolteacher surprised everyone by voting against the bill.

The Ober Act follows the Smith Act in making it a felony for any person to "advocate, abet, advise or teach" the overthrow of the Government of the United States (or of Maryland) or to conspire to do so. What is exceptional under this statute is that mem-

* For further passages from Justice Douglas's dissent see Chapter 10.

bership in a "subversive" or "foreign subversive" organization
becomes a crime punishable by a maximum fine of $5,000 or a
maximum jail sentence of five years, or both. Anyone convicted
under this law is also ineligible to vote or to hold public office
in the State of Maryland.

The Act makes mandatory a drastic loyalty oath for candidates
for public office and all government employees in the State, including teachers in public schools and in private educational institutions receiving financial support from the State, such as Johns
Hopkins University and St. John's College. An institution which
refuses to carry out this provision of the law is denied further aid
from the State treasury. Candidates for president and vice-president of the United States do not have to sign the oath; but their
loyalty must be vouched for by "those persons who file the certificate of nomination for such candidates."

The required oath reads as follows: "I am not a person who
commits, attempts to commit, or aids in the commission, or advocates, abets, advises or teaches by any means any person to commit, attempt to commit, or aid in the commission of any act
intended to overthrow, destroy or alter, or to assist in the overthrow, destruction or alteration of, the constitutional form of the
Government of the United States, or of the State of Maryland, or
of any political subdivision of either of them, by revolution, force
or violence.

"I am not a member of a subversive organization. . . . I am
not a member of a foreign subversive organization. . . . Under
the penalties of perjury I hereby certify, affirm, and declare that
all the statements hereinabove contained are true and correct, and
that I have made no material misstatement or concealment of
fact and no material omissions of fact."

More than 150 years ago Alexander Hamilton stated the fundamental objection to the loyalty oath; he denounced it as being "a
subversion of one great principle of social security, to wit: that
every man shall be presumed innocent until he is proved guilty."
Such an oath, he declared, was designed "to invert the order of
things, and instead of obliging the state to prove the guilt . . . it

was to oblige the citizen to establish his own innocence to avoid the penalty. It was to excite scruples in the honest and conscientious, and to hold out a bribe to perjury." His conclusion was that loyalty oaths are unconstitutional "and repugnant to the true genius of the common law." [160]

Plainly, test oaths tend to denigrate the individual affected. As a U.S. Court of Appeals put it as far back as 1868, they impose upon him "a severe penalty, which interferes with his privileges as a citizen; affects his respectability and standing in the community; degrades him in the estimation of his fellowmen, and reduces him below the level of those who constitute the great body of the people of which the government is composed." [161]

Shortly after the Maryland Ober Act became law two suits were instituted against the Attorney General of the State to prevent its enforcement. Judge Joseph Sherbow of the Baltimore Circuit Court heard the cases and in a vigorous opinion pronounced the Act unconstitutional in its entirety. Judge Sherbow asserted that the statute was in conflict with the First and Fourteenth Amendments of the United States Constitution, that it was a violation of due process because of inherent vagueness, and that it embodied a bill of attainder. He also found that the loyalty affidavits mandatory on candidates for public office were inconsistent with the State Constitution, which forbids any oath from officeholders other than that required by the Constitution itself.

The upper courts, however, reversed Judge Sherbow's thoughtful decision and declared the Ober Act valid in its major provisions. But they held that the Maryland legislature exceeded its power in prescribing a loyalty oath for those who were running for Congress. And they insisted on some simplification of the required loyalty affidavit for candidates for public office within the State of Maryland. Unfortunately, the influence of the Ober Act has extended far beyond the borders of Maryland and several other States have enacted statutes similar to it.

California has been noteworthy for its insistence on loyalty oaths. In 1950 the State legislature passed the Levering Act making it mandatory for every state employee down to the last janitor to swear to an oath that "I do not advocate, nor am I a member of any party or organization, political or otherwise, that now advocates the overthrow of the Government of the United States or of the State of California by force or violence or other unlawful means." This Act ordains a unique and arbitrary form of conscription by stating: "All public employees are hereby declared to be civil defense workers subject to such civilian defense activities as may be assigned to them by their superiors or by law." Having thus transformed all public employees into civil defense workers, the Act then provides that all civil defense workers must take the loyalty oath.

The California legislature voted the Levering Act in 1950 with full knowledge that it was illegal, owing to the fact that the State Constitution prohibited oaths other than the traditional ones to the State and Federal Constitutions. This legal defect was not cured until two years later when on Election Day of 1952 the people of California adopted an amendment to the State Constitution authorizing additional loyalty oaths. At the same time they voted an additional amendment making the Levering Act, in effect, an official part of the Constitution and adding a new and unusual provision—paragraph (b) below.

The amendment reads: "No person or organization which advocates the overthrow of the Government of the United States or the State by force or violence or other unlawful means or who advocates the support of a foreign government against the United States in the event of hostilities shall: (a) Hold any office or employment under this State. . . . (b) Receive any exemption from any tax imposed by this State or any county, city or county, city, district, political subdivision, authority, board, bureau, commission or other public agency of this State."

In 1950 the California legislature implemented provision (b) by passing a law requiring all persons, except householders, and all organizations claiming any exemption from a property tax to file a loyalty declaration that they do not advocate violent overthrow of the government, or support of a foreign government in case of war.* This oath is to be repeated each year as a condition for obtaining the tax exemption. The law automatically applies to religious, charitable and educational institutions, and to individual veterans. More than ten churches and religious associations refused to sign the declaration and brought suit to challenge the measure as unconstitutional.

The First Unitarian Church of Los Angeles, under the leadership of the Reverend Stephen H. Fritchman, made a most persuasive case against the law and one that holds against all loyalty oaths: "The new California statute requiring a declaration of political opinion from churches and other institutions, in return for tax exemption, is a frontal assault on freedom of religion as guaranteed by the First Amendment of the United States Constitution. The use of the taxing power to command declarations of opinion seems to the members of the First Unitarian Church of Los Angeles, as to many Quakers, Universalists and other religious people, to be an improper invasion of the rights of conscience. . . .

"There are few persons who could not individually subscribe to the particular contents of the declaration in the present statute, but there is no assurance that this would be the final statement required. Once the right of the state to invade the church is granted by the signing of this present declaration, the entire issue is lost. . . .

"This is not alone a problem for religious organizations. The issue today affects also people who have no church or temple associations. Test oaths or declarations have a habit of reaching further and further into the individual citizen's life. We should remember that in our own generation Nazi Germany ended by requiring a loyalty pledge of political conformity in order for a citizen to buy a loaf of bread, as a reading of the Nuremberg trial reports makes tragically clear. The pattern of Assembly Bill No. 923, if not stopped now, will reach beyond teachers, public officials and churches. It will reach every single citizen at every

* In its mania for loyalty oaths the California legislature enacted in 1953 two more laws of this variety: the Dilworth and Luckel Acts. See Chapter 10.

point of his life, and American freedom of opinion and conviction will have disappeared. It is against this disaster that we are standing today."

During 1955, court decisions in California—far from clarifying the issue—only resulted in a legal snarl. Three decisions held the tax exemption oath unconstitutional; whereas two other decisions found it constitutionally valid. All five cases are in process of being appealed to the higher courts; and presumably one or all of them will eventually reach the U.S. Supreme Court.

Such is the craze for loyalty oaths in California that a smart businessman not unnaturally decided that it was time to cash in on it. According to the *Christian Science Monitor* for May 31, 1955, his firm is selling "an individual 'loyalty kit' for those who have not been required to sign an oath but who wish to do so anyway. The red-white-and-blue certificate, suitable for framing, contains pictures of Lincoln and Washington and the statement that the signer is not now and never has been a member of the Communist Party. James Casselman, president of Loyalty Enterprises, offers this 'opportunity to demonstrate your patriotism' at the price of $1."

In 1953 New York, Putnam and Westchester Counties in New York State carried the loyalty oath idea to a new extreme when they asked every juror serving for the first time to state whether he is or has been "a member of or affiliated with the Communist Party or with any group or organization which advocates the overthrow of the U.S. Government by force." In 1955 Governor Averell Harriman of New York vetoed a bill which extended this requirement to the whole State.

In 1954 the sovereign State of Indiana, in order to ensure its safety beyond all peradventure of a doubt, put into effect a statute making it mandatory for professional boxers and wrestlers to take a non-Communist oath before appearing in the ring.

During the same year of fear Georgia outdid itself by passing an Act requiring all State employees to fill out under oath an unprecedented "Security Questionnaire." In addition to the standard inquiries about membership in the Communist Party or any organization advocating the overthrow of the U.S. Government by force and violence, the Georgia legislature included the question: "List all groups, societies or organizations of which you are, or have been a member." This covers, of course, all political, social and religious organizations. One wonders what will happen if a secret Republican postmaster is turned up in Democratic Georgia.

In 1955 Assemblyman Eugene Toepel of Wisconsin capped the climax on loyalty oaths by introducing a bill into the State legislature requiring tavernkeepers to sign a special oath. Mr. Toepel explained that he had thought up the measure "because in most 'cloak and dagger stories' subversive elements gathered in taverns." [162]

In regard to penalties for "subversive" utterance the State of Tennessee leads the nation. There in 1951 the legislature, in the name of freedom, passed a statute making the death sentence a possibility for unlawful advocacy. Michigan comes second in this form of patriotism, having enacted a law in 1950 providing life imprisonment for those speaking or writing "subversively."

Besides adopting drastic new legislation, many States have revived old anti-sedition or anti-anarchy laws enacted during the period of hysteria after the First World War. In 1950 Pennsylvania indicted Steve Nelson, a Communist Party leader, under its drastic anti-sedition Act of 1919 making it a crime "to incite or encourage any person to commit any overt act with a view to bringing the Government of this State or the United States into hatred and contempt."

Found guilty in 1952 and savagely sentenced to twenty years in the penitentiary, Mr. Nelson appealed his case.* In 1954 the Pennsylvania Supreme Court reversed the conviction and declared the statute unconstitutional on the ground that the Federal Smith Act has superseded State legislation on the subject of sedition and preempted the field. Pennsylvania's Attorney General,

---

* Nelson was also convicted in 1953 under the Smith Act for conspiring to advocate violent overthrow of the Government, and was sentenced to five years in jail.

supported by thirty States with anti-sedition laws, appealed this decision to the U.S. Supreme Court. U.S. Attorney General Brownell backed the States in their appeal.

Meantime, in 1951 the State of Massachusetts indicted Dr. Dirk J. Struik, Professor of Mathematics at the Massachusetts Institute of Technology, and Harry W. Winner, a businessman from Malden, for violating an anti-anarchy Act of 1919 by supposedly conspiring "to advocate, advise, counsel and incite the overthrow by force and violence" of the Commonwealth of Massachusetts and the United States Government. The disposition of these cases depends on the decision of the U.S. Supreme Court in the Pennsylvania Nelson case.

The vague language of sedition laws lends them readily for use in all sorts of prosecutions. In 1954, just four months after the U.S. Supreme Court ordered an end to segregation in public schools, the Commonwealth of Kentucky unearthed a previously untested 1920 sedition law and used it to indict seven white persons who favored racial equality. Those indicted had helped a Negro veteran and his family purchase and settle into a house in an all-white community just outside Louisville. The indictments, which charged sedition and conspiracy to promote communism, were brought after a bomb exploded under the house, partially wrecking it.

This appalling case received little attention in the national press. It originated when a Negro family, Mr. and Mrs. Andrew Wade IV, wanted to buy a house, and sought the help of a white couple, Carl Braden, a copy-reader on the Louisville *Courier-Journal*, and his wife Anne, a member of the Louisville branch of NAACP. A protracted search for housing in the Louisville area had netted the Wades nothing. In Negro sections, no suitable dwellings were available; and in white neighborhoods the Wades had been curtly refused. Would the Bradens buy a suburban bungalow and resell it to the Wades? The Bradens agreed; a house was bought; and the transfer completed.

On May 13, as the Wades began moving into the new house, Ku-Klux-Klan-like elements opened their campaign. An angry mob of whites, including the real-estate broker, called on the Bradens, and threatened them and their children with violence unless the Wades vacated the house within forty-eight hours. Two nights later, rocks were thrown through the window of the Wade home; a cross was burned on a nearby lot; and rifle shots were fired into the house.

The local newspaper, *Shively Newsweek*, published a series of anti-Negro stories and letters; threatening mobs gathered near the Wade home; and the Bradens received constant abusive and threatening telephone calls. The county police set a twenty-four-hour watch on the Wade home. A Wade defense committee was also formed, of white and Negro volunteers. One of the volunteers was Vernon Bown, a white truck driver who worked nights and who moved into the house to help guard Mrs. Wade and her child during the day. Another white volunteer was Lewis Lubka, a union shop steward in the General Electric Plant. Both were later indicted.

On June 22 the county police withdrew their day guard from the house. On Saturday, June 27, about 12:30 a.m., just after the Wades had returned from an outing, a bomb exploded under their bedrooms, tearing out one side of the house. Fortunately the Wades had not yet gone to bed, and so escaped injury or death. As the Louisville *Courier-Journal* pointed out, the crime of murder was "only accidentally avoided."

When the grand jury investigation opened on September 15, the Commonwealth Attorney, A. Scott Hamilton, contended that the explosion was part of a Communist plot to foment racial discord; and the white supporters of Wade came under heavy attack. Some of them had been members of the Progressive Party and leftist organizations. They were queried only briefly about the bombing; instead, the probers questioned their associations, their membership in organizations, the literature they read. The *Courier-Journal's* comment on the grand jury probe was: "Mr. Hamilton has produced not the slightest evidence to uphold his theory of a Communist plot. He has paid very little attention to the alternative and much more likely theory that the bombing was the work of hoodlums who resented a Negro's purchase of a house in a white area." [163]

When the grand jury investigations ended, however, the Communist-plot theory was fully blown. On October 1, indictments for sedition were returned, charging six white persons with crimes. Besides Mr. and Mrs. Braden, those indicted were Vernon Bown, who was also charged with the actual bombing, although he had been out of town for two days at the time of the explosion; I. O. Ford, a retired riverboat captain who was Bown's roommate; and two social workers, Miss Louise Gilbert, and Miss Larue Spiker, who had pleaded for good will for the Wades.

In November the grand jury returned additional indictments, charging the Bradens, Bown, Ford, and Lewis Lubka with conspiring to damage property to achieve a political end, "to wit . . . communism." Meanwhile, the police raided the homes of five of the defendants (four of them without warrants), and confiscated a large amount of literature and personal papers which the prosecution claimed was subversive. It was this literature, interpreted à la mode for the prosecution by ten "expert witnesses" imported especially for the occasion, which laid the foundation for the conviction of Carl Braden, first of the accused to be tried. The ten witnesses included such wandering minstrels as Manning Johnson, Maurice Malkin and Benjamin Gitlow, none of whom knew Braden, but all of whom painted ominous pictures of the Red menace.

The defense strenuously contested this trial based on anti-Communist phobia and on speculation as to a man's reading habits. Braden's counsel maintained that no inventory was made of the items of literature seized, and that unsystematic storage of the books and papers left their source open to question. These objections were of no avail. The jury found Braden guilty on December 13. The judge sentenced him to fifteen years in jail and a $5,000 fine, and set his bail at the excessive figure of $40,000.

Following his conviction, Braden remained in jail for seven months until, with the aid of the Emergency Civil Liberties Committee, he was able to raise the necessary $40,000. Prosecution of the other Louisville defendants was postponed pending the outcome of Braden's appeal. This, like the Massachusetts cases, depends on the ruling of the U.S. Supreme Court in the Nelson case.

In spite of all the anti-subversive measures of the past decade on the national, state and local levels, the Red-hunters remain unsatisfied. As Dean Lawrence Chamberlain says in his study of the situation in New York State: "It is noteworthy that those who press most vigorously for additional legal restrictions derive the least sense of protection from each new law and thus are obliged to seek ever more sweeping repressive measures." [164]

The fact is that these laws accomplish so little in the way of exposing any real dangers to the community that legislators, evidently under the impression that Communists have preternatural means of concealing their thoughts and activities, feel obliged to go to further and further extremes, ever expanding the meaning of subversion, disloyalty and other such terms. "In the end," says Professor Gellhorn, "the failure of legislation to banish the fears that started the whole spiral is rarely taken as showing that the fears were perhaps ill founded. It is taken as showing, rather, that more and more remains to be done." [165]

State legislatures, in addition to enacting new anti-subversive, anti-freedom laws and resurrecting old ones, have instituted investigating committees that have aped the worst practices of Congressional committees. Taking the lead in violations of the Bill of Rights and the onslaught on cultural freedom have been the California Tenney Committee, the Illinois Broyles Commission, the Ohio Un-American Activities Committee, the Massachusetts Committee to Curb Communism, the New Hampshire Commission on Subversive Activities and the Washington Canwell Committee. Fortunately, none of these committees has been voted permanent status.

In California the Fact-Finding Committee on Un-American Activities, of which Senator Jack B. Tenney was chairman from 1941 to 1949, set a record for scandalous behavior. Mr. Tenney, a piano player and song writer, started out in politics as a left-winger. In 1938, speaking at a meeting of the Hollywood Anti-

Nazi League where the dissolution of the Dies Committee was called for, Tenney asserted: "Fellow subversive elements, I have just heard that Mickey Mouse is conspiring with Shirley Temple to overthrow the government and that there is a witness who has seen the 'Red' card of Donald Duck. When the Dies Committee stoops to calling President Roosevelt a Communist, and says that Mrs. Roosevelt is a front for subversive elements, then I think the rest of us should be flattered to be put in that category." [166]

Like so many other "radical" Americans in recent times, Mr. Tenney suddenly decided on a quick transition from Left to Right. A year after the above speech he was already turning against his former associates; three years after, he was heading up the legislative investigating committee.

That committee bore down especially heavily on teachers in schools and colleges; on actors, directors and script writers in the motion picture industry; and on workers for civil liberties. When Tenney investigated a high-school course on marriage and family relations at the small town of Chico, he promptly reported that the books used "either wittingly or unwittingly follow or parallel the *Communist Party* line for the destruction of the moral fibre of American youth. Disrespect for parents, religion and the law of the land is subtly injected throughout the hedonistic content." [167] The Chico affair, Tenney concluded, was part of "a carefully laid Communist plan for the corruption of America's coming generation." [168]

The California press reacted violently to this typical Tenney investigation and headlined the theme, "Tenney fears Sex may be Un-American."

The Tenney Committee also compiled and published its own list of 175 alleged Communist-front organizations. The accuracy of this list may be judged by the fact that it included the American Civil Liberties Union.

Regarding the ACLU, the Tenney Committee stated in its 1943 report: "The *American Civil Liberties Union* may be definitely classed as a Communist front or 'transmission belt' organization. At least 90 percent of its efforts are expended on behalf of Communists who come into conflict with the law. While it professes to stand for free speech, a free press and free assembly, it is quite obvious that its main function is to protect Communists in their activities of force and violence in their program to overthrow the government." [169]

Mr. Ernest Besig, Director of the Northern California Branch of the Civil Liberties Union, wrote to Senator Tenney denying these charges, pointing out that no member of his executive committee had been called upon to testify and requesting that his organization be given a hearing by the Senator's committee. A long correspondence ensued, but the request was never granted.

Like its Congressional prototypes, the Tenney Committee was continually attempting to punish or banish the unrelenting dissenter. "Efforts were made to prevent association with him, to forbid lawyers defending him in his troubles with the law, to cause his employer to discharge him and his union to expel him. People were warned that they should not rent him a hall for a meeting, or join any organization of which he was a member, or read any book or attend any play or motion picture written by him, or even espouse any cause espoused by him." [170]

Senator Tenney finally made the same mistake as Joseph Mc-Carthy. His anti-communism became so hysterical that he began to smear even conservative elements in the community as Communists. At the end he was antagonizing everybody except the rabid Right. Ministers and church groups issued protests against the committee's procedures. Influential newspapers joined in the attack. And in 1949 such strong pressures were brought from different directions on the California Senate that it forced Tenney to withdraw entirely from the committee in June of that year and appointed Senator Hugh M. Burns as chairman in his place.

Senator Tenney's political position deteriorated even further when he later sought out the support of the fascist-minded Gerald L. K. Smith. In the 1954 primaries the Republican Party of California deserted Tenney and put up Mrs. Mildred Younger to run for the State Senate against him. Tenney's supporters thereupon entered a totally unknown Mrs. Hazel Younger in an attempt to confuse the situation and split the vote. The ruse did not work, however, and Mrs. Mildred Younger swamped Tenney in the primary. But on Election Day she was defeated in turn by her Democratic opponent.

In New Hampshire—where the FBI reported in 1950 that there were forty-three members of the Communist Party—the State legislature, alarmed by such a grave Red menace to a commonwealth traditionally Republican, passed in 1951 a Subversive Activities Act; and in 1953—annoyed that so little subversion had been uncovered—it directed the State Attorney General to inquire into violations of this law. The measure declares that the Communist Party is a foreign-controlled conspiracy aimed at overthrowing the United States Government by force and violence; and prescribes heavy penalties for any person who belongs to the Communist Party or some other subversive organization, and for any person who teaches, advocates or otherwise promotes the violent overthrow of constitutional government.

In 1954 State Attorney General Louis C. Wyman called for questioning Dr. Paul Sweezy, formerly an economics teacher at Harvard University and co-editor of the independent Socialist magazine, *Monthly Review*. At his first hearing Dr. Sweezy answered questions to the effect that he was a Marxist and Socialist, that he had never been a member of the Communist Party or attended its meetings, and that he had never advocated overthrow of the government by force. But at the same time he stated: "I shall respectfully decline to answer questions concerning ideas, beliefs, and associations which could not possibly be pertinent to the matter here under inquiry and/or which seem to me to invade the freedoms guaranteed by the First Amendment to the United States Constitution (which of course applies equally to the several States)." [171]

At his second hearing Sweezy refused to answer questions concerning a lecture on Socialism which he had recently given at the University of New Hampshire. He asserted that in this talk he did not advocate violent overthrow and that questions by the Attorney General relating to the lecture constituted an invasion of the

First Amendment. A few weeks later a New Hampshire judge declared Dr. Sweezy in contempt of court and sentenced him to jail. Sweezy was then released on $1,000 bail and appealed his case to the State Supreme Court. A particularly serious angle in this case is that under New Hampshire practice a man finally found guilty of contempt of court stays in jail until he answers the original questions.

In Florida in 1954, the State Attorney for Dade County, George A. Brautigam and the Senior Circuit Judge of the County, George E. Holt, ably assisted by the Miami *Daily News,* instituted a virtual reign of terror in Miami. After Damon Runyon, Jr., had denounced a number of persons in a lurid series of articles in the *Daily News,* State Attorney Brautigam started to summon these individuals for questioning by a grand jury. When they invoked the Fifth Amendment in refusing to answer a series of accusatory questions, Judge Holt declared twenty-eight of them in contempt of court and sentenced all to a year in jail.

He took this action in cooperation with Mr. Brautigam, who had confined his questions to a time prior to the two years prescribed by the Florida Statute of Limitations. The judge held that since no witness could be prosecuted for any crime committed prior to the two-year period, the invocation of the Fifth Amendment against compulsory self-incrimination was invalid. When in November 1954 the Florida Supreme Court reversed the contempt convictions, State Attorney Brautigam announced that he would seek the indictment of the individuals concerned under Florida's special anti-sedition law.

In 1955 in Massachusetts the Special Commission to Study and Investigate Communism, Subversive Activities and Related Matters opened up new territory for State legislative committees when it issued a blacklist of eighty-five Massachusetts residents who it claimed "creditable evidence" showed were members of the Communist Party, Communists or subversives. The Commission printed a long account of each person's misdeeds and subversive associations. A special statute passed by the State legislature authorized the Commission's inquiry. Already in 1951

Massachusetts had made membership in the Communist Party illegal.

The municipalities have also done their bit in the great crusade against subversion. There have been a number of "run-them-out-of-town" statutes in various localities throughout the country. These ordinances require all known Communists to leave the city. Other ordinances have required Communists to register with the police. One city—Cumberland, Maryland—frankly made it a crime to sell or give away "Communist" literature on the city streets. More subtle and sophisticated Detroit closed down newsstands displaying Communist publications on the grounds that the stands were a nuisance on the public thoroughfares. In Oklahoma City persons possessing "Communist literature" were arrested for disorderly conduct.

Municipalities have also put increasing obstacles in the way of dissenters hiring meeting halls or staging street demonstrations. School buildings have become less and less accessible for meetings. For instance, in 1951 the New York City Board of Education barred all organizations believed to be Communist, totalitarian, subversive or fascist from holding meetings in public schools.

We go back to the First World War for the classic case on street meetings. It happened in New York City in 1918 when a Socialist stood on a street corner in the Bronx and started to read aloud the Declaration of Independence. Just after he had read, "Whenever any Form of Government becomes destructive of these ends, it is the Right of the people to alter or to abolish it," a policeman arrested him. The Socialist protested: "But I didn't say that. Thomas Jefferson said it." "Where's that guy?" demanded the cop. "We'll get him too!"

In October 1952, when I was running for U.S. Senator from New York on the American Labor Party (ALP) ticket, I encountered obstacles in making scheduled speeches in two cities. At Syracuse, where I was due to speak in the War Memorial Building on "Back to the Bill of Rights," the county authorities canceled the arrangements at the last moment after protests by the local press and American Legion. I was forced to give my speech at the small and inadequate headquarters of the ALP.

A week later at Kingston I was unable to obtain any hall at all in which to speak. First, the Hotel Stuyvesant canceled a reservation made by the local ALP and refunded a deposit of $15. Then the ALP hired a hall in the YMCA building; but in two or three days the YMCA canceled that reservation. Finally, the ALP tried to obtain a room in the Municipal Auditorium; but the Mayor of the city thereupon discovered that it was against the policy of the municipal Common Council to permit political meetings in the Auditorium.

The consequence was that I did not make my scheduled Saturday night talk in Kingston, but instead read aloud the Bill of Rights, by the light of a street lamp, from the steps of the County Courthouse in the center of the city. I had a small audience of about twenty-five persons, almost all of them ALP members or sympathizers. I prefaced the reading by saying: "Fellow citizens, I have been denied my right to make a speech tonight. I would like to read to you the most precious part of the United States Constitution. That is the Bill of Rights, for which every American should be willing to give his life."

A favorite device of city authorities has been to prevent a meeting they do not like by suddenly informing the owner of the hall where it is scheduled that his building violates the local statute against inadequate fire exits or too narrow staircases or some other structural insufficiency. Since a mayor can revoke the license of a hall for such defects, the owner is inclined to heed such a warning and cancel the meeting.

Long a scandal, with little relation to anti-Communist hysteria, has been a dangerous disregard by municipal police for the protections of the Bill of Rights. This includes illegal search and seizure, false arrest and various types of police brutality such as solitary confinement or beating in order to obtain incriminating evidence. Needed corrections are better trained police, fullest publicity on abuses, and civil suits against policemen for lawless conduct.

In 1955 a U.S. Court of Appeals in New York State granted a prisoner, Santo Caminito, serving a life term for murder, a new trial because of mistreatment by the New York City police. Judge Jerome N. Frank, delivering the opinion of the Court, stated: "The police interrogated him almost continuously for twenty-seven hours with but a brief interval for rest in a cell so badly equipped as to make sleep virtually impossible for a man already harried by the questioning. During this long period, the police, in effect, kidnapped him; they kept him incommunicado, refusing to allow his lawyer, his family and his friends to consult with him. . . . The confessions obtained by these loathsome means were no more evidence than if they had been forged. . . .

"Repeated and unredressed attacks on the constitutional liberties of the humble will tend to destroy the foundations supporting the constitutional liberties of everyone. The test of the moral quality of a civilization is its treatment of the weak and powerless." [172]

THE DRIVE AGAINST CULTURAL FREEDOM

The drive against freedom in the United States since the Second
World War has extended to nearly every field of cultural endeavor. Art, science, education, literature, publishing, journalism,
religion, the theatre, motion pictures, radio and television have
all suffered. The attack on non-conformity is in essence an anti-
intellectual, anti-cultural movement. The demagogue feeding on
the fears and frustrations of the public realizes that his greatest
enemy is the spread of knowledge and understanding. Accordingly he is against intellectuals of every sort and ridicules them
as "eggheads."

The demagogue is mortally afraid of people thinking, because
he knows that thought can pierce his pretensions. He stands with
the patriotic American mother who complained to her friends
that the U.S. Army was subjecting her son to Communist propaganda. "They're always telling him, 'Think for yourself,'" she said.
For the conformists there is now an Eleventh Commandment,
"Thou shalt not think."

The numberless attacks on cultural freedom during the postwar years almost defy cataloguing. I shall take up first those
which involve censorship—by government officials, individual
busybodies, or pressure groups with some particular ideological
axe to grind. Such censorship has as its object not only the suppression of the cultural production immediately involved, but

also a general intimidation of the mind which will result in *self-censorship*.

In 1950 the San Diego, California, City Council rejected as an inscription for a war memorial the Four Freedoms enunciated by President Franklin D. Roosevelt. The inscription was intended for a plaque at a new Veterans Memorial Building. The Council took its action after Admiral William H. Standley, a former U.S. Ambassador to the Soviet Union, protested that "Freedom from want is a Russian communistic slogan," and that "Freedom from fear is a political slogan." The Admiral magnanimously did not object to freedom of speech and freedom of worship.

In the same year Monogram Studio of Hollywood canceled the filming of a script dealing with the life of Hiawatha, fifteenth-century Onondaga Indian Chief immortalized in Longfellow's classic poem. The studio thought the production might be construed as Communist propaganda. To quote *The New York Times:* "It was Hiawatha's efforts as a peacemaker among the warring Indian tribes of his day, which brought about the Confederation of the Five Nations, that gave Monogram particular concern, according to a studio spokesman. These, it was decided, might cause the picture to be regarded as a message for peace, and therefore helpful to present Communist designs." [173]

In point of fact the movie industry, under the influence of the Motion Picture Producers and Distributors of America * with its Production Code, has for many years suppressed scripts and cut pictures that strayed from the glorification of orthodox morality, portrayed "excessive and lustful kissing," or were too controversial politically. The Production Code, a sixteen-page manual of "Dont's" and "Be Carefuls," was drawn up in 1930 by a Jesuit priest and a Catholic layman. This Code, reflecting the viewpoint of the Roman Catholic Church, should be abolished.

One of the most shameful acts of censorship was the withdrawal in 1938, under pressure from Will Hays as President of the Motion Picture Producers and Distributors, of a script by Sidney

* In 1945 the name of this organization was changed to the Motion Picture Association of America.

Howard based on Sinclair Lewis's powerful anti-fascist novel, *It Can't Happen Here*. Metro-Goldwyn-Mayer canceled the movie version of the book at the last minute after most of the casting had been completed and Lionel Barrymore had been engaged to play the central role of Doremus Jessup, the anti-fascist newspaper publisher. Mr. Lewis himself denounced the ban against a movie dramatization of his book as "a fantastic exhibition of folly and cowardice," and a violation of free speech and free opinion.

The atmosphere in the motion picture industry has become more and more saturated with fear and suspicion since the Second World War; and particularly since 1947, when the big movie producers surrendered to the pressures of the witch-hunt and fired ten actors and directors cited for contempt of Congress for not answering the Un-American Activities Committee's questions. Since then, actors or other movie employees who have held leftist or even mildly liberal views or who have been active in an organization on the Attorney General's blacklist have lost or been in danger of losing their jobs.

As Miss Lillian Ross said in a special article for *The New Yorker* Magazine: "Almost the only motion-picture star who is taking conditions in his stride is Lassie, a reddish-haired male collie, who is probably too mixed up emotionally over being called by a girl's name to worry about the box office. Lassie is working more steadily, not only in films but on the radio, than anyone else in Hollywood. 'We'd be in a hole if we didn't have Lassie,' I heard an M-G-M man say. 'We like Lassie. We're sure of Lassie. Lassie can't go out and embarrass the studio. Katharine Hepburn goes out and makes a speech for Henry Wallace. Bang! We're in trouble. Lassie doesn't make speeches. Not Lassie, thank God!'" [174]

When motion picture directors, producers and writers are not censoring themselves, other people are trying to do it for them. During the past decade attempts have been made—successful in some localities—to ban: *The Bicycle Thief*, a realistic Italian picture offensive to prudes; *Lost Boundaries*, which portrays racial discrimination against a Negro doctor; *Pinky*, another film critical of anti-Negro prejudice in America; *The Birth of a Nation,* an early movie depicting the Reconstruction period in the South and biased against the Negro; *Salt of the Earth,* which tells the story of a New Mexico miners union carrying through a long-drawn-out strike; *The Moon Is Blue,* based on a Broadway theatre hit in which the heroine visits two bachelors' apartments, participates in some sophisticated conversation, but emerges with her virtue intact; *Latuko,* a documentary on an African tribe, sponsored by the American Museum of Natural History; *Oliver Twist,* film version of the novel by Charles Dickens; and *The Miracle,* an Italian movie about a psychologically disturbed peasant girl who interprets her love affair as a miraculous religious visitation from on high.

The Motion Picture Division of the New York State Board of Regents refused a license for *Latuko* because it included several scenes in which nude African natives appeared. Mr. Alexander M. White, President of the sponsoring Natural History Museum, stated: "The primary object of this film is to educate and enlighten the audience as to the manner in which primitive people are living in Africa today. If nudity is objectionable *per se,* many of the great masterpieces of painting and sculpture should be withdrawn from exhibition. It is the museum's judgment that there is nothing inherently indecent in portraying these African natives as they actually live." [175]

Jewish groups boycotted *Oliver Twist* on the ground that the portrayal of Dickens's famous character, Fagin, was anti-Semitic; Negro groups protested the revival of *The Birth of a Nation* because it fanned racial prejudice; and Catholic groups tried to have *The Miracle* suppressed on the claim that it was offensive to the Christian religion. Taking an active part in the campaign against *The Miracle* were the Catholic Welfare Conference, the Catholic War Veterans, the Holy Name Society and the National Legion of Decency of the Roman Catholic Church, which denounced the film as "a sacrilegious and blasphemous mockery of Christian religious truth." [176]

The Legion of Decency is the most powerful of the pressure

groups that operate in the field of the motion picture. Founded in 1934, the Legion insists on strict enforcement of the 1930 Production Code and began issuing classified lists of movies early in 1936. The five classifications include general clearance—A-1—for "morally unobjectionable" pictures, a B rating for those which are "morally objectionable in part for all," and a C rating for those which are "condemned." The Legion of Decency wields great influence on the more than 30,000,000 American Catholics, millions of whom take an annual pledge to support it. It is easy to understand, therefore, why movie producers will make considerable alterations in their scripts or will cut finished films in order to obtain an A-1 rating or avoid the C rating. Thus the Legion is able to exercise an unofficial censorship over the movie industry.

Under such severe Catholic pressure, the New York State Board of Regents, which had twice cleared *The Miracle,* finally revoked the license for the showing of the film on the ground that it was sacrilegious. But in the end this censorship boomeranged decisively against its originators. For in 1952 the U.S. Supreme Court reversed the ban on *The Miracle,* showing how dangerous it was to base censorship on such a vague term as "sacrilegious"; and in the same decision came out for the first time with a clearcut statement bringing the movies under the protection of the Bill of Rights. "Expression by means of motion pictures," said the Court unanimously, "is included within the free speech and free press guaranty of the First and Fourteenth Amendments." [177]

In radio and television, as in the movies, any actor who has become "controversial" is usually eased out of his job. In nine cases out of ten a "controversial" performer is one who belongs or has belonged to an organization on the U.S. Attorney General's blacklist or sometimes is merely "reported" to be or have been a member. Widely publicized, although unproved, charges against individuals working in radio and TV have repeatedly served to make them so "controversial" that they lose their jobs.

The most pernicious single element in this situation has been the book *Red Channels, the Report of Communist Influence in Radio and Television,* published in 1950 by the weekly newsletter,

Counterattack. Ex-FBI agents issue this periodical devoted to exposing alleged Reds, Pinks, fellow-travelers, dupes and super-dupes. *Red Channels* has created havoc with the careers of the 151 actors, dancers, singers, musicians, composers, writers and others listed in it for "Communist" activities or associations. The book makes no pretense of presenting established facts; instead it starts off each listing under an individual's name with the phrase "Reported as." Most radio and television companies have used *Red Channels* as a blacklist for dismissing or refusing to employ the persons named.

The appointment late in 1953 of Senator McCarthy's friend, Robert E. Lee, to the Federal Communications Commission, which regulates the radio and television industry, was an additional factor in making the various companies in this field even more nervous about letting dissenters appear on programs. The FCC can make trouble for a station by holding up or refusing altogether to renew its license. Early in 1954 when I had been invited to take part in a television debate in New York City, the producer at the last minute tried to bring about my withdrawal, and was perfectly frank in saying that he was afraid my appearance would antagonize Mr. Lee and Joe McCarthy. I declined to withdraw and the program went through as scheduled.

The censorship that blights movies, radio, and television is no less crippling in the theatre. In 1953 a New York production of Aristophanes's farce, *Congress of Women,* written almost 2400 years ago, was presented "in an expurgated version allegedly because of fears that the play might be labeled pro-Communist." [178] Robert Klein, director of the production, protested that the Board of Directors of the Academy of Dramatic Arts deleted the following two passages for political reasons:

> PRAXAGORA: *The rule which I dare to enact and*
> *declare*
> *Is that all shall be equal, and equally share*
> *All wealth and enjoyments, nor longer endure*
> *That one should be rich, and another be poor,*

> *That one should have acres, far-stretching and wide,*
> *And another not even enough to provide*
> *Himself with a grave: that this at his call*
> *Should have hundreds of servants, and that none at all.*
> *All this I intend to correct and amend:*
> *Now all of all blessings shall freely partake,*
> *One life and one system for all men I make. . . .*
> >   BLEPYRUS: *'Tis those that have most of these*
> >   *goods, I believe,*
> *That are always the worst and the keenest to thieve.*
> >   PRAXAGORA: *I grant you, my friend, in the days*
> >   *that are past,*
> *In your old-fashioned system, abolished at last;*
> *But what's he to gain, though his wealth he retain,*
> *When all things are common, I'd have to explain.*[179]

Another significant incident of 1953 was the sudden cancellation in New York of a regular performance of the hit musical *Wonderful Town,* starring Rosalind Russell, because the producer did not like the views of the *National Guardian,* a progressive newsweekly, which had bought a bloc of tickets for its spring theatre benefit. The playwright Elmer Rice, Chairman of the National Council on Freedom from Censorship, objected to the action on the grounds that "theatregoers must now pass political tests set up by producers. . . . The theatre will suffer, ideas will no longer be freely expressed, dramatists and producers will operate not with the conscience of intellectual freedom, but only with a view of obtaining the approval of self-appointed censors." [180]

During the same year two members of the Georgia State legislature denounced as Red propaganda another popular musical, *South Pacific,* by Richard Rodgers and Oscar Hammerstein 2nd, which had just completed a successful run in Atlanta. State Representative David C. Jones and State Senator John D. Shepard claimed the play advocated inter-racial marriage; and that they would introduce "appropriate legislation to prevent the showing of movies, plays, musicals or other theatricals which have an underlying philosophy inspired by Moscow." [181]

The two legislators were especially offended by the song, "You've Got to Be Taught," the lyrics of which read: "You've got to be taught to be afraid of people whose skin is a different shade. . . . You've got to be taught before it's too late . . . to hate all the people your relatives hate." [182] Mr. Jones opposed what he considered the message of this song, saying: "We in the South are a proud and progressive people. Halfbreeds cannot be proud. In the South we have pure blood lines, and we intend to keep it that way." [183]

Occasionally, the self-appointed defenders of purity and patriotism in culture have resorted to outright force in order to protect their conception of Americanism. This happened in the infamous Peekskill riots of 1949. On August 27 of that year Paul Robeson's outdoor concert at Peekskill, New York, was broken up by mob violence. The mob, led by 100-percent patriots of the American Legion and the Veterans of Foreign Wars, beat up persons coming to attend the concert, overturned cars, and burned chairs, programs, song books and the concert platform. Effective police protection for the concert was deliberately withheld.

Robeson's sponsors and supporters, determined to go through with their concert, scheduled another one for September 4. The concert took place, with an attendance of 15,000, but then a mob of some 10,000 assaulted them as they left. To quote the *Peekskill Evening Star:* "Nearly 150 persons were injured Sunday afternoon, at least six seriously, when hundreds of automobiles and scores of buses carrying jeering Paul Robeson supporters, ran a gauntlet of stone-throwing demonstrators. . . . Incensed demonstrators assembled at points along Hillside Avenue, out of sight of the police. In the ensuing rioting, hundreds of cars had windshields and windows shattered. Eight cars were reported overturned and destroyed, four of them in Putnam County. Peekskill Hospital was jammed as the injured began pouring in late Sunday afternoon." [184]

Although these two Peekskill riots expressed the hatred of

fanatical and misguided patriotism for the alleged Communist groups behind the Robeson concerts, deep-lying prejudices of an anti-Jewish and anti-Negro character were important factors in the outbreaks. Since a majority of the people, including local government officials, in the neighborhood of Peekskill quite evidently either justified or condoned the violence, it is not surprising that no one was ever brought to book for the riots. In the United States, governmental authorities sworn to uphold "law and order" can quickly forget their duty when they are called upon to safeguard some unpopular element in the community.

In the realm of art the once liberal New School for Social Research has joined the ranks of the censors by covering with white monkscloth one of four notable murals painted in its dining room by the famous Mexican artist, José Clemente Orozco. When in 1930 Orozco painted these murals depicting the great social movements astir in the world, his work received wide acclaim and was highly prized by the New School. One mural showed the Mexican Revolution in full bloom, another Gandhi's non-violent movement to free India from British rule, a third the Chinese Revolution led by Sun Yat-sen. The fourth mural of course had to be about the Russian Revolution; and here the realistic Orozco not unnaturally included portraits of Lenin and Stalin.

Twenty-one years later, in 1951, the new barbarians, including teachers and students at the New School, began to harass the School authorities with protests against the painting about Soviet Russia, alleging that it gave particular offense because it was in the cafeteria where large numbers of people had their meals. The School answered by installing below the offending mural a copper plaque which said that the sentiments expressed in the picture were exclusively Orozco's. But the vituperation continued; and in 1953 the New School finally surrendered and placed the white cloth over the painting. This is "a period of great unease about Russia," explained the publicity director in masterly understatement.

In Detroit in 1952 a controversy flared up over the work of another great Mexican painter. Eugene I. Van Antwerp, a former mayor of the city, led a campaign to have Diego Rivera's "Age of Steel" frescoes in the Detroit Institute of Arts removed or covered up. The volunteer art purgers charged that the murals, executed in 1922 and commissioned by the late Edsel Ford, contained Communist propaganda, represented Detroit workingmen as ugly, and were blasphemous and decadent. The city's Common Council let the paintings stand after the Detroit Art Commission in a special report refuted the complaints and defended the frescoes as among the best of Rivera's work.

It will be recalled that in 1933 in New York City a noted fresco by Diego Rivera did not fare so well. This was a large mural portraying human intelligence in control of the forces of nature, which John D. Rockefeller, Jr., had engaged Rivera to paint in the Great Hall of the RCA Building in Rockefeller Center. After the actual painting had begun, the Rockefellers objected to the inclusion of a figure of Lenin joining the hands of a soldier, a worker and a Negro, for the reason that this symbolic group "might very easily offend a great many people."

Rivera claimed that the head of Lenin was included in the original sketch, but the Rockefellers insisted that they had not recognized it as such. Rivera then offered to balance the portrait of Lenin with one of Abraham Lincoln, surrounded by John Brown, Nat Turner, William Lloyd Garrison and perhaps Harriet Beecher Stowe. After the Rockefellers had refused to accept this compromise and Rivera had refused to take out Lenin, Mr. Rockefeller terminated Rivera's contract and had the unfinished painting destroyed.

Rivera later reproduced the whole mural in the Palace of Fine Arts in Mexico City, entitling it "Man at the Crossroads." I saw the fresco when I visited Mexico in 1951 and noticed that Rivera had made one alteration from his original conception. He had painted in a figure of John D. Rockefeller, well known as a complete teetotaler, sipping a glass of champagne and holding the hand of a glamorous female. This, Rivera told me when I interviewed him for the *Daily Compass*, was his "revenge."

The West Coast has also been notable for controversies over

the social comment in art. In California, Congressmen and patriotic organizations combined in a movement to do away with Anton Refregier's murals in the Rincon Annex Post Office in San Francisco. Representative Herbert Scudder, Republican of California, introduced a resolution into Congress calling on the Federal Government to remove the Refregier paintings from the walls of the post office. He asserted that the murals were "artistically offensive and historically inaccurate; and . . . cast a derogatory and improper reflection on the character of the pioneers and history of the great State of California." [185] Mr. Scudder's resolution was finally shelved.

In Los Angeles in 1951 alarmed citizens and an agitated City Council talked ominously of "Communist infiltration" when second prize in a municipal art exhibition went to a picture entitled "Surge of the Sea" in which there was a sailboat with an emblem imagined to resemble the hammer and sickle. In the special investigation that followed, the offending painter, Rex Brandt, explained to his solemn interrogators that the insignia on the sail was simply the racing class symbol of the boat. As one observer remarked, the local Philistines might as well have gone into high dudgeon "against the new moon, which when crossed by a wisp of cloud, might appear to the idiot's eye to be making Communist propaganda." [186]

In 1954 Los Angeles patriots started a campaign to remove from the city's Police Department building Bernard Rosenthal's stylized metal figure sculpture of a family group. Members of the City Council suddenly blossomed forth as art critics; and one of them denounced the sculpture as "raceless, faceless, gutless." A local taxpayer brought suit in order to have the offending sculpture removed, but a wise judge dismissed the case.

In Norwalk, Connecticut, however, the art censors won out when in 1955 the Board of Education voted to ban from a school building murals by Mrs. Anita P. Willcox, illustrating harbor scenes in Norwalk history. The Veterans of Foreign Wars and local McCarthyites had objected to the paintings because Mrs.

Willcox, wife of Henry Willcox,* had attended a peace conference in Communist China, had had her passport seized by the U.S. State Department, and was a "known subversive."

Nothing better illustrates the decline of cultural freedom than what has been happening to books and book publishing. Nineteen fifty-three was the year during which Senator McCarthy and his minions developed such a burning interest in literature. Owing to pressures, direct or indirect, resulting from McCarthy's investigations, many American libraries banned controversial volumes. A number of the titles eliminated were the same as those burned by Nazi storm troopers in the days of Adolf Hitler. The Senator charged that among the approximately 2,000,000 books in the State Department's overseas libraries there were 30,000 by Communist authors. Some of the writers whom he put in this category were John Dewey, Elmer Davis, Robert M. Hutchins, Sherwood Anderson, Louis Bromfield, Edna Ferber, Carl Van Doren and Mark Van Doren.

Unbalanced by McCarthy's rantings, the State Department issued a drastic order to the United States Information Agency in direct charge of the overseas libraries: "No material by any Communists, fellow-travelers, et cetera will be used under any circumstances." [187] No definition was ever given of the term "et cetera," a phrase so broad and vague that it could be stretched to cover almost any author or book that some narrow-minded bureaucrat did not personally approve.

During the period early in 1953 when McCarthy's blasts were attaining hurricane volume the Information Agency was shipping abroad monthly an average of only about 3,400 books instead of the previous norm of about 120,000. Meanwhile, following confidential State Department directives, several hundred books by more than forty authors were removed from the overseas libraries. Secretary of State Dulles disclosed that when word came to Washington that eleven of these volumes had been literally burned, a directive immediately went out to stop this type of disposal.

* See Chapter 11.

Typical books proscribed in the State Department purge were *Washington Witchhunt*, by Bert Andrews, conservative special correspondent for the *New York Herald Tribune; Mission to Moscow*, by Joseph E. Davies; *Union Now*, by Clarence Streit; *The Stilwell Papers*, by the late General Joseph Stilwell; *The Loyalty of Free Men*, by Alan Barth, able editorial writer on *The Washington Post; Middletown* and *Middletown in Transition*, two classic sociological studies by Helen and Robert Lynd; *A Rising Wind— A Report on the Negro Soldier in the European Theatre of War*, by the late Walter White, Executive Secretary of the NAACP; the *Selected Works of Thomas Paine*, because they were edited by the left-wing novelist, Howard Fast; and the detective stories of Dashiell Hammett, because of the author's radical political orientation.

It was this burgeoning book-burning movement sparked by the McCarthy Committee that led President Eisenhower to remark in a speech at Dartmouth College in June 1953: "Don't join the book-burners. Don't think you are going to conceal faults by concealing evidence that they ever existed. Don't be afraid to go in your library and read every book as long as any document does not offend our own ideas of decency. That should be the only censorship.

"How will we defeat communism unless we know what it is? What it teaches—why does it have such an appeal for men? Why are so many people swearing allegiance to it? It's almost a religion, albeit one of the nether regions." [188]

The U.S. Information Agency has never recovered from McCarthy's wild onslaughts of 1953. It automatically bars from the overseas libraries three types of books: those by avowed Communists, those by invokers of the Fifth Amendment, and those by individuals convicted of crimes relating to the security of the United States. The USIA uses a fourth category in its censorship activities, that of the "et cetera" or "additional data" cases. This "graylist" consists of all authors against whom any sort of derogatory information has been brought, and therefore includes hun-

dreds of names. The USIA will not purchase books by any person
on this list until he has been cleared.

On the graylist in 1954 were such authors, artists or composers
as Henry Seidel Canby, Aaron Copland, Malcolm Cowley, Adolph
Dehn, Dorothy Canfield Fisher, Martha Foley, Ernest Hemingway, Julian Huxley, Saul K. Padover, Dorothy Parker, Frederick
L. Schuman, Roger Sessions, Edgar Snow, and Victor Yakhontoff.
In order to avoid adverse publicity, the Information Agency suddenly removed Hemingway from the list when a *New York Times*
reporter began asking embarrassing questions.

Chief of the Agency's service which controls the overseas libraries is Franklin L. Burdette. He discovered one day that paper-
bound volumes of Thoreau's *Walden* were scheduled for shipment
to some of the libraries. Mr. Burdette decided that *Walden* was
"socialistic" and had the shipment canceled.

Somewhat earlier in the spring of 1953 I myself had become
directly involved in an ugly book-burning incident. On April 12
in Chicago a mob broke into a meeting being held by the Chicago
Council of American-Soviet Friendship on the anniversary of
President Franklin D. Roosevelt's death. The mob attacked and
injured more than a dozen persons; seized the books and pamphlets on sale; trampled some of them in the meeting hall, and
then carried the rest out into the street. There, before the police
finally went into action, the rioters tore the literature to pieces,
throwing some of it on a bonfire and scattering the rest to the
winds.

Among the volumes destroyed were two copies of my book,
The Peoples of the Soviet Union, which afterwards got me into
trouble with Senator McCarthy; nineteen copies of a later work,
Soviet Civilization; 350 copies of my pamphlet, *Soviet Aggression,
Myth or Reality?;* and 126 copies of my pamphlet, *Effects of
American Foreign Policy.* At least one of the copies of *Peoples of
the Soviet Union* was thrown on the fire. An eyewitness of the
riot brought me back the charred remains of it.

On April 25 I wrote a letter of protest to Senator Robert C.

Hendrickson, Chairman of the Subcommittee on Civil Rights *
of the Senate Judiciary Committee, and requested that his Subcommittee "investigate thoroughly this outrageous action in defiance of law and order, to determine whether it constituted a
violation of the Federal Civil Rights Acts; to discover why the
Chicago police stood by and permitted this raid, riot and book-
burning to take place; and to find out whether those responsible
for the outbreak can be prosecuted under some law." At the same
time, I sent Senator Hendrickson as Exhibit A the charred copy
of *The Peoples of the Soviet Union.*

The Senator replied on May 6 and said: "I am presently organizing a Subcommittee staff, and expect to consider your problem
at an early meeting of the membership." I did not hear from
Senator Hendrickson again until two months later when, on July
7, he wrote that "our Subcommittee is tentatively scheduled to
meet on July 17, to consider an early hearing." *The New York
Times* ran a story to the same effect. On July 20 Senator Hendrickson wired me that the meeting of his Subcommittee had to be
postponed, but that he expected it to be held at any moment.

On July 26, as I informed Senator Hendrickson by telegram,
Mr. Nicholas Lotushinsky, manager of the People's Auditorium
where the Chicago rally was held, suddenly died of a heart attack.
Lotushinsky had been badly beaten by the mob; and his doctor
said that his physical injuries and severe mental strain were
primary factors in his unexpected death.

But I never heard again from the Senate Subcommittee on
Civil Rights; and so far as I know, it never even discussed the
Chicago riot. Thus, not only the City of Chicago, and the State of
Illinois, but also the Federal authorities were unwilling to assess
responsibility and take action regarding a violent outbreak violating freedom of assembly and involving the wanton destruction
of property.

My book, *The Peoples of the Soviet Union,* was still stirring up
controversy in 1954 and 1955 when some super-patriots in Cali-

---

* In 1955 the name of this Subcommittee was changed to Subcommittee on Constitutional Rights.

fornia attempted to have this study, along with fourteen other titles, removed from certain public school libraries. The educational authorities finally "cleared" all fifteen volumes for use.

Meanwhile, the large majority of publishers, fearful of public disapproval or of investigation by some Congressional committee, have not been idle in attempting to purify themselves by letting controversial works go out of print, declining to publish books of a liberal or radical nature, and bringing pressure on employees under fire to resign. In some cases even printers and binders have refused to take part in the manufacture of books which they consider subversive or dangerous.

The drive against "subversive" literature holds alarming threats to freedom of opinion and inquiry, and often to economic security; but it is not without its amusing aspects. Thus, in the fall of 1953, Mrs. Thomas J. White, a member of the Indiana Textbook Commission, demanded that the story of Robin Hood be removed from school textbooks because it promoted Communist Party doctrines. Mrs. White charged that "there is a Communist directive in education now to stress the story of Robin Hood. They want to stress it because he robbed the rich and gave it to the poor. That's the Communist line. It's just a smearing of law and order and anything that disrupts law and order is their meat." [189]

The Sheriff of Nottingham, England, William J. Cox, immediately entered the controversy and denied that Robin Hood was a Red. Said Mr. Cox: "If Robin Hood were alive today, we'd probably call him a gangster. Then it would be my duty to go out after him—just like my predecessor 700 or 800 years ago. But that outlaw was no Communist. That doesn't mean to say that I think he was the finest person in the world. . . . The Communists may claim a lot of things, but they can't claim Robin Hood. We're really proud of him." [190]

Mrs. White also urged that references to Quakers be eliminated from books. "Quakers don't believe in fighting wars," she warned. "All the men they can get to believe that they don't need to go to war, the better off the Communists are. It's the same as their crusade for peace—everybody lay down his arms and they'll take over." [191]

In 1954 the proud purgers of literature scored one of their most resounding triumphs when they pressured the Girl Scouts of America, with an enrollment of 2,000,000, into major revisions of the 1953 edition of the *Girl Scout Handbook*. An article by Robert Le Fevre, a Florida newscaster, had initiated the controversy. Le Fevre charged that the *Handbook* promoted "socialized medicine" (because it contained a paragraph describing the work of the United States Public Health Service), spoke favorably of the League of Women Voters and, worst of all, had a suspicious "internationalist" tone.

The issue snowballed to ominous proportions when the Le Fevre article and another piece critical of the *Handbook* were entered in the Appendix of the *Congressional Record*. The worried Girl Scouts quickly decided to issue a revised *Handbook* with a number of "corrections" to "clarify" certain passages. Before this could be done, however, the Illinois Department of the American Legion passed a resolution condemning the Girl Scouts on the ground that the *Handbook* contained "un-American" literature. The Illinois Commander especially criticized favorable references to the U.N., "in view of the fact that the United Nations Charter was the handiwork of that arch traitor Alger Hiss." [192]

The Girl Scouts then immediately printed and sent out a leaflet to correct the 100,000 copies of the old edition of the *Handbook*. This leaflet listed the sixty changes that were to go into the forthcoming impression of August 1954. The corrections eliminated the phrase "citizens of the world," all mention of the League of Women Voters, any reference to housing as an activity of the United States Government and much of the material on the United Nations, including any reference to the Declaration of Human Rights.

The "clarifications" also altered the phrase "one world" to "my world"; struck out the word "world" entirely in more than twenty places; substituted "Tea—India" for "Tea—China"; and replaced "Service is your way of making this a better world in which to live" with "Service is your way of making a contribution to the community." Perhaps most amazing of all, the new impression of the *Handbook* contained a complete blank page, representing thirty lines cut out of the section entitled "My World."

After these various corrections and deletions had been announced, the Illinois branch of the Legion magnanimously rescinded its vote of censure.

This absurd episode of the *Girl Scout Handbook* is less important for itself than for what it shows about the objectives of the American witch-hunters. Those who attacked the *Handbook* did not make the familiar claim that it was spreading Communist propaganda. Their main charge was that it gave space to facts and views which tended to support a liberal attitude in international relations. This brings out the point that the anti-freedom drive today is not merely against Communist ideas, but against *all* ideas diverging from a confused right-wing orthodoxy.

Censorship imposed by private groups can have powerful effect, as can that wrought by Congressional inquiry. But occasionally, too, the Executive arm of the Government moves ponderously into the act. The U.S. Post Office Department, for instance, can be counted upon frequently to complicate life and literature by some egregious act of censorship. Thus in 1951 the Post Office refused to deliver a rare edition of Aristophanes's classic comedy, *Lysistrata,* to Mr. Harry A. Levinson, a book dealer in California. Post Office officials claimed that the book was "plainly obscene, lewd and lascivious in character"; that it was "well calculated to deprave the morals of persons reading same and almost equally certain to arouse libidinous thoughts in the mind of the average normal reader"; and that the evil effect of the play "was intensified and heightened by the indecent and lascivious character of the illustrations" by the Australian artist Norman Lindsay.[193]

Aristophanes wrote the farce in a vain effort to end the Peloponnesian War between Athens and Sparta. The central theme is how the women of the two city states banded together in a plot to cease sexual relations with their men until a peace treaty was signed.

Mr. Levinson brought suit to compel delivery of the book. This action challenged as unconstitutional under the First Amendment the so-called Comstock Act of 1873, which gives the Postmaster General the right of pre-censorship or prior censorship. That is, without granting the defendant a court test and jury trial, the Postmaster General has the discretion of banning from the mails any literature or art judged by him to be obscene. Although the Post Office Department won the first round in the *Lysistrata* case, it apparently became fearful that the higher courts would reverse the decision and curb its censorship powers under the Comstock Act. Accordingly, it dropped the controversy early in 1955, agreed to deliver the offending copy of *Lysistrata,* and weakly explained that, after all, the volume was not for "general distribution."

On the political front the Post Office Department became particularly active in 1951 when it proceeded on a wide scale to stop delivery of publications such as the Soviet newspapers, *Pravda* and *Izvestia,* coming through the mails from the Soviet Union. The Department based its action on a ruling by the U.S. Attorney General in 1940 that under the Foreign Agents Registration Act of 1938 only persons in the diplomatic service or registered agents of foreign powers could receive publications from abroad containing "political propaganda."

Although the Post Office authorities at their discretion made certain exceptions for a few scholars and educational institutions, its censorship move prevented hundreds of Americans from receiving Soviet publications. Among those publicly protesting were two anti-Communist stalwarts, George Sokolsky, who writes a daily column for the Hearst papers, and David J. Dallin, a prolific anti-Soviet author.

Mr. Sokolsky commented: "If we are opposed to an Iron Curtain, it makes no sense to establish a Star-Spangled Curtain." [194] Mr. Dallin acknowledged that some of the readers of Soviet publications are American Communists. "The great majority, however," he said, "comprise non-Communist and anti-Communist newspapers and magazines, researchers, scholars and writers, as well as libraries, scientific foundations, etc. What is the point of depriving these people of this important source of knowledge and weapon in the Cold War?" [195]

The National Council on Freedom from Censorship also entered the fray when its Chairman, Elmer Rice, wrote the Postmaster General that he should "authorize delivery of all Soviet publications without discretion to anyone who requests or subscribes to them. . . . If your position is sustainable, it would seem to place political commentators, many of whom rely on Soviet publications for background material, completely at the will of Post Office officials." [196]

In 1955 it was revealed that the U.S. Government had extended its censorship of foreign mail, at least at the port of Boston, to British pacifist and other non-Communist materials being sent to the United States from England. Inspectors of the U.S. Customs Mail Division in Boston were processing some 150,000 sacks of mail a year and consigning large quantities of it to the incinerator as "Communist propaganda." Destroyed by fire in this way were the *Peace News* of London, addressed to the American Friends Service Committee, the educational agency of the Quakers, and pamphlets sponsored by two English organizations, the Movement for Colonial Freedom and the Union of Democratic Control.

In 1954 the Post Office Department assumed the role of defender of the faithful when it declared "non-mailable" Avro Manhattan's book, *Catholic Imperialism and World Freedom*, a study critical of the Catholic Church. Published in London in 1952, this volume had circulated freely in America for two years. Under pressure from Catholic groups, the Post Office Department then banned the book under a clause in the Foreign Agents Registration Act, which defines political propaganda as including materials designed to "promote in the United States racial, religious or social dissension." The Solicitor of the Department reversed this ruling when *The Churchman*, a liberal religious journal, protested.

The United States Army, ever alert in the detection of subversion, felt obliged in 1955 to take on the function of literary critic in order to safeguard the Republic. This became evident in

How to Spot a Communist, a manual prepared by the First Army and circulated by the Watertown (Massachusetts) Arsenal and the Continental Air Command. The study stated: "While a certain heaviness in style and preference for long sentences is common to most Communist writings, a distinct vocabulary provides the second and more easily recognized feature of the 'Communist Language.'

"Even a superficial reading of an article written by a Communist or a conversation with one will probably reveal the use of some of the following expressions: integrative thinking, vanguard, comrade, hootenanny, chauvinism, book-burning, syncretistic faith, bourgeois-nationalism, jingoism, colonialism, hooliganism, ruling class, demagogy, dialectical, witch-hunt, reactionary, exploitation, oppressive, materialist, progressive." [197]

The Army pamphlet also asserted that another good clue to spotting a Communist was to see if a person kept raising such controversial issues as McCarthyism, violation of civil rights, police brutality, racial or religious discrimination, immigration laws, anti-subversive statutes, any legislation concerning labor unions, the fluoridation of water, the Federal military budget or peace.

After a scornful column by Murray Kempton in the *New York Post* and a biting editorial in *The New York Times,* the First Army beat a hasty retreat and withdrew *How to Spot a Communist.* First Army headquarters announced that the booklet "was not appropriate for the purpose for which it was intended when originally issued by Intelligence personnel." [198]

Magazines and newspapers published within the United States have long been subject to various sorts of proscription. Here again a serious problem is censorship by the Post Office, which often refuses to deliver periodicals that it considers obscene or subversive, and which sometimes brings a criminal action against the publisher. In addition, public libraries here and there have refused to receive magazines regarded as subversive, such as *The Nation, The New Republic, Negro Digest* and *Soviet Russia Today.* Worst of all is the fact that in 1948 the public schools of

New York City dropped *The Nation* because it printed Paul Blanshard's informative articles concerning the Catholic Church.
These were later included in Blanshard's book, *American Freedom and Catholic Power*, which has sold more than 225,000
copies.

A comic interlude in censorship took place when the Student's
Union store at the University of California stopped selling the
National Guardian after the students protested that it was communistic. The store management explained that its policy was to
ban any publication if three students complained about it. Forth-
with the requisite number of complaints was registered against
Life, Time, the *Reader's Digest,* the *Saturday Evening Post,* and
Hearst's *San Francisco Examiner.* At this point the store abruptly
changed its policy and decided to handle all of these publications,
as well as the *National Guardian.*

In New York City in 1954 the police arrested Ammon Hennacy,
associate editor of a monthly newspaper called *The Catholic
Worker* and author of *Autobiography of a Catholic Anarchist,* for
selling both the periodical and his book without a license. Convicted by a Manhattan magistrate and fined $10, Mr. Hennacy
told the court it was against his principles to pay the fine and so
was sent to jail for five days instead. The New York Administrative Code makes it unlawful to peddle without a license, but ex-
empts persons selling newspapers and periodicals. Hennacy won
his case on appeal.

Like the municipal police, the U.S. Congress has a deep and
abiding interest in literature. In 1952 a group of official snoopers—
the House Select Committee on Current Pornographic Materials,
with Representative E. C. Gathings, Democrat of Arkansas, as
Chairman—became very busy looking into a sphere of writing long
exploited by prurient priers. This Committee, with a much-publi-
cized display of purity and righteousness, made an investigation
of comic books, "cheesecake" or "girlie" magazines, and pocket-
size paper-bound books. The Committee concentrated on the last-
named category and said in its report: "This type of writing has

now reached a stage where it has become a serious menace to the social structure of the nation." [199]

The report then attacked the liberal legal philosophy that has developed in the United States over the past few decades in regard to the censorship of literature, asserting that it "serves as the basis for excuse to print and circulate the filthiest, most obscene literature without concurrent literary value to support it ever known in history." [200]

To all manifold activities for the censorship of literature in the United States, the American Library Association's 1953 manifesto, "The Freedom to Read," gave a telling answer: "The freedom to read is essential to our democracy. It is under attack. Private groups and public authorities in various parts of the country are working to remove books from sale, to censor textbooks, to label 'controversial' books, to distribute lists of 'objectionable' books or authors and to purge libraries.

"These actions apparently rise from a view that our national tradition of free expression is no longer valid; that censorship and suppression are needed to avoid the subversion of politics and the corruption of morals. . . . Most such attempts rest on a denial of the fundamental premise of democracy: that the ordinary citizen, by exercising his critical judgment, will accept the good and reject the bad. The censors, public and private, assume that they should determine what is good and what is bad for their fellow citizens. . . .

"Suppression is never more dangerous than in such a time of social tension. Freedom has given the United States the elasticity to endure strain. Freedom keeps open the path of novel and creative solutions, and enables change to come by choice. Every silencing of a heresy, every enforcement of an orthodoxy, diminishes the toughness and resilience of our society and leaves it the less able to deal with stress. . . . The freedom to read is guaranteed by the Constitution. Those with faith in free men will stand firm on these constitutional guarantees of essential rights and will exercise the responsibilities that accompany these rights." [201]

Beginning with 1952, yet another Congressional committee

burgeoned as a major menace to cultural freedom. This was the House of Representatives Special Committee to Investigate Tax-Exempt Foundations and Comparable Organizations. In 1952 this Committee, of which the late Representative Eugene E. Cox of Georgia had been chairman, investigated a large number of American foundations for possible subversion, but uncovered little that even Congressional extremists could call "un-American." In 1954, however, the new chairman, Representative B. Carroll Reece, Republican of Tennessee, and some of his colleagues, feeling that they had been cheated of their share of the headlines, decided to open up the inquiry again.

This time the Special Committee concentrated on a few of the larger foundations, such as the Carnegie, Ford, and Rockefeller Foundations. The Committee rendered a verdict before hearing the evidence by announcing prior to this second investigation that American foundations had taken part in a vast plot to swing the United States to the Left through radical teaching in colleges and universities. Among other things, according to the Committee, grants had been used for the heinous aim of directing American education "toward an international viewpoint." The Ford Foundation summed up the Committee charges as meaning that the foundations "have engineered a giant conspiracy, subverting our people, our institutions and our Government to produce the major political, social and economic changes of the past fifty years." [202]

After the Committee had heard a number of witnesses hostile to the foundations, Mr. Pendleton Herring, President of the Social Science Research Council, came on the stand and started to demolish the anti-foundation evidence. At this point Chairman Reece abruptly called off the public hearings and told the foundations that they could rebut by mail. The Carnegie Foundation, undoubtedly expressing the sentiments of the other foundations under attack, issued a statement protesting this procedure and accusing the Committee of making "completely unfounded charges" based on a "shocking combination of innuendo and implication."

When several leading newspapers such as the *New York Herald*

Tribune, The New York Times and *The Washington Post* gave the case of the foundations full coverage and ran editorials critical of the Special Committee, Mr. Reece suddenly discovered another sinister conspiracy on the part of the foundations and claimed they had put pressure on the newspapers deliberately to misrepresent him and his Committee.

At one point in the hearings, the Committee's associate research director, Thomas McNiece, gave a most convincing demonstration both of his own ignorance and of the biased nature of the Committee investigation. McNiece was in the witness chair and had been reading excerpts from Government reports to prove the communistic wickedness of the foundations. A Democrat member of the Committee, Representative Wayne L. Hays of Ohio, objecting to this procedure, read Mr. McNiece some excerpts from anonymous authors and asked him if he could identify the sources of the quotations. Unhesitatingly the witness replied that the passages were "closely comparable" to Communist literature he had read and "paralleled very closely communistic ideals."

Representative Hays then revealed that the excerpts were from encyclicals by Pope Leo XIII in 1891 and by Pope Piux XI in 1931. One of Pope Leo's statements read: "But all agree, and there can be no question whatever, that some remedy must be found, and quickly found for the misery and wretchedness which press so heavily at the moment on a very large majority of the poor. . . . A small number of the very rich have been able to lay upon the masses of the poor a yoke little better than slavery itself." [203]

Pope Pius said: "Every effort must therefore be made that fathers of families receive a wage sufficient to meet adequate ordinary domestic needs. If in the present state of society this is not always feasible, social justice demands that reforms be introduced without delay which will guarantee every adult working man such a wage." [204]

In December 1954 the Republican majority of the Special Committee on Foundations issued a report that approved the thesis with which the investigation had started. "Some of the larger foundations have directly supported 'subversion' in the true meaning of that term—namely, the process of undermining some of our vitally protective concepts and principles. They have actively supported attacks upon our social and governmental system and financed the promotion of socialism and collectivist ideas." Furthermore, the report alleged, these foundations have promoted "'internationalism' in a particular sense—a forum directed toward 'world government' and a derogation of American 'nationalism.'" [205]

The Committee report also assailed the Rockefeller Foundation, the Carnegie Corporation and the Russell Sage Foundation for financing or materially supporting the publication of the fifteen-volume *Encyclopedia of the Social Sciences*, issued 1930-1935. The charge was that this notable *Encyclopedia*, of which Professor E. R. A. Seligman of Columbia was Editor-in-Chief and Dr. Alvin Johnson, Director of the New School, Associate Editor, had a strong "left" slant and that twenty-one authors who had written articles for it had at the time been Socialist, Marxian or connected with "Communist-front" organizations.

In a letter to *The New York Times* Dr. Johnson made a dignified rebuttal of these accusations and pointed out that there was now great need for a new encyclopedia. "Can we find the money for such an encyclopedia? No. The only source for funds for such an enterprise is the foundation, and the reckless clay-pigeon shooting of the Reece Committee has made the foundations gun-shy." [206]

On the basis of its exposures, the Committee finally recommended that foundations "should be very chary of promoting ideas, concepts and opinion-forming material which run counter to what the public currently wishes, approves and likes"; that the tax-free status of foundations should be re-examined by Congress and curtailed; and that the law should be revised to prohibit foundation support not only of communism and fascism, but also of "socialism, collectivism or any other form of society or government which is at variance with the basic principles of ours." [207]

The minority report of the two Democrats on the Committee to Study Foundations exposed the inner workings of the group: "Each step of the proceedings of this Committee placed an ugly

stain on the majestic record of the United States House of Representatives and the great tradition of the American people. . . .
The hard truth is that, by the manner in which the proceedings
of the Committee were conducted and by the self-evident bias
of the majority report, the Committee has failed in the most basic
way to carry out the mandate of Congress. The results of the
proceedings are of no value to the Congress, and it was therefore
a complete waste of public money. . . . As the matter now
stands, the tax-exempt foundations of this nation have been indicted and convicted under procedures which can only be described as barbaric." [208]

Dr. Robert M. Hutchins commented on the Special Committee's
work with characteristic pungency: "Congressman Reece was
scoffed at. It was agreed that his investigation was a farce. I
think he had good reason to be satisfied with himself. I think he
won. Without firing a single serious shot, without saying a single
intelligent word, he accomplished his purpose, which was to
harass the foundations and to subdue such stirrings of courage,
or even of imagination, as could be found in them. . . . If there
ever was a foundation that was willing to be controversial, that
was willing to take risks and venture capital in areas about which
people have strong prejudices, it learned its lesson by the time Cox
and Reece got through." [209]

Another alarming development in the sphere of culture during
the past decade has been a growing effort to break down the
traditional separation of church and state in America.* Article I
of the Bill of Rights starts off with the statement: "Congress shall
make no law respecting an establishment of religion or prohibit-
ing the free exercise thereof." Our Founding Fathers were determined that this Republic should not have an official state
religion functioning in an interlocking directorate with the Government. It is manifest that for the U.S. Government to give any

* To deal with this issue, there was founded in 1948 a special national organization, Protestants and Other Americans United for Separation of Church and State, with headquarters at Washington, D.C.

one religion a special official status is to violate the Constitution.

The separation of church and state has always extended to the sphere of public education. Yet in recent times religious groups, particularly the Catholic Church, have been making strenuous attempts to smuggle religious teaching into the public educational system. In 1945 a courageous American woman, Mrs. Vashti C. McCollum of Champaign, Illinois, mother of three sons, started a suit against the School Board of that city to stop religious instruction in tax-supported public schools. During two years of litigation in the courts she stood out staunchly against the hostility of vengeful "Christian" neighbors and malicious treatment by much of the press.

In her absorbing book, *One Woman's Fight*, Mrs. McCollum describes what happened when on Halloween night, 1945, her doorbell rang and she opened her front door. "I was met by a shower of everything the victory gardens had to offer that year. Rotten tomatoes smashed against the walls, splattered in my hair and over my clothes. Huge cabbage plants, roots, mud and all, came careening through the open door and into the living room. . . . Our pet kitten disappeared, too, that night. Poor pagan pussycat, even she had to pay for belonging to a family of nonconformists!" [210]

Hundreds of abusive letters poured in, carrying such messages as: "You slimy bastard, may your rotten soul roast into hell. Your filthy rotten body produced three children so that you can pilot them all safely to hell"; [211] and "I hope you lose every cent you and your husband have and are tared [sic] and feathered and rode out of town on a broom stick." [212] Mrs. McCollum estimated, however, that three-fifths of the letters she received about her case were favorable.

In 1948 Mrs. McCollum won her battle in the U.S. Supreme Court 8-1. The heart of the majority opinion was: "Here not only are the State's tax-supported school buildings used for the dissemination of religious doctrines. The State also affords sectarian groups an invaluable aid in that it helps to provide pupils for their religious classes through the use of the State's compulsory public school machinery. This is not separation of church and state." [213]

Balked in the endeavor to bring religious teaching directly into public education, the religious zealots thought up the idea of "released time," in which children are freed from regular classes one hour a week in order to receive religious instruction in institutions of their faith apart from school property. In 1952 the Supreme Court declared, in a case arising in the State of New York, that this innovation was constitutional under the circumstances involved. As the dissenting opinions of Justices Black, Frankfurter and Jackson brought out clearly, the decision was inconsistent with the principle established in the McCollum case.

In the words of Justice Black: "In the New York program, as in that of Illinois, the school authorities release some of the children on the condition that they attend the religious classes, get reports on whether they attend, and hold the other children in the school building until the religious hour is over. . . . The State thus makes religious sects beneficiaries of its power to compel children to attend secular schools. Any use of such coercive power by the State to help or hinder some religious sects or to prefer all religious sects over non-believers or vice versa is just what I think the First Amendment forbids." [214]

In 1954 the movement to make theistic religion official gained fresh ground when Congress amended the Pledge to the Flag by inserting the words "under God." Thus the last part of the pledge now reads: "One nation, under God, indivisible, with liberty and justice for all." During the same year the first U.S. postage stamps, in three-cent and eight-cent denominations, appeared bearing the motto, "In God We Trust." In 1955 Congress passed a bill requiring that this same inscription be placed on all U.S. paper money.

Unfortunately, discrimination against certain religious groups still prevails in many parts of the United States. Small dissident sects like Jehovah's Witnesses have a hard time; and even members of so powerful a group as the Catholic Church have suffered considerably from religious prejudice in those communities where they constitute a minority.

Freedom of religion under the American Constitution implies freedom *from* religion. In his dissent in the released time case, Justice Jackson asserted: "The day that this country ceases to be free for irreligion it will cease to be free for religion—except for the sect that can win political power." [215] Yet serious prejudice and discrimination persist in this country against those who believe in no religion or who, like myself, give allegiance to an anti-supernaturalist philosophy such as Humanism, with its stress on the welfare and happiness of all mankind upon this earth. Also in a number of States legal discriminations still exist against admitted atheists. And many Americans who do not believe in God fear social ostracism if they acknowledge this openly.

Discriminations against the unorthodox in religion or philosophy extend even to the sphere of military service. In dealing with conscientious objectors who oppose war on the grounds of religious training and belief, the Selective Service Act of 1948 limited draft exemptions to those who have faith in a Supreme Being. This excludes members of Humanist or Ethical Culture religious groups who reject belief in God or the supernatural. Hence freedom of conscience is violated by the law. Several cases challenging it are now in the courts.

These unfair and unreasonable discriminations against those who are dissenters in regard to religion undoubtedly reflect the fact that popular feeling in America is very hostile towards the free expression of anti-religious sentiments. In a recent public-opinion survey, Samuel A. Stouffer, Professor of Sociology at Harvard, found that 60 percent of the general public would be opposed to allowing a speech in their community against churches and religion, whereas only 34 percent of "community leaders" would be opposed. The same percentages of general public and community leaders would be in favor of removing a book against churches and religion from the public library. Eighty-four percent of the public, Professor Stouffer reported, and 71 percent of community leaders would not permit an opponent of religion to teach in a college or university. [216]

The curtailment of cultural freedom which I have described in this chapter points up once more the indivisibility of civil liberties. Interference with freedom of opinion in the field of politics, whether affecting the rights of Communists or anyone else, sooner or later spreads to the realm of literature, art and culture in general. In no sphere have the repressive effects been more far-reaching than in education, to which I now turn.

10

THE ASSAULT ON ACADEMIC FREEDOM

As philosophers from Plato down to John Dewey have repeated, the most important element of all in the moulding of a people's mind is education. The anti-democratic, anti-intellectual demagogues of today also realize this. That is why they have made such mighty efforts to stimulate heresy-hunting and thought control in the schools, colleges and universities of the United States. They proceed on the sound assumption that what happens to American education will be a primary factor in what eventually happens to America.

Few schools, colleges or universities in this country have been, even in the best of times, 100 percent faithful to the principles of academic freedom. Since World War II the situation has grown much worse. During the 1948 elections several college teachers lost their jobs because they supported the Progressive Party and its presidential candidate, former Democratic Vice-President Henry A. Wallace. In 1953 W. Lou Tandy, Professor of Economics and Sociology at the Kansas State Teachers College, was dismissed for signing a petition to President Eisenhower asking that he pardon the eleven Communist leaders jailed as a result of the first Smith Act trial. This was particularly outrageous because the First Amendment guarantees "the right of the people . . . to petition the Government for a redress of grievances."

In a special study of seventy-two colleges and universities throughout the United States, *The New York Times* reported in

May 1951: "A subtle creeping paralysis of freedom of thought and speech is attacking college campuses in many parts of the country, limiting both students and faculty in the area traditionally reserved for the free exploration of knowledge and truth. These limitations on free inquiry take a variety of forms, but their net effect is a widening tendency toward passive acceptance of the *status quo*, conformity and a narrowing of the area of tolerance in which students, faculty and administrators feel free to speak, act and think independently. . . . Such caution, in effect, has made many college campuses barren of the free give-and-take of ideas. . . . At the same time it has posed a seemingly insoluble problem for the campus liberal, depleted his ranks and brought . . . an apathy about current problems that borders almost on their deliberate exclusion." [217]

The *Times* survey showed that members of the college community were inhibited in discussing controversial issues and unpopular ideas because they feared social disapproval; criticism by friends, the college authorities or legislative bodies; being labeled pink or Communist; being rejected for study in graduate schools; and being investigated by Government or private business so that post-graduate employment might be adversely affected.

In June of the same year a college teacher wrote the *New York Herald Tribune* telling how he had asked his students in an English course whether they would like to publish a pamphlet on some current problem. The answers were negative: "The FBI would get you"; "You would be called a Communist"; "They would say you were un-American"; "You would lose your job if you expressed yourself"; "I am looking for security, not trying to change anything"; "Don't stick your neck out, McCarthy will investigate you." [218]

In 1952 the *Times* reported that repression of thought in educational institutions had extended to the banning of factual information about the United Nations and UNESCO. "Some school systems," the *Times* article stated, "have discarded the use of teaching materials relating to the United Nations or its specialized agencies because of highly vocal minority groups.

Much of the growing opposition comes from self-styled super-patriotic organizations or critical individuals. These groups and individuals charge that the United Nations or its educational branch, UNESCO, is subversive or tainted with atheism and communism. They maintain that UNESCO is propagandizing for world government and, through revision of textbooks, is undermining nationalism." [219]

The controversy over this matter in educational circles has been most acrimonious in Los Angeles where an ultra-conservative faction has bedeviled the community by pushing the view that UNESCO is nothing more nor less than a conspiracy to put across Soviet-dominated world government. In 1953 the issue became so hot that the city's Board of Education rejected a $335,000 grant for a special teachers training program from the Ford Foundation's Fund for the Advancement of Education, because the Foundation was considered too "internationalist" in outlook and "left" in sympathies.

Later in the same year Dr. O. Meredith Wilson, Secretary of this same Education Fund, pointed out: "Even in the business of education the intellect has become suspect. If a man does not conform, even to stereotypes, he is branded as an egghead and a brain-truster. Businessmen and employers talk about the importance of college degrees, at the same time shying away from Phi Beta Kappa keys." [220]

The McCarran-Walter Immigration Act of 1952 had already written current suspicion of intellectuals and higher education into law by repealing the nonquota immigrant status of foreign professors which had been in existence for more than twenty-five years. Under this exemption to immigration regulations, the United States had admitted 2,869 professors during the years 1925-1948. Ministers of religion enjoyed the same exemption; and in the same period 8,364 of them had entered this country. The 1952 statute retained the special provision as relating to clergymen, but dropped it in regard to professors.

Another adverse sign of the times for those seeking a genuine education was the circulation, from 1948 to late in 1954, of a personnel pamphlet issued by the Socony-Vacuum Oil Company and entitled *So You Want a Better Job*. This pamphlet advised young people just out of college how to make good and noted: "Personal views can cause a lot of trouble. Remember, then, to keep them always conservative. The 'isms' are out. Business being what it is, it naturally looks with disfavor on the wild-eyed radical or even the moderate pink. On the other hand . . . you will find very few business organizations who will attempt to dictate the political party of their employees." [221] Socony-Vacuum withdrew this statement after *The Daily Princetonian*, student newspaper at Princeton University, severely criticized it.

In 1954 the play-it-safe trend in educational institutions was highlighted when the authorities at West Point and Annapolis forbade cadets and midshipmen respectively to participate in intercollegiate debates on whether the United States should recognize the People's Republic of China. An Army spokesman in Washington stated: "It is Department of the Army policy not to have United States Military Academy cadets involved in debate on such a controversial subject, on which in any event national policy has already been established." [222]

The Navy took the position that if the Annapolis team were assigned to argue in favor of U.S. recognition of Communist China, this would be tantamount to upholding "the Communist philosophy and party line." The Navy spokesman added: "The Academy's young men are being trained to be naval officers, and to argue the Communist doctrine would make them liable to misrepresentation, as well as providing the Reds a tremendous propaganda device." [223]

At a press conference President Eisenhower made clear that he disagreed with the decisions of the superintendents at West Point and Annapolis and would have left the matter to the judgment of the students themselves.

Roanoke College in Virginia also refused to enter a team on the affirmative side of the question: "Should the United States recognize Red China?" The debate director at Roanoke gave as the reason that the College feared its students might subject themselves to investigation in later life. One of the Roanoke debaters explained he did not want to take a chance that the thing would "kick back" on him if one day he entered the Government service. In Nebraska three State-supported teachers colleges ruled out the same debate topic.

Interference with student freedom is not limited to restrictions on expressions of opinion. In 1954 the U.S. Department of Defense bore down heavily on college and university students by requiring all those in ROTC training courses to take a special loyalty oath. This new regulation obliged the enrollee to name any organization on the U.S. Attorney General's so-called subversive list of which he was or had been a member, whose meetings or social activities he had attended, whose literature he had distributed, or with which he had been "identified or associated . . . in some manner."

A student admitting to any such associations could not be formally enrolled in the ROTC program, but could participate on an informal basis. This meant that he was not permitted to borrow the necessary textbooks and drill equipment or to march in uniform. And he was stigmatized in the eyes of his fellow-students because he must march alone or with others similarly disqualified.

Owing to the volume of protests over the workings of this loyalty oath, the Defense Department in April 1955 retreated to some extent. It announced that in the future the special oath would be continued only for Juniors and Seniors in the Army and Air Force ROTC, since they have reached a more advanced stage of training, and for Naval ROTC students. Mandatory for all other ROTC students would be merely the routine oath: "I do solemnly swear (or affirm) that I will support and defend the Constitution of the United States against all enemies, foreign or domestic; that I will bear true faith and allegiance to the same; and that I take this obligation freely, without any mental reservation or purpose of evasion; so help me God." [224]

One of the unhappier aspects of education in America at present is that both teachers and students fear—and with justification— that Government agents are planted in courses to take note of any unorthodox ideas. In 1943 when I was a member of the Cornell University staff in charge of the Intensive Study of Contemporary Russian Civilization, one of the most brilliant and likable students turned out to be a Government agent who reported regularly to Washington on what was said in the lectures and discussions. The staff had been so impressed by this man that it had asked him to return as an assistant the following year.

In 1953 Dean Carl W. Ackerman of the Columbia School of Journalism strongly protested against this sort of snooping, mentioning in particular the FBI, the Central Intelligence Agency, the Secret Service and the Civil Service. Dean Ackerman said in part: "The practical problem which confronts deans, professors, schoolteachers and students today is political freedom to discuss public affairs in classrooms or at lunch or during a 'bull' session without fear that someone may make a record which may be investigated secretly, upon which he may be tried secretly, and also convicted secretly, either by a governmental official or a prospective employer." [225]

Teachers in general in the United States today are being treated as a species of second-class citizens whose loyalty is considered so questionable that strict control of their ideas must be maintained and special legislation passed to guard the community against them. More than twenty States have put through special laws requiring teachers in public schools and colleges to sign a loyalty oath. Many of these statutes call for the dismissal of any teacher associated with an organization on the U.S. Attorney General's blacklist.

Legislators, government officials and educational administrators have more and more been taking the attitude: "Beware of the teacher! He is almost sure to be a doubtful character, probably trying surreptitiously to lead your child astray with Communist propaganda and secretly spreading subversion in the classroom. Watch out for teachers above all others and immediately report to the authorities any suspicious conduct, remarks or associations."

I have had personal experience of such tactics, since many efforts have been made to persuade Columbia University to dismiss me as a lecturer in philosophy. In 1952, for instance, when I was running for the U.S. Senate on the ALP ticket, *The New Leader* which styles itself a "liberal" magazine, published an editorial bitterly attacking me as a Communist and inviting Dwight Eisenhower, then President of the University, to help me "lead a new political life unencumbered by membership on the faculty of a 'capitalist' university." [226] In 1953 *Counterattack* took up the cry and devoted its entire issue of May 15 to summarizing my many "subversive" writings, speeches and associations. It told its readers to write President Grayson L. Kirk of Columbia asking for my dismissal in order "to preserve academic freedom." There has been no sign that the Columbia authorities have been impressed by all this.

In 1950 the ultra-suspicious Board of Regents of the University of California initiated one of the worst imbroglios ever to confound the academic world. The Board suddenly demanded that all teachers and other employees in the institution sign a special non-Communist test oath. A widespread revolt against this oath took place and thirty teachers refused to sign. Within a year a California Court of Appeals handed down a decision that the Regents' oath was invalid because loyalty oaths for teachers in a State institution were provided for by a new law, the Levering Act.* The Supreme Court of California upheld this ruling.

Meanwhile, the battle had raged on at the University between principled professors and dictatorial governing authorities. Before the courts declared the loyalty oath illegal, twenty-six teachers were dismissed by the University, thirty-seven resigned in protest and fifty-five courses were dropped from the curriculum. During the same period forty-seven teachers refused offers of appointment at the University.

The issue, well publicized on both sides, took on national importance and aroused educators throughout the country. Among those who made public protests against the University of California oath were 292 Princeton teachers, under the leadership of Dr. Gordon A. Craig, Professor of History; fifty Columbia teach-

* See Chapter 8.

ers, under the leadership of Dr. John H. Randall, Jr., Professor of Philosophy; and all twelve professors at the Institute for Advanced Study, including Albert Einstein and J. Robert Oppenheimer.

In 1953 the California legislature, dissatisfied with the Levering Act, passed two new oath laws affecting teachers. The first, the Dilworth Act, calls on all public school employees, on pain of dismissal, to answer questions put by any public agency regarding their political beliefs and associations. The second, the Luckel Act, makes the same requirement for all other public employees. Under both Acts the questioning always comes down to whether an individual is or has been a member of the Communist Party. An outstanding case under the Luckel Act is that of Professor Harry C. Steinmetz, a teacher of psychology for twenty-three years at San Diego State College, who was dismissed in 1954 for refusing to answer questions about his political convictions. He appealed to the U.S. Supreme Court when the California Supreme Court approved his dismissal.

One of the most disturbing aspects of the assault on academic freedom is that fear-ridden fanatics or plain busybodies in many communities send in to local school principals, superintendents and boards of education a continuing mass of derogatory, anonymous and unsupported information about teachers. Sometimes this "information" comes from officials in State or Federal Governments. On the basis of such unreliable and unevaluated data, according to *The Denver Post* in its timely series of articles on "Faceless Informers in Our Schools," at least 1,000 teachers in public schools and colleges throughout the United States during 1952, 1953, and 1954 were put on suspect lists as disloyal or subversive.

The *Post* reports: "The fact that stands out above all others about the anti-subversion drive directed at the schools is this: In the vast majority of the cases, the informers or accusers have utterly refused to face the accused, or to come forward with supporting evidence or proof." [227]

The professional informer and Government witness, Harvey Matusow, revealed in his book *False Witness* that the Board of

Education of New York City employed him as a consultant for ten days in 1952 for the purpose of helping to identify Communists in the city schools. The book reproduces a letter to Mr. Matusow from Superintendent of Schools William Jansen in which Mr. Jansen states: "It may be that you have some information that would be of great value to us concerning New York City teachers who are members of the Communist Party." [228] Another letter reproduced is from Mr. Saul Moskoff, Assistant Corporation Counsel in charge of investigating communism in New York City schools. Mr. Moskoff avers: "I find that Mr. Harvey M. Matusow is in possession of important information which will be of material assistance to the Board of Education." [229] Later, in conferences with Moskoff, Matusow made false allegations about the Communist associations of a number of teachers.

The use by high educational authorities in New York City of an informer like Matusow, now a self-confessed perjurer, well demonstrates the disreputable quality of the whole academic witch-hunt.

In March 1953 Richard E. Combs, Chief Counsel for the California Senate Committee on Un-American Activities, boasted before the Jenner Committee that the Committee's work had led, in the space of one year, to the removal of some 100 teachers from California college and university faculties. Mr. Combs was pleased about the cooperation of the educational authorities: "The Committee deemed it expedient to indicate to the university administrators the necessity, particularly in the larger institutions, of employing full-time people who had a practical experience in the field of counter-Communist activities, ex-FBI agents, and ex-Navy and military intelligence men. That has been followed. On the major colleges and campuses in California such persons are working and have been for almost since last June. They maintain a liaison with our committee." [230]

In addition to these various troubles, teachers have had to endure for a number of years the high-handed investigations of Congressional committees. When teachers have exercised their constitutional prerogatives and refused to answer, on the grounds of the First or Fifth Amendments, questions concerning political beliefs or associations put by House or Senate investigators, they have usually been summarily dismissed by the school, college or university employing them. Only a few educational institutions have stood firm for the rights of their employees.

One of America's most revered teachers, Ralph Barton Perry, Professor Emeritus of Philosophy at Harvard University, has spoken out strongly against the tendency of colleges and universities to dismiss automatically members of their staffs who get into trouble with Congressional committees. "By so doing," he states, "the institutions virtually turn over to government their authority to hire and fire. A refusal to testify does not constitute grounds for dismissal, even when it constitutes sufficient evidence for the charge of contempt. The institution will take account of other considerations, and reach its own decision on educational grounds.

"There is no reason why the institution should serve as the executioner—the instrument by which to penalize those who have offended the committees, or against whom the committees have obtained what they consider to be unfavorable evidence. . . . The issue here is the autonomy of the educational institution as regards the employment of its staff. It has a duty to resist all 'pressures,' whether they come from Congressional committees or from public clamor or from its own alumni." [231]

In teacher dismissals brought about by Congressional investigations it has hardly ever been charged that the victims are professionally incompetent or have violated classroom standards by trying to indoctrinate their pupils with some sort of political propaganda. And rarely has a Congressional committee disclosed anything about a teacher that shows him guilty of any crime. Instead the committees ask insulting questions that *imply* political crime, subversion or outright treason; and often the self-respecting teacher has invoked some section of the Bill of Rights and declined to answer such loaded questions.

In commenting on the prevailing psychology among teachers, Dr. Robert M. Hutchins writes in *Look* Magazine: "Whittaker

Chambers and Prof. Sidney Hook of New York University, both of whom proclaim themselves devotees of academic freedom, say, 'Don't worry; only a few teachers have been fired.' What has this got to do with it? The question is not how many teachers have been fired, but how many think they might be, and for what reasons. It is even worse than that: Teachers are not merely afraid of being fired; they are afraid of getting into trouble, with resultant damage to their professional prospects and their standing in their communities. You don't have to fire many teachers to intimidate them all. The entire teaching profession of the United States is now intimidated." [232]

Let us consider at this point, as typical of the witch-hunt in education, what happened when the House Committee on Un-American Activities held hearings in Philadelphia during 1953 and 1954. In the fall of 1953, the Committee, with the expressed purpose of investigating "subversion" in education, subpoenaed a considerable number of teachers in the Philadelphia public schools. Out of thirty-three who testified before the Committee in Philadelphia or Washington, thirty-two invoked the Fifth Amendment, and one the First, in refusing to answer questions, all of which pertained to past activities and associations from 1939 to 1950. The Philadelphia Superintendent of Schools, Mr. Louis P. Hoyer, had also asked these teachers similar questions which in general they had not answered.

Mr. Hoyer suspended thirty of the thirty-three who had appeared before the Un-American Activities Committee. Later the Board of Public Education sustained the charges against twenty-six and dismissed them from their jobs. All of the twenty-six, prior to their appearance before the Committee, had had "satisfactory" ratings by their individual school principals. These ratings were based on personality, preparation, instruction techniques and pupil reaction. It is obvious that the twenty-six were fired primarily because of their refusal to cooperate with a Congressional committee that was violating their constitutional rights.

The one victim who relied on the First Amendment in refusing to answer the Un-American Activities Committee's questions was

Mrs. Goldie E. Watson, a Negro teacher who had taught in the Philadelphia school system for twenty-three years and had always been rated as competent. In her testimony before the Board of Education she told how two representatives of the Un-American Activities Committee, a Mr. Fuoss and a Mr. McKillip, had come to interview her at her home. They informed her that everything would be all right and that the Committee would not even subpoena her if she would "cooperate." When she asked what this meant, Mr. Fuoss explained: "That you will name other people as Communists."

After this interview Mr. Fuoss called her several times on the phone and promised job security and promotion if she would only "cooperate." As Mrs. Watson told the Board: "I couldn't do it. And it would have been the lowest type of moral courage and morals for me to have permitted myself to become a stoolpigeon and informer because I had been informed on. I wouldn't do it. I could not have returned to my classroom under these circumstances. . . . Because for me to have participated in that inquisitorial inquisition . . . would have been showing that I did not believe in the Constitution." [233]

At the same hearing before the Board of Education Superintendent Hoyer explained why suddenly after twenty-three years Mrs. Watson had become an unsatisfactory teacher: "On the form, the State form provided for rating teachers, there are a number of items that enter into the competency or incompetency of a teacher. And among those items are three which I have checked as being unsatisfactory.

"The first of these is the item of civic responsibility. . . . I am of the opinion that Mrs. Watson gave evidence of a very unsatisfactory concept of civic responsibility in her appearance before the Committee of the Congress. I consider it the duty of any citizen . . . and . . . especially the duty of a teacher to so cooperate with such a body of Congress. That Mrs. Watson did not do. And I therefore consider her as incompetent and unsatisfactory on the basis of civic responsibility.

"I also have considered her judgment extremely faulty. . . .

This is another item which appears on this report. And that is because of the position which she took in this connection.

"I marked also the item of appreciation and ideals, particularly the ideals part of that combination, because she gave evidence of extremely unsatisfactory ideals with regard to the duties and responsibilities of American citizenship in her appearance before the Committee." [234]

Mrs. Watson not only lost her teaching job, but was later cited for contempt of Congress by the House of Representatives and indicted for this alleged crime. She is one of the few teachers in America who has chosen to run the risk of a year in jail by standing on the First Amendment and thereby making a court test of the powers of a Congressional committee. She intends to fight her case up to the U.S. Supreme Court.

In recent years teachers in many a city throughout the United States have had the same sort of unhappy experience as the Philadelphia schoolteachers. New York City, which ought to provide leadership as regards academic freedom, has done the opposite so far as teachers in public schools and public colleges are concerned. Indeed, New York's Board of Education and Board of Higher Education have actually spearheaded the nation-wide witch-hunt against teachers, and during the six years from 1950 through 1955, drove out of the city's educational institutions, through one means or another, more than 250 teachers.

The U.S. Supreme Court is at present working out its decision in the test case of Dr. Harry Slochower, who in 1952 was dismissed from his post as Associate Professor of Literature and German at Brooklyn College for invoking the Fifth Amendment before the Jenner Committee.

New York's downward trend started sixteen years ago, in 1940, when Bertrand Russell, one of England's most eminent thinkers, was forced out of his professorship of philosophy at the College of the City of New York. A censorious faction led by Episcopal Bishop William T. Manning had demanded that Russell be ousted on the grounds that his books were "lecherous, salacious, libidinous, lustful, venereous, erotomaniac, aphrodisiac, atheistic, irreverent, narrow-minded, untruthful, and bereft of moral fibre." [235]

City College and the Board of Higher Education stood their ground in defending the appointment. But Mayor Fiorello H. La Guardia, a fighting liberal on most issues, struck from the city's budget the position which Russell was to have filled; and the city's Corporation Counsel, W. C. Chanler, refused to take an appeal from a lower court decision voiding Russell's appointment.

New York City's anti-freedom policies reached a climax in 1955. At that time the Board of Education, three years after hiring the notorious informer, Harvey Matusow, adopted 7-1 a resolution authorizing the Superintendent of Schools to "require" teachers to inform on their colleagues. Those who failed to do so would be liable to dismissal for "unbecoming conduct and insubordination." This was the first action of the kind taken by a public body in the whole of the United States. The American Civil Liberties Union opposed the resolution on the grounds that "questions about another teacher's views or associations are always to be considered improper because they immediately subvert that sense of freedom which is the life center of the academic process." [236]

In September 1955 the Board of Education suspended three schoolteachers, a school clerk and a principal for their refusal to inform on their associates. The outcome of these cases is still in doubt.

New York State, which during the administrations of Governors Alfred E. Smith, Franklin D. Roosevelt and Herbert H. Lehman had established a notable record for liberalism, fell to the level of New York City when in 1949 the legislature passed the Feinberg Law (See Chapter 8) to bring about the exposure and expulsion of all "subversives" from the public schools. Under this blunderbuss measure a special investigative official is appointed in each of the State's 2,536 school districts, and is required to submit annually to the Board of Regents "a report in writing on each teacher or employee. Such report is required to state either that there is no evidence . . . or that there is evidence of subversiveness." [237]

Justice Douglas's dissent from the U.S. Supreme Court's decision declaring the Feinberg Law constitutional describes the evil effects of the statute: "The very threat of such a procedure is certain to raise havoc with academic freedom. Youthful indiscretions, mistaken causes, misguided enthusiasms—all long forgotten—become the ghosts of a harrowing present. Any organization committed to a liberal cause, any group organized to revolt against an hysterical trend, any committee launched to sponsor an unpopular program becomes suspect. . . .

"The law inevitably turns the school system into a spying project. Regular loyalty reports on the teachers must be made out. The principals become detectives; the students, the parents, the community become informers. Ears are cocked for tell-tale signs of disloyalty. The prejudices of the community come into play in searching out the disloyal. This is not the usual type of supervision which checks a teacher's competency; it is a system which searches for hidden meanings in a teacher's utterances.

"What was the significance of the reference of the art teacher to socialism? Why was the history teacher so openly hostile to Franco Spain? Who heard overtones of revolution in the English teacher's discussion of *The Grapes of Wrath*? What was behind the praise of Soviet progress in metallurgy in the chemistry class? Was it not 'subversive' for the teacher to cast doubt on the wisdom of the venture in Korea?

"What happens under this law is typical of what happens in a police state. Teachers are under constant surveillance; their pasts are combed for signs of disloyalty; their utterances are watched for clues to dangerous thoughts. A pall is cast over the classrooms. . . . Supineness and dogmatism take the place of inquiry. A 'party line'—as dangerous as the 'party line' of the Communists—lays hold. It is the 'party line' of the orthodox view, of the conventional thought, of the accepted approach. A problem can no longer be pursued with impunity to its edges. Fear stalks the classroom. The teacher is no longer a stimulant to adventurous thinking; she becomes instead a pipeline for safe and sound information." [238]

Justice Black, concurring in Justice Douglas's dissent, asserted in part: "This is another of those rapidly multiplying legislative enactments which make it dangerous—this time for schoolteachers —to think or say anything except what a transient majority happen to approve at the moment. Basically these laws rest on the belief that government should supervise and limit the flow of ideas into the minds of men. The tendency of such governmental policy is to mould people into a common intellectual pattern. . . .

"Public officials cannot be constitutionally vested with powers to select the ideas people can think about, censor the public views they can express, or choose the persons or groups people can associate with. Public officials with such powers are not public servants; they are public masters." [239]

State and municipal educational institutions are of course more vulnerable to political influence than private ones and are subject to the operation of suppressive legislation such as the Feinberg Law and State Acts requiring loyalty oaths of teachers or all State employees. These are major reasons for the fact that the few colleges and universities in America which have maintained a principled position in the face of mounting pressures are private educational institutions such as Amherst, Columbia, Harvard, Sarah Lawrence, Smith, and the University of Chicago.

As a Harvard graduate I have been proud that President Nathan M. Pusey and the governing bodies at my alma mater showed no disposition to yield to the demands of Senator Joseph McCarthy to dismiss two teachers, Dr. Wendell T. Furry, Associate Professor of Physics, and Leon J. Kamin, a teaching fellow, because in 1953 they refused on grounds of the Fifth Amendment to answer questions before the Senate Permanent Subcommittee on Investigations. McCarthy went into a rage over Harvard's stand; claimed that the University was "a real privileged sanctuary" for "Fifth Amendment Communists"; and told a New York teacher who had invoked the Fifth Amendment: "You can get a letter of recommendation from your Communist cell and get a job from Mr. Pusey." [240] At the same time the Senator threatened to introduce a bill in Congress that would end gift-tax exemptions on contributions to educational institutions which employed "Fifth Amendment Communists."

When the McCarthy Committee recalled Furry and Kamin to testify again in 1954, both men invoked the First Amendment instead of the Fifth in declining to become informers by answering questions about persons other than themselves. Owing to this action, they were indicted for contempt of Congress in December 1954. Mr. Kamin had already left Harvard to take a research post at McGill University in Montreal; but Dr. Furry had continued in his regular position. After Furry's indictment, President Pusey made clear in a public statement that the University would nonetheless retain him as a teacher.

In 1949 Harvard had already demonstrated its adherence to principle by dismissing in no uncertain terms the complaint of Mr. Frank B. Ober, a graduate of the Harvard Law School and author of Maryland's vicious Ober Act.* Mr. Ober had refused to subscribe to the Law School Fund because the University continued to employ two teachers who, he claimed, were guilty of "giving aid and comfort to communism." These were Dr. John Ciardi, Assistant Professor of English, who had spoken in opposition to the Ober Act at a Progressive Party meeting in Maryland; and Dr. Harlow Shapley, Professor of Astronomy, who had been chairman of a peace conference held at the Waldorf-Astoria Hotel in New York City.

Dr. James B. Conant, President of Harvard from 1933 to 1953, answered Mr. Ober briefly, but turned the main job over to Mr. Grenville Clark, a well-known lawyer and a member of the Harvard Corporation. Mr. Clark dealt with Ober's charges in two letters, saying in part: "You want the authorities to keep a 'closer watch on what its professors are doing.' On this point you evidently want a watch kept pretty much all the time—presumably day and night, in term and in vacation. For you say that 'most of the damage is done outside of the classroom' and that 'it is not reasonable to close one's eyes to such extra-curricular activities.' . . .

"For Harvard to take the course you recommend would be to repudiate the very essence of what Harvard stands for—the search

*See Chapter 8.

for truth by a free and uncoerced body of students and teachers. And it would be to make a mockery of a long tradition of Harvard freedom for both its students and its faculties. . . . Harvard, like any great privatelv supported university, badly needs money; but Harvard will accept no gift on the condition, express or implied, that it shall compromise its tradition of freedom. . . . I affirm again that your plan implies an extensive system of detection and trial. . . . The harm done by the effort necessary to discover even a single clandestine Party member would outweigh any possible benefit." [241]

Mr. Clark referred to and quoted from the statement on academic freedom made by the late President A. Lawrence Lowell of Harvard in his Annual Report of 1916-1917. This statement, all the more notable because it was issued during the tensions of the First World War, remains a landmark in the development of academic freedom in America. I quote it at length:

"In spite of the risk of injury to the institution, the objections to restraint upon what professors may say as citizens seem to me far greater than the harm done by leaving them free. In the first place, to impose upon the teacher in a university restrictions to which the members of other professions, lawyers, physicians, engineers, and so forth, are not subjected, would produce a sense of irritation and humiliation. In accepting a chair under such conditions a man would surrender a part of his liberty; what he might say would be submitted to the censorship of a board of trustees, and he would cease to be a free citizen. The lawyer, physician, or engineer may express his views as he likes on the subject of the protective tariff; shall the professor of astronomy not be free to do the same? Such a policy would tend seriously to discourage some of the best men from taking up the scholar's life. It is not a question of academic freedom, but of personal liberty from constraint, yet it touches the dignity of the academic career.

"That is an objection to restraint on freedom of speech from the standpoint of the teacher. There is another, not less weighty, from that of the institution itself. If a university or college censors what its professors may say, if it restrains them from uttering something that it does not approve, it thereby assumes responsibility for that which it permits them to say. This is logical and inevitable, but it is a responsibility which an institution of learning would be very unwise in assuming. It is sometimes suggested that the principles are different in time of war; that the governing boards are then justified in restraining unpatriotic expressions injurious to the country. But the same problem is presented in wartime, as in time of peace. If the university is right in restraining its professors, it has a duty to do so, and it is responsible for whatever it permits. There is no middle ground. Either the university assumes full responsibility for permitting its professors to express certain opinions in public, or it assumes no responsibility whatever, and leaves them to be dealt with like other citizens by the public authorities according to the laws of the land."

Though Harvard in my opinion has one of the best records on academic freedom of any university in the United States, both Presidents Conant and Pusey made one important and unfortunate qualification to Harvard's stand. Both stated, when they were rebuffing inquisitorial demagogues, that they would not sanction a member of the Communist Party as a teacher at Harvard because, to quote Dr. Pusey, "He does not have the necessary independence of thought and judgment."

This position yields decisive ground to the inquisitors because it abandons the basic principle of judging teachers, whether their orientation be left-wing, right-wing or anything else, according to individual professional competence; and substitutes the unacceptable criterion of what varying implications can be drawn from membership in an unpopular political organization. Thereby the doctrine of guilt by association is established in academic life; and the gates are opened to that general witch-hunt among American teachers which Drs. Conant and Pusey deplore.

For once we accept the premise that members of the Communist Party are *ipso facto* unfit to be teachers in American educational institutions, we set in motion an unceasing inquisition which has for its purpose the ferreting out of all Communists, open or secret, in the teaching profession. This frantic enterprise then spreads to ever widening circles and necessarily leads to the questioning of so-called fellow-travelers, of individuals who may be or may have been members of an organization blacklisted by the U.S. Attorney General, of independent progressives and radicals who have spoken their minds freely, and of anyone about whom malicious gossip is circulated. Such goings-on are bound to create an atmosphere of apprehension among teachers.

What Justice Black says about public officials in the field of education exceeding their legitimate powers also applies to the trustees, presidents and administrative authorities of private educational institutions. Academic freedom in American education means that just as Congress, under the First Amendment, "shall make no law abridging the freedom of speech," so officials in school, college and university shall adopt no rules and take no action abridging the intellectual freedom of teachers, scholars and students.

Educational authorities violate this principle of academic freedom as soon as they dismiss teachers or subject them to any kind of pressure because of their political or other beliefs, or because of their organizational or personal associations. It is proper of course to drop teachers if it can be shown concretely that they lack professional competence, have used their classrooms for propaganda purposes, or have been guilty of moral turpitude or of some other grave misconduct.

But the charges brought against alleged subversives in the educational system are simply that they hold certain proscribed ideas or are, or have been, associated with certain proscribed organizations. Since, as I have pointed out, the witch-hunt gets going as soon as Communist Party members as such are barred from teaching positions, let us consider whether such action is justified.

The main argument for automatically dismissing Communists is that the American Communist Party exercises such strict discipline over its members, forcing them to follow the "party line" in all spheres of thought and activity, that they can have no real intellectual freedom and are therefore necessarily disqualified as teachers. A secondary argument is that Communist teachers are under orders to push the cause of communism whenever possible and accordingly inject Communist propaganda into their lectures and classroom instruction. These arguments do not stand up under the analysis of reason.

In the first place, the American Communist Party does not have the power to "force" its members to do anything, as is shown by the large numbers who have withdrawn from the organization. Tens of thousands of men and women have joined and left the Communist Party since it was founded in 1919. The conclusion is inescapable that, as Professor Alexander Meiklejohn has phrased it, "They do not accept Communist beliefs because they are members of the Party. They are members of the Party because they accept Communist beliefs." [242] When they find themselves in substantial disagreement with those beliefs, they can choose to resign and do resign. This fact alone proves that Communist Party members do not inevitably lose their intellectual freedom.

In the second place and supporting this first point, the evidence indicates that people who join the Communist Party, however unwise that step proves, may even be more independent intellectually than the average person. Certainly to espouse communism in America has been a far cry from comfortable conformity to orthodoxy, and has always been a hazard from the viewpoint of social repute, occupational security and personal relations.

Hence I must agree with Professor Meiklejohn's further observation: "Why, then, do men and women of scholarly training and taste choose Party membership? Undoubtedly, some of them are, hysterically, attracted by disrepute and disaster. But, in general, the only explanation which fits the facts is that these scholars are moved by a passionate determination to follow the truth where it seems to lead, no matter what may be the cost to themselves and their families." [243]

In the third place, there is a basic element of political bias and downright hypocrisy in the argument against Communist teachers that I have cited. For every church, every civic organization, every political party imposes some measure of discipline on its members in the sense that they are expected to subscribe to the fundamental tenets of the group concerned. The Audubon Society would not tolerate as a member a man dedicated to shooting down as many birds as possible; nor the National Association for the Advancement of Colored People a man who agitated for racial segregation. Although Communist Party discipline is unusually severe, so is that of the Roman Catholic Church, which has an over-all philosophy as inclusive and rigorous as that of the Communists.

The fact, then, that a teacher belongs to an organization which to one degree or another requires discipline of its members is neither sufficient reason, nor indeed a reason at all for dismissing him. Actually, Communist teachers have been fired throughout America, not because of this trumped-up discipline issue, but because they hold ideas on economics and politics to which the educational authorities object. Those authorities, while loudly proclaiming their devotion to intellectual freedom, are determined to suppress such freedom if it moves in a radical direction. It is their intention not only to get rid of all Communists and "fellow-travelers," but also to make sure that teachers are in favor of the "free enterprise" system, the anti-Communist crusade and orthodoxy in general. This is "brain-washing" with a vengeance.

Who ever heard of a teacher being fired for supporting capitalism, the Cold War against Soviet Russia, the Republican Party or the Catholic Church? Although leading educators have recommended the study of communism in schools and colleges, they make clear that the treatment of the subject should not be impartial, but must discredit communism by pointing out its evils. The powers-that-be in American education, then, take pains to establish, as Justice Douglas has said, their own "party line" to which the teacher is expected to conform, while at the same time they insist that anyone who follows a leftist "party line" is thereby derelict in seeking and imparting the truth.

In the fourth place, as to Communist teachers spreading leftist propaganda among their students, I know of no case involving the dismissal of a "subversive" teacher where that charge has even been made, let alone proved. Here again the argument smacks of hypocrisy. For there are no teachers anywhere, Communist or otherwise, who are able to be so completely impartial that they never bring into their teaching their personal opinions on controversial questions. Nor would such an attitude be desirable, since it would lay cramping restrictions on the teacher's intellectual freedom in lectures and discussion.

Dr. Broadus Mitchell, Professor of Economics at Rutgers University, has well summed up this situation: "The truth is that teachers, like other mortals, have intellectual and moral commitments, and perhaps arrive at them more cautiously than some others do. If we are to pillory teachers for their attachment to beliefs, philosophical, political, religious—equating these with closed minds and unworthy acceptance of authority—the waiting-line behind the stocks must be long and number some very respectable characters." [244]

What is objectionable is a teacher's turning his classroom primarily into an echo chamber for his own views or neglecting to present objectively both sides of controversial issues. Then indeed he may be rightly accused of propagandizing. But little evidence has been adduced that Communist teachers in America do this. And, indeed, the very lack of such evidence has led to the additional accusation that Communist teachers are so diabolically clever that they instil their insidious propaganda without the innocent pupil or the vigilant school principal ever knowing about it.

Despite these various considerations about Communist teachers, the drive to oust them and other teachers with left-wing associations or views has gone on unabated. Only a few *local* teachers unions, such as the Teachers Union of New York City, the Philadelphia Teachers Union and the Los Angeles Federation of Teachers, have maintained without compromise the traditional position on academic freedom. Professional organizations of nation-wide scope that have stood firm are the American Association of University Professors, the American Philosophical Association, and the American Psychological Association.

On the other hand, the general movement undermining teachers' rights has been aided and abetted by some of the main educators' groups, such as the National Education Association, the most powerful school organization in the United States; the Association of American Universities, composed of university administrators; and the American Federation of Teachers, AFL, representing teachers from school to university level. Each of these bodies has voted that Communists have no place in the educational system of the United States.

Yet in all the hullabaloo over Communists, we cannot afford to forget that teachers dissenting from *any* form of orthodoxy stand in danger. While freedom of teaching in the natural sciences has made considerable progress and laws against the teaching of evolution have become a dead letter since the famous trial of science instructor John T. Scopes in Tennessee in 1925,* the situation as regards teaching in the social sciences, philosophy and religion is less healthy.

For example, in 1955 Willard J. Graff, Superintendent of Public Schools in Springfield, Missouri, took the position that there was no place for agnostics or atheists in the school system when he ousted Leslie Hill as a teacher of science in Pipkin Junior High School. A pupil in science class had asked Mr. Hill if he believed in God. Hill said, "No," and told his students that he would discuss the matter informally after class with any who wished to stay. A number of them did remain, and Hill frankly answered their questions.

When Superintendent Graff asked Hill to resign, Hill refused and reminded him, "We have freedom of religious beliefs in this country." [245] Hill also said that he had always taught his students the scientific attitude, counseling them: "Think for yourselves instead of believing what I tell you or other teachers tell you. Everyone should weigh the evidence for himself." [246] Nonetheless Mr. Graff dismissed Leslie Hill who, though eligible under the Constitution for any elective office in American political life, suddenly became ineligible to teach in a high school.

* This trial, in which attorneys William Jennings Bryan and Clarence Darrow were the leading protagonists, has been recently dramatized in a first-rate Broadway play entitled, *Inherit the Wind.*

To summarize, the sad truth is that American educators in general have been so preoccupied by the Communist issue during the decade following the Second World War that they have neglected their paramount responsibility of maintaining and developing a first-rate educational system. At a time when there is an enormous shortage of teachers—reliably estimated as at least 300,000—in the United States, the educational authorities have considerably lessened the available supply by driving out of the profession men and women whose competence is admitted, but who have clashed with a Congressional committee or become suspect in some way as "subversives."

Agitated legislators—through the passage of loyalty oath statutes and witch-hunt laws—and frightened educational administrators have put a premium on conformity among teachers and have drastically curtailed the exercise of academic freedom. These developments have discouraged independent thought on controversial subjects among both teachers and students; and have deterred increasing numbers of young people from entering the teaching profession, with its peculiar occupational hazards.

No profession has a finer tradition in the battle for human liberty than the teachers'. They can claim as theirs the noblest of all freedom's martyrs—the Greek teacher of philosophy, Socrates— and many another hero of the intellect in the history of the West. America's approximately 1,500,000 teachers have the responsibility of preserving their great tradition of freedom of thought and expression. And beyond that they have the obligation of contributing their best efforts to the general struggle on behalf of the Bill of Rights. Owing to the central function of teachers in our society, their voice, their influence, their perseverance may well prove decisive in that struggle.

11

CONFORM—OR LOSE YOUR JOB

One of the most significant measures of the gravity of the postwar civil liberties crisis is that political dissenters are so generally dismissed from their jobs and frequently blacklisted for future employment. The practice of firing people for their opinions and associations has spread more and more from the Federal Government to State and municipal governments, to education, to the entertainment industry, to the press and to private enterprise in general. The sort of injustices and inanities operating in the Federal loyalty-security program, which began as a limited and temporary emergency measure, have extended to well-nigh every sphere of work, and promise to become a permanent feature of American life.

As we saw in the last chapter, public schools and public colleges throughout the United States have almost without exception dismissed teachers who invoked the Fifth Amendment in declining to answer the questions of Congressional committees. Private colleges and universities, with a few honorable exceptions, have taken the same position. In 1947 the motion picture studios which employed the Hollywood Ten fired all of them when they refused to answer Congressional questions on the grounds of the First Amendment.

Federal, State and municipal authorities have all followed the general policy of dismissing, or more infrequently, of suspending, employees "guilty" of non-cooperation with the Congressional Inquisition. Senator McCarthy's Committee repeatedly brought direct influence to bear in this regard. For instance, when in 1953 Edward Rothschild, a bookbinder at the U.S. Government Printing Office, stood on the Fifth Amendment in refusing to answer questions about Communist Party affiliations, McCarthy turned to his Chief Counsel, Mr. Cohn, and said:

"Mr. Counsel, will you call the head of the Government Printing Office and tell him of this testimony? I assume he will be suspended. I can't conceive of his being allowed to go back to the Government Printing Office and allowed to handle secret material." [247] At once, David Schine, staff consultant, "hustled to a telephone booth in the corner of the big hearing room in the Senate Office Building. It wasn't long before McCarthy told reporters word had come back from Phillip L. Cole, deputy public printer, that Rothschild had been suspended immediately without pay." [248]

After Mr. Albert Shadowitz had relied on the First Amendment in declining to answer questions put by the McCarthy Committee in its abortive inquiry at Fort Monmouth, a Committee agent promptly telephoned Shadowitz's employer and demanded that he dismiss the recalcitrant witness. When the employer argued that Shadowitz was a valuable worker and supported his family on the wage he received, McCarthy's man pointed out that this attitude would be bad for the firm's Government contracts. Not long afterwards Shadowitz was discharged.

In 1954 the Jenner Committee heard some picturesque testimony from William P. Gandall, who had been a sergeant in the U.S. Army during World War II and had served under Captain William Jenner, who later was elected to the Senate. Gandall claimed that Jenner had started to "ride" him while they were both serving overseas, and that he was still doing it. The witness invoked the Fifth Amendment in refusing to answer some of Chairman Jenner's questions. Senator Jenner at once sent transcripts of the testimony to all officers of Universal Pictures where Gandall was employed and complained to the Chairman of the Board over the telephone. Gandall testified before the Committee on a Friday. Universal Pictures fired him the following Monday afternoon.

Radio and television, as I earlier pointed out, are as sensitive as the movies to the employment of "controversial" persons, with the *Red Channels* blacklist ° continuing to play a central role in the dismissal of performers. The judgment on *Red Channels* rendered by the dramatist, Robert E. Sherwood, remains definitive: "We are all too familiar with defamation used as a conventional weapon in political strife, and defamation in the rantings of racial and religious bigots; but defamation conducted as a commercial enterprise belongs in a category of contemptibility all by itself."[249]

This defamation ruined one of America's most accomplished actors, J. Edward Bromberg. After his listing in *Red Channels*, neither Broadway, nor Hollywood, nor TV nor radio would hire him. He went abroad to seek work and at last found a job. But the long ordeal had been too much for him, and he died a broken man in 1952. His body was brought back to America for burial, and the lines were long at his funeral. Later, a memorial service was held. But there, circulating among his friends, were those who had come not to pay respects, but to spy. And soon actors and actresses were being blacklisted for attending the memorial service of J. Edward Bromberg.

Other blacklisted actors whose premature deaths seemed at least partly attributable to their distress at being outcasts in their profession were Roman Bohnen, Mady Christians, John Garfield, Canada Lee and Philip Loeb. The last-named, who for several years played the popular TV role of "Papa Goldberg," was in 1952 found "too controversial" for continued employment. Years of union work in Actors' Equity, appearances (polite but negative) before Congressional committees, and a long listing in *Red Channels* destroyed his livelihood, and his prospects. An all-but-hopeless family problem was added strain. In 1955 Philip Loeb, registered under a false name in a New York hotel, took his own life.

John Crosby, in his *New York Herald Tribune* column "Television and Radio," hit hard at what he calls "the blacklist

° See Chapter 9.

racket." "God knows," he writes, "how many blacklists there are,
but they run into the dozens, all different. The closest thing to a
master list is in the hands of one of the largest advertising agencies. When in doubt, people call that agency. How do you get
on a blacklist? Well, some actors have got on by having foreign
names. Others by having names resembling those of other actors
who once appeared at benefits which turned out to be under the
auspices of left-wingers. . . .

*Actors have been blacklisted for having appeared in Arthur
Miller's plays—as if Mr. Miller's politics had anything to do with
their working or not. Actors have been blacklisted for having
worked at the Phoenix theatre, which is supposed to have some
left-wingers around. And actors have been blacklisted for nothing
at all—and have been unable to find out what the trouble is." 250

Dancers, musicians and singers have also felt the effects of
blacklist and boycott. For instance, Paul Draper, one of the most
talented dancers America has produced, and his able associate,
Larry Adler, the harmonica player, were subjected to an intensive
campaign. These two finally decided to strike back, and in 1948
brought suit against a woman in Connecticut who had called them
Communists. In 1950 the trial resulted in a hung jury; and Draper
and Adler emerged with even more mud sticking to them than
before.

Counterattack has steadily added new names from the entertainment world to the original list published in Red Channels.
And one of the surest ways to get on this expanding blacklist is to
denounce the immoral business of blacklisting. Meanwhile, as an
outgrowth of Red Channels, a new organization with the same
objectives was founded in 1953. It is called Aware, Inc.: An Organization to Combat the Communist Conspiracy in Entertain-
ment-Communications. The president of Aware is Godfrey P.
Schmidt, Professor of Law at Fordham University.

Like Counterattack and Red Channels, Aware takes the position that performers guilty of some sort of Communist association
can "cleanse" themselves by publicly confessing and recanting
their wrong-doing before one of the Congressional investigating

committees, usually the House Committee on Un-American Activities. In this process of getting "cleared" the accused individual must also turn informer and yield up to the proper authorities the names of associates who may be concealing their "subversive" connections, past or present.

Aware has valuable contacts within AFTRA, the American Federation of Television and Radio Artists (AFL), several of whose members are directors of Aware and report to it what is going on in the trade union. For this reason, "AFTRA has lived, literally, under a reign of terror for years. Members have been afraid to speak at meetings, afraid to vote against the administration, in some cases afraid even to attend meetings, because their livelihoods were in danger. Established performers, whose records have included nothing except that they have run for office against the administration, have been blacklisted." [251]

Finally on July 4, 1955 the New York Local of AFTRA in self-defense passed almost 2 to 1 a resolution deploring the circulation of smear lists by Aware; and also condemned Aware "for interfering in the internal affairs of our Union" by attacking "an entire slate of candidates for AFTRA office." "Such attacks," AFTRA stated, "are calculated to, and have in fact served, to injure members in jobs and to deprive them of economic opportunity and security in their professional life; and to undermine the democratic process of elections in the Union." [252]

But the Congressional vigilantes, working closely with the private vigilantes, were not going to let their confreres down. And on July 12 Congressman Walter's House Committee on Un-American Activities, determined to quell the rebellion against the blacklisters, announced that it was soon coming to New York City to unmask communism in the theatre. On July 21 AFTRA's national board, jittery over the pending investigation, decided to rush through a mid-summer referendum on whether local boards of the organization were to be authorized to "fine, censure, suspend or expel" any member who failed or refused to tell a Congressional committee if he is or was a member of the Communist Party. Though 60 percent of AFTRA's membership did not return

ballots, those who did vote backed the new rule overwhelmingly.
This unhappy result was announced just before Walter's circus
opened up.

The Walter Committee put on the rack twenty-three actors and
other entertainers, asking them the same stale old questions about
Red plots and affiliations. Twenty-two of the witnesses defied the
Committee and refused to answer questions they deemed violative of their constitutional rights. Only one actor confessed political sin, namely, that he had been a member of the Communist
Party during 1946-1947. And it turned out that he had already
voluntarily reported everything about it to the FBI. The Committee hearings were a dismal failure.

As to singers, the outstanding *cause célèbre* has been that of
Paul Robeson, the famed Negro baritone. Unable to keep on earn-
ing a living in the United States because of his radical sympathies,
Mr. Robeson could have continued his career in Europe where he
enjoys great popularity. But in 1950 the U.S. State Department
revoked his passport on account of his political views; and he has
not been able to go abroad since that time.

In 1951 *Counterattack* took the initiative in forcing the retirement of D. Angus Cameron, who for eight years had been brilliant editor-in-chief of Little, Brown & Company of Boston, an
old and conservative publishing firm. *Counterattack* ran an article
charging that Little, Brown was a Communist-front publisher because it had printed, under Mr. Cameron's editorship, a number
of books by alleged Communists or Communist sympathizers.
The Scripps-Howard newspapers took up the refrain and created
a further furor over the issue.

Little, Brown replied in a handsome brochure, asserting that
the accusations were absurd and showing that the "objectionable"
titles were only a tiny percentage of their total list. However, the
publishing house was sufficiently intimidated to tell Mr. Cameron,
who had been president of the Progressive Party in Massachusetts, that he must henceforth limit his political and cultural activities to those approved by the Company's Board of Directors.
As a man of principle, Mr. Cameron would not accept these terms

which curtailed his rights as an American citizen. He resigned from the firm, and later became co-partner in the publishing house of Cameron & Kahn in New York City.

The first important case which centered upon interference with the right to work and which also reached the U.S. Supreme Court was that of Dr. Edward K. Barsky, whose license to practice medicine was suspended in 1951 for six months by the New York State Board of Regents. This was owing to his conviction for contempt of Congress as Chairman of the Joint Anti-Fascist Refugee Committee, which had declined to turn over its records to the House Un-American Activities Committee. Dr. Barsky appealed his case to the Supreme Court, which in April 1954 upheld his suspension 6-3. The dissents of Justices Frankfurter and Douglas, however, bring out the dubious character of this decision.

Declared Justice Frankfurter: "It is one thing thus to recognize the freedom which the Constitution wisely leaves to the States in regulating the professions. It is quite another thing, however, to sanction a State's deprivation or partial destruction of a man's professional life on grounds having no possible relation to fitness, intellectual or moral, to pursue his profession." [253]

Justice Douglas stated: "The right to work I had assumed, was the most precious liberty that man possesses. Man has indeed as much right to work as he has to live, to be free, to own property. . . . The Bill of Rights does not say who shall be doctors or lawyers or policemen. But it does say that certain rights are protected, that certain things shall not be done. And so the question here is not what government must give, but rather what it may not take away. . . .

"Neither the security of the State nor the well-being of her citizens justifies this infringement of fundamental rights. So far as I know, nothing in a man's political beliefs disables him from setting broken bones or removing ruptured appendixes, safely and efficiently. A practicing surgeon is unlikely to uncover many state secrets in the course of his professional activities. When a doctor cannot save lives in America because he is opposed to

Franco in Spain, it is time to call a halt and look critically at the neurosis that has possessed us." [254]

This same neurosis was also responsible for purges in the medical profession on the other side of the continent. In late 1951 and early 1952 the House Un-American Activities Committee held hearings in Los Angeles and questioned various physicians about their political affiliations. Several doctors who refused to answer the questions were dismissed from their hospital staffs. In 1953 the conservative Los Angeles County Medical Association, an affiliate of the American Medical Association, passed a resolution declaring membership in the Communist Party or any activity aiding the goals and purposes of that Party incompatible with membership in the Association.

In 1954 Dr. Phil Sampson, President of the Association, requested the California State Un-American Activities Committee to conduct an inquiry into subversion among Los Angeles physicians. The Committee, under the chairmanship of State Senator Hugh M. Burns, a Democrat, naturally obliged and announced that it would investigate a "Communist plot to control the medical profession."

But it soon became obvious that the real plot had been hatched jointly by the Committee and the Los Angeles Medical Association for the purpose of getting rid of dissenters in the Association and discrediting any form of low-cost, prepaid group medical insurance plan. Accordingly, the Committee subpoenaed a number of doctors who were known to favor some kind of group practice, and spent much time looking into the Community Medical Center, the only consumer-controlled, low-cost, interracial health center in California.

The Committee hearings also helped lay the groundwork for a new bill which Senator Burns introduced into the State Senate early in 1955. This measure called for the revocation of the license of any person coming under the Business and Professions Code if "on any ground whatsoever" he refused to answer certain questions concerning political opinions and associations put to him by any committee of the United States Congress or the California legislature. This dragnet bill covered approximately 500,000 individuals, including all doctors, nurses, lawyers, druggists, beauticians, bartenders, barbers, plumbers, professional boxers, undertakers and 150 other categories of business or professional people. Owing to the loud public outcry against this measure, Senator Burns finally dropped it.

In January 1955 the California State Supreme Court, 4-3, extended the doctrine of the Barsky case to private employment by upholding the right of the Cutter Laboratories, a drug manufacturing company, to discharge a unionized employee because she was believed to be a member of the Communist Party. Cutter Laboratories was of the opinion in 1947 that the employee, Mrs. Doris Walker, was a Communist, but did not fire her until 1949 when, as president of her union local, she was engaged in bitter negotiations with the company over a new contract.*

The majority decision stated: "From the array of Congressional and legislative findings which have been quoted above, if not from the common knowledge of mankind, it must be accepted as conclusively established that a member of the Communist Party cannot be loyal to his private employer as against any directive of his Communist master. . . . The employer is not obligated to await a governmental decree before taking steps to protect himself or to exercise his right to discharge employees who upon the established facts are dedicated to be disloyal to him, to be likewise disloyal to the American labor union they may purport to serve, and who constitute a continuing risk to both the employing company and the public depending upon the company's products." [255]

The minority opinion pointed out: "By judicial fiat, but without the temerity to declare that Communists are deprived of civil rights, the court abrogates not only the right of employers and unions to contract for the employment of Communists, but the right of Communists as a class to enter into binding contracts. . . .

* In 1955 Cutter Laboratories came into prominence during the nation-wide controversy over methods of manufacture and distribution of the Salk anti-polio vaccine.

If the threat of Communist activity makes an employment contract with a known Communist illegal as against public policy, does it not also invalidate other contracts? Thus, can a landlord break his lease with a Communist on the ground that his building may be sabotaged? Can a buyer refuse to accept and pay for goods purchased from a Communist on the ground that they may conceal cleverly concealed defects? Can a seller refuse to deliver goods sold to a Communist on the ground that they may be used to promote Communist activities? . . . If contracts with Communists are illegal, cannot Communists themselves violate them with impunity?"[256]

The U.S. Supreme Court is reviewing the Walker-Cutter case and is expected to render a decision during 1956. The CIO took the unusual step of filing an amicus brief on behalf of Mrs. Walker.

In December 1954 a Federal District Court in Washington, D.C., ruled that the General Electric Company had a constitutional right to oust a worker, John Nelson, who had relied upon the Fifth Amendment in refusing to answer the Jenner Committee's questions concerning "subversive" connections. Mr. Nelson and his trade union, the United Electrical, Radio and Machine Workers of America, had claimed that the dismissal violated the union's collective bargaining contract with General Electric. The Court held that the contract gave the company the right to dismiss an employee for "obvious cause" and that invoking the Fifth Amendment came within this provision.

The General Electric Company had previously announced a new security program. Each job applicant is asked to affirm that he is not a present or past member of the Communist Party or of any organization listed as subversive by the U.S. Attorney General. If he cannot truthfully so state, he is subject to special investigation and may be refused employment. The American Civil Liberties Union criticized these regulations on the ground that security programs, while they might sometimes be needed for "sensitive" positions in industry, should be formulated and administered by the U.S. Government and not by private firms.

The ACLU added: "While we understand GE's proper concern

for national security, we feel that its workers . . . and applicants, recognizing the emphasis on security, will so carefully watch what they say and with whom they associate as to add to the already heavy pressures placed on the traditional American principles of freedom of speech and association. There is already so much of a drift toward loyalty oaths in various sections of American life, that unless this trend is arrested, these principles of free speech and association which form the heart's core of American freedom will be severely damaged." [257]

How to defend American freedom was the last thing the U.S. Defense Department was thinking about when in 1954 it "proposed to require every defense worker with access to any classified information to fill out a questionnaire naming under penalties of perjury every person he had ever associated with, *no matter how many years back,* who, at any time in his entire life, had ever belonged to any of the . . . organizations on the Attorney General's list." [258] [Italics mine—C.L.] If it appeared that the worker knew too many "subversives," he would be dismissed.

Owing to strong protests on the part of the CIO and its President, Walter P. Reuther, the Defense Department withdrew this so-called "stoolpigeon" question, but continued to insist that its industrial security questionnaire ask the worker whether he is or has been associated with organizations on the Attorney General's list.

Mr. Reuther had another worry. For he had reported to the CIO delegates: "Your officers are also particularly concerned lest the information on these questionnaires come into the hands of employers who might utilize the 'derogatory' information thus gained by them against militant union men." [259]

Business concerns have increasingly insisted that their employees be free of the taint of association with an organization on the U.S. Attorney General's subversive list. For example, the American Telephone and Telegraph Company requires each employee to sign a "Citizenship" form that includes the question: "Are you now or have you ever been a member of any organization which

has been designated, under the Executive Order, by the United
States Attorney General . . . as of this date?" [260]

It is no wonder, then, that in 1955 a private non-profit organization, the Girl Scouts Council of Ulster County, New York, took
the cue and asked all of its prospective counselors to fill out an
affidavit promising that they are not now and never will be members of any organization planning to overthrow the U.S. Government by force and violence. For the information of the job applicant a copy of the Attorney General's subversive list was attached
to each affidavit.

A number of private businesses have set up their own informal
security systems by engaging American Business Consultants,
owners of the notorious weekly, *Counterattack*, to provide inside
information on "subversive" employees. Business Consultants
charges a minimum fee of $5,000 a year for this service. Some-
times *Counterattack* runs a sensational story about how the
Communists have infiltrated a certain company. Then Business
Consultants follows this up with an offer to sell "protection service" to the firm, which, rather than risk another smear article, hires
the Consultants.

An unusual case, in which a top business executive instead of
a rank-and-file employee lost his job, was that of Henry Willcox,
professional engineer and president of the Willcox Construction
Company of New York City. Mr. Willcox had founded the firm
in 1921 and had provided most of its initial capital. In 1952 he
took a two months' trip to Communist China with his wife.
Promptly cracking down on this exercise of the right to travel,
the U.S. State Department announced that the Willcoxes would
be severely dealt with, and seized their passports when they returned to New York.

Before Mr. Willcox got back to America, however, his friends
and associates in the Construction Company had voted him out
of office and out of the corporation, without his knowledge and
without giving him any opportunity to be heard. They later explained to him that after FBI agents had visited them, and unfavorable comments had appeared in the press about his trip,

they decided that the firm could not survive unless he was retired. Specifically, a $6,000,000 contract with the New York City Housing Authority, on which the firm was low bidder, had been "unaccountably" held up—only to be duly awarded as soon as Willcox was out.

Another case deserving of special note centered around the farfetched action of the Washington, D.C. Police Department in refusing to renew the license of William Shonick, a second-hand piano-dealer. Mr. Shonick had earlier been purged as a music teacher from a Maryland high school on loyalty grounds. In 1954 the police claimed that because Shonick had attended meetings of two organizations rated as subversive by the U.S. Attorney General, and because he had invoked the Fifth Amendment before a Congressional committee, his character was such as to make him unfit to sell pianos. Shonick took his case to the Board of Appeals and Reviews of the District of Columbia Department of Licenses and won a favorable recommendation from the Hearing Examiner. This is a good omen for civil liberties, since many American municipalities require special licenses for the practice of a wide range of occupations and professions.

Among the professional people particularly subject to witchhunt pressures have been lawyers. Throughout the United States competent attorneys hesitate to take on the defense of Communists or other radicals because they fear the loss of other clients and a reaction against their business in general. I know several lawyers who have wanted to step into left-wing cases as a matter of principle, but whose partners vetoed the idea on the grounds that it would handicap or even ruin the firm.

In 1950 after the tumultuous trial of the first eleven Communists under the Smith Act, the presiding judge, Harold R. Medina, found all five of the defense counsel guilty of contempt of court, and took the unusual course of sentencing them to jail for terms ranging from three to five months. The five attorneys served their sentences, but had great difficulty in resuming their law practices afterwards, in the face of efforts by the State authorities to disbar them temporarily or permanently.

The effect of the whole proceedings on other lawyers was wide-spread. After Steve Nelson, Pennsylvania Communist leader, had been indicted in 1950 under Pennsylvania's anti-sedition law,* not one of some eighty attorneys he approached was willing to represent him. Typical was the reaction of a "liberal" lawyer in Pittsburgh. According to Mr. Nelson, he said: "Nelson, I can't help you. I'm not going to ruin my business. Be sensible. A man can't be a lawyer in this town by getting in trouble with the judges who are against you and your friends. Besides, I'm not a youngster any more. I used to stick my neck out, but I'm not the foolish idealist I used to be." [261]

Just before his trial was to take place, Nelson finally obtained the names of three lawyers who would take his case, provided that they had a month or two in which to prepare it. However, the judge in charge was unwilling to postpone the trial. Fifteen minutes before the trial was to begin a fourth lawyer, whose name had been provided by the judge and recommended by the prosecuting attorney, agreed to defend Nelson. But Nelson, after talking with him, found him incompetent and unacceptable. The upshot of all this was that Steve Nelson took on the responsibility of being his own counsel.

In September 1954, for the first time on record, a lawyer was disbarred for invoking the Fifth Amendment. A Florida State Court ruled that Leo Sheiner, a Miami attorney, could no longer practice law in Florida because he had relied on the Amendment in appearances before a County grand jury, the Senate Internal Security Committee and a State judge. The American Bar Association, instead of coming to the defense of Mr. Sheiner and the Bill of Rights, filed an amicus brief in support of Florida's action and indicated that it favored ejecting from membership any lawyer who took the Fifth Amendment. The liberal National Lawyers Guild, on the other hand, filed a brief in support of Sheiner. And in July 1955 the Florida Supreme Court over-ruled the disbarment.

Not unnaturally the drive to oust "controversial" persons from

* See Chapter 8.

jobs has extended to the sphere of religion, where there exists a long tradition of political and social dissent stemming from the militant preaching of the ancient Hebrew prophets and the ethics taught by Jesus in the New Testament. We have already seen that in 1953 the House Committee on Un-American Activities, under the chairmanship of Representative Velde, started an investigation of Communists in the churches, but gave it up because of the extremely adverse public reaction.*

In the meantime, individual clergymen were under local fire for their social and political views. In 1947, in the Episcopal Church of the Holy Trinity in Brooklyn, a campaign was started to force out the rector, Reverend John Howard Melish, and his son, the assistant rector, Reverend William Howard Melish. Dr. Melish, Senior, had served brilliantly as pastor of the parish for forty-five years. Finally, however, he was challenged by some of the congregation and vestrymen who had become restive over his liberal views and positively alarmed over the younger Melish's social-mindedness, particularly his activities and speeches on behalf of international peace and American-Soviet understanding.

William Howard Melish, like his father a man of outstanding integrity and civic spirit, is a Harvard graduate and had succeeded me in 1946 as Chairman of the National Council of American-Soviet Friendship. His troubles at Holy Trinity began shortly after U.S. Attorney General Tom Clark, late in 1947, first made public his list of subversive organizations and included in it the National Council. The situation was aggravated in 1948 when both of the Melishes supported former Vice-President Henry A. Wallace for President on the Progressive Party ticket.

In January of 1949 the vestry of Holy Trinity Church voted 9 to 2 to petition the bishop of the diocese, James P. DeWolfe, to put an end to Dr. Melish's rectorship. They accused the Melishes of holding views that gave aid and comfort to the enemies of America, and predicted that the two clergymen would lead the Church to ruin. Bishop DeWolfe immediately called the younger Mr. Melish into conference and told him that if he would resign as

* See Chapter 4.

assistant rector, the tempest would blow over and the petition in all probability be withdrawn. After conferring with his father, Mr. Melish replied that this proposal violated Christian and democratic principles, and that he could not accept it.

Meanwhile, 321 families in the parish, representing 70 percent of the membership, subscribed to the following statement: "We, the undersigned members of Holy Trinity parish, are completely opposed to the action of the vestry in asking for the resignation of our pastor, Dr. John Howard Melish. We have the strongest affection for Dr. Melish and approve the policy he has consistently followed for the past forty-five years of his rectorship. We state that the vestry in this action in no way represents our sentiments."

Since this made clear that the parish opposed the vestry's position, and since the regular election of vestrymen was due to take place at the annual parish meeting in April, the reasonable and democratic course would have been for the vestry and the bishop to defer action until after that meeting. But they pushed ahead relentlessly in total disregard of the opinions and rights of the Holy Trinity congregation. Early in March Bishop DeWolfe handed down his judgment granting the petition of the anti-Melish vestrymen and dissolving the pastoral relation between Dr. John Howard Melish and the Church.

The whole issue went to a court trial on April 18, 1949, the very date of the annual meeting. That same evening the parish of Holy Trinity met in formal session and overwhelmingly voted in a new slate of vestrymen who in general supported the Melishes. Although this result was reported to the court the next day, it did not prevent the judge from ruling in favor of the ex-vestrymen and the dismissal of Dr. Melish. The higher courts affirmed this decision when the Melishes and the parish appealed; and in 1951 the U.S. Supreme Court declined to review the case.

Yet in the end the principled and persevering stand taken by the Holy Trinity congregation and the Melishes, father and son, resulted in substantial victory. Dr. Melish, Senior, seventy-five years old when the courts finally upheld his dismissal, intended shortly to retire in any event; and the action of the old vestry and Bishop DeWolfe did not reach to the position of assistant rector held by the younger Melish, whose ouster had all along been the primary object of the reactionary attack. William Howard Melish continued in this post for a time and then was appointed Acting Minister by the vestrymen. In this capacity he is able to perform almost all the duties of rector without officially assuming that title.

In 1955 a sizable group—more than fifty—of religious dissenters belonging to a fundamentalist Protestant sect called the Church of God of the Union Assembly, were promptly fired when they disclosed the identity of their religion on a questionnaire their employers had demanded they fill out. This happened in Dalton, Georgia. An unusual part of Church of God doctrine is that workers should all join trade unions. The CIO has taken these cases of discharge for religious affiliation to the National Labor Relations Board.

To summarize the findings and implications of this chapter, we can state that to a degree unique in the history of the United States those holding unpopular opinions face the loss of their jobs and the possibility of being unable to earn a living. For many, the iniquitous principle of "Conform or lose your job" may come to mean "Conform or starve." Unfortunately, although dismissing a person for political reasons clearly violates the spirit of the Bill of Rights, that document affords legal protection in a relatively small proportion of cases.

The practice of dismissal for dissent has gone far beyond industries producing for the country's defense to businesses and professions that have no relation to national security; it has extended from the firing of Communists to the ousting of liberals, progressives, New Dealers, and civil libertarians who uphold their constitutional rights. There is literally no field of employment which is exempt from this drive against freedom to work. And the evil effects cannot be evaluated merely by the totals of those unfairly dismissed. For the whole working population is to some extent disturbed or intimidated by hearing about and reading about the well-publicized discharges which take place or are threatened. If dismissal for dissent becomes an established pattern in this country, minority voices will be more effectively silenced than ever before.

12

THE DECLINE OF THE
CIVIL LIBERTIES UNION

The United States is noted among the countries of the world for the large number and general efficacy of private, charitable, educational or pressure groups working on behalf of one cause or another. These organizations as a rule attempt to raise funds for their programs; and to influence public opinion and government policies through meetings, radio and television, newspaper releases, letters to the press, pamphlets, books or other written materials.

It is a telling sign of the precarious state of civil liberties in America since the First World War that public-spirited citizens have felt called upon to found numerous organizations for defense of the Bill of Rights; and that despite all the efforts of these organizations, the cause of civil liberties is today more gravely threatened than ever before. In 1955 more than fifty national groups active in defending civil liberties were associated with the National Civil Liberties Clearing House, a voluntary educational association with its office in Washington, D.C.

Many organizations concerned with civil liberties concentrate on some special aspect of the struggle for freedom. Typical of these groups are the National Association for the Advancement of Colored People, the Association on American Indian Affairs, the American Jewish Committee, the American Committee for the Protection of the Foreign Born, the Authors League of America, the Committee to End Sedition Laws, the American Association of University Professors, the Central Committee for Conscientious Objectors, the Workers Defense League, and the Fund for the Republic.

The leading organizations with an over-all function are the American Civil Liberties Union (ACLU), founded in 1920 and now possessing more than twenty active affiliates and more than 33,000 members; the Civil Rights Congress (CRC), with a left-wing orientation, founded in 1946 to succeed the International Labor Defense and the National Federation for Constitutional Liberties; and the Emergency Civil Liberties Committee (ECLC), founded in 1951 to take prompt and militant action and to fill in the gaps left by the faltering Civil Liberties Union.

In this chapter I shall give particular attention to the Civil Liberties Union, because the history of this organization during the sixteen years from 1939 through 1955 throws considerable light on the general decline of civil liberties during the same period. Since I was a member of the ACLU Board of Directors from 1931 to 1954 and an active participant in its constant internal battles, I am able to tell the story of how America's principal civil liberties organization went far in compromising the cause of civil liberties. I shall be sorry if my account offends some of those involved; but I believe it is essential to record these facts about the ACLU, both for the sake of historical truth and in order to show the pitfalls that may in these times beset a liberal organization.

The ACLU was an outgrowth of the National Civil Liberties Bureau which came into existence shortly after the United States entered the First World War. Roger N. Baldwin, Director of the Bureau, became the first Director of the Civil Liberties Union and remained in that position until 1950. Working with him as Chairman of the organization until 1940 was Dr. Harry F. Ward, Professor of Christian Ethics at Union Theological Seminary. Mrs. Lucille Milner, an experienced social worker, became the first Secretary and held that post until 1945.

In its very first year the ACLU entered militantly into the defense of the victims of the anti-Bolshevik hysteria following the First World War. It supported the constitutional liberties of liberals and radicals arrested and thrown summarily into jail in Attorney General Palmer's raids. Because it stood up for the rights of "Reds," it became itself the target of virulent attacks by government officials, malevolent newspapers and the whole wolf-pack of reactionaries.

Telling about the pressures exerted against the ACLU in those days, Mrs. Milner writes in her book, *Education of an American Liberal:* "Active support of the Union's work might mean social ostracism or economic ruin and possibly imprisonment. It took a very brave lawyer to join with us in defense of civil liberties cases in the courts. Even so rock-ribbed an American institution as the *Atlantic Monthly* felt the pressure of the Iron Heel and declined to print our advertisement soliciting members. . . . The Overman Committee of the United States Senate, created originally to investigate German propaganda in the United States, published a list of individuals, furnished by the Military Intelligence Bureau, accused of 'radicalism.' The alphabetical blacklist, which began with Jane Addams of Hull House and ended with Lillian Wald of the Henry Street Settlement, two great American public servants, contained the names of most of the men and women serving in the Union's work." [262]

In this early period the ACLU took on free speech battles on behalf of Communists, Socialists, members of the IWW (The Industrial Workers of the World), birth control advocates and many others. It defended Mrs. Margaret Sanger, courageous exponent of planned parenthood; Sacco and Vanzetti, finally executed in a famous frame-up case with international repercussions; and John T. Scopes, science instructor who violated Tennessee's law against the teaching of evolution. The Union also helped materially in the successful campaign to win pardons for Tom Mooney and Warren Billings, California labor organizers framed and sentenced to life imprisonment for their alleged guilt in the bombing of a 1916 Preparedness Day parade in San Francisco.

The Civil Liberties Union grew steadily in prestige and influ-

ence, and at the end of its first decade was generally recognized
as the foremost organization working for the defense of the American Bill of Rights.

In 1931 the Board of Directors of the ACLU elected me as a
member and I served in that capacity for twenty-three years. Outstanding on the Board when I joined it were Roger N. Baldwin,
the able and hard-working Director; Morris L. Ernst, subtle and
soft-spoken lawyer who became J. Edgar Hoover's personal attorney; the late Arthur Garfield Hays, another lawyer, straightfor-
ward and usually uncompromising in his support of civil liberties;
the Reverend John Haynes Holmes, liberal minister and founder
of the Community Church in New York City; Dorothy Kenyon,
brilliant woman attorney and an early suffragette; and Chairman
Harry F. Ward, sensitive teacher and writer, an excellent presiding officer and one of America's greatest crusaders for freedom.

Three or four years later there became members of the Board
Osmond K. Fraenkel, a liberal New York lawyer and a veritable
Rock of Gibraltar for free speech principles; Elmer Rice, noted
playwright with a burning passion against the censorship of literature; Norman Thomas, Socialist Party leader who constantly put
partisan politics above civil liberties; and Mary Van Kleeck, untir-
ing social worker and Director of Industrial Studies at the Russell
Sage Foundation.

Up to 1944 the Board met regularly for lunch every Monday,
except during the summer and Christmas holiday seasons; beginning with that year the luncheons took place every other week.
At these meetings we discussed and decided upon fundamental
issues and cases involving every aspect of civil liberties. The constitutional rights of workers, trade union organizers, capitalist
manufacturers, newspaper owners, Catholics, Jehovah's Witnesses,
atheists, teachers, writers and publishers all came within our pur-
view. And we were active in opposing both legislation and Congressional committees that violated the Bill of Rights. The scope
of the Civil Liberties Union, at least up to the Second World War,
was as broad as the entire sphere of civil liberties.

Every Director had his say at Board meetings and the discussions were always interesting and often exciting. It was a rare luncheon which did not see disagreement develop among the members; and the debates, though necessarily short, were for the most part stimulating and enlightening. The Directors were continually educating one another as to the true meaning of civil liberties. Not infrequently motions were passed by a majority of one or two. The ACLU Board never became a rubber stamp for the approval of the program offered by its dynamic Director; and you always felt that your vote really counted. We talked a lot, fought a lot, at these Board meetings; yet from week to week we put through an enormous amount of business.

When I first became a Director of the ACLU, discussions were carried on in a spirit of good humor and fair play. But as the years went by and the fateful issue of communism and Communists increasingly entered into our considerations, some of our debates assumed an acrimonious tone. The first controversy that I recall arousing hard feelings on the Board centered around a serious clash in 1934 between Communists and Socialists at a mass meeting in Madison Square Garden. The Socialist Party and a number of trade unions had called this rally in order to protest against the attack on the Vienna workers by the Austrian Government headed by Chancellor Dollfuss.

Communist Party members and sympathizers came to the meeting in large numbers, causing disturbances throughout the hall and demanding that their leaders be allowed to speak. When one of these leaders, Clarence Hathaway, mounted the platform with the apparent intention of trying to speak, he was beaten up by the Socialists and ejected from the Garden. Owing to the continuing noise and disorder, the meeting finally had to be adjourned before the scheduled program was concluded.

The Board of the ACLU appointed a Special Commission of Inquiry to look into the riot. I was a member of this Commission and signed its public report (March 1934) forthrightly condemning the Communists. This report stated: "It is undisputed that the Communists participated in the Madison Square Garden meeting for the announced purpose of preventing two speakers from being heard and of demanding places for two of their own speakers on the program. The immediate responsibility for breaking up the meeting rests, therefore, squarely upon the Communist Party leadership."

At the same time the report criticized the Socialists for searching Communists at the entrance to the Garden and taking away from them copies of the *Daily Worker,* and for assaulting Mr. Hathaway physically. Norman Thomas was furious over this mild criticism of the Socialists and absurdly claimed that the report was a sop to Communist sympathizers on the ACLU Board. In making his remarks, he did not speak, but shouted, as if he were himself on the platform at Madison Square Garden. From that day until my last Board meeting early in 1954, Mr. Thomas carried on a remorseless vendetta against alleged Communist infiltration of the Civil Liberties Union—a vendetta that was actively supported by other members of the Board and that year after year distracted the ACLU from its central task of defending civil liberties.

In 1938 another serious controversy developed among the Directors concerning a National Labor Relations Board order that the Ford Motor Company cease and desist from the distribution of two anti-union publications to its employees. The NLRB had ruled that the placing of the pamphlets in the hands of the individual workers constituted "interference, coercion and restraint" in the exercise of the employee's rights of self-organization. I was one of the ACLU Directors who felt that in this case the NLRB was interfering with Henry Ford's right of free speech, a position later upheld by a Federal Court of Appeals. After protracted debate, the Civil Liberties Union Board decided to petition the NLRB "to clarify its order so as to make clear the distinction between language as part of a coercive course of conduct and language merely expressing the employer's views of trade unions or trade union leadership." [263]

Our heated discussion over this issue arose from the fact that since its very founding the ACLU had championed the rights of labor, and some of its Directors found it difficult to realize that in borderline cases breaking fresh ground the National Labor Relations Act might be interpreted in such a way as to jeopardize the civil liberties of *employers*. So rarely had the free speech of capitalists ever been threatened that our Board was slow to adjust to the new situation. The Board members who opposed criticism of the NLRB were not, then, communistically motivated, any more than the members of the NLRB itself.

Early in 1939, with dangerous tensions increasing in the international arena and with Congressman Dies's House Committee on Un-American Activities extending its witch-hunt at home, the Communist issue came more and more to the fore on the Board of the Civil Liberties Union. Norman Thomas, energetically seconded by Morris Ernst, the late Roger William Riis and others, pressed the Board to abandon its traditional policy of confining itself to the American Bill of Rights. This group, at first a small minority, wanted the ACLU to take a stand against anti-democratic forms of government, including the Government of the Soviet Union.

At a special meeting on March 6, 1939, the Directors overwhelmingly defeated this move and in April issued a leaflet, *Why We Defend Free Speech for Nazis, Fascists and Communists*, which declared: "The Union does not engage in political controversy. It takes no position on any political or economic issue or system. It defends without favoritism the rights of all comers, whatever their political or economic views. It is wholly unconcerned with movements abroad or with foreign governments."

Meanwhile, irresponsible witnesses at public sessions of the Dies Committee branded the ACLU as a Communist front. And in a report issued early in 1939 the Committee itself said: "From the evidence before us we are not in a position to definitely state whether or not the Civil Liberties Union can properly be classed as a Communist organization. But the statement of the United Mine Workers to the effect that the Civil Liberties Union is serving as a forerunner and trail blazer for the active and insidious activities of the Communist is borne out by the evidence we have heard thus far. We strongly urge that this organization be investigated." [264] Presumably this last sentence was meant for the Department of Justice.

On October 14, 1939, Representative Dies brought renewed pressure on the ACLU when he attacked a two-day National Conference on "Civil Liberties in the Present Emergency." The Civil Liberties Union had issued the call for this meeting. Dies told the press that many of the organizations sponsoring the Conference were Communist fronts. He added that he would be interested to know whether the Conference had adopted any resolution condemning communism. The Conference passed no such resolution.

Meanwhile, the ACLU had been trying to obtain an assurance from Mr. Dies that it could have a hearing before his Committee to present its side of the case. The top leadership of the Union reached an understanding that if at such a hearing the Committee asked its representative any improper questions, he was to refuse to answer on grounds of the First Amendment so that a constitutional test could be made. This is why Dr. Ward, when he testified on October 23 before the Committee as Chairman of the American League for Peace and Democracy, did not raise the constitutional issue. For he had agreed that the Civil Liberties Union had higher standing in public opinion than the League and was more likely to be successful in a possible appeal to the U.S. Supreme Court.

Towards the end of Dr. Ward's session with the Committee, the matter of a hearing for the ACLU came up. It was then that Representative Dies unexpectedly declared, according to the printed record: "This Committee found last year, in its reports, there was not any evidence that the American Civil Liberties Union was a Communist organization. That being true, I do not see why we would be justified in going into it. I mean, after all, they have been dismissed by unanimous report of the Committee as not a Communist organization." [265]

The strange and suspicious thing about this statement was that the Committee had made no such report. Its only report about the ACLU, as quoted on the previous page, was hostile.

Why, then, did Martin Dies suddenly revise so drastically the opinion of his Committee, and give the Union a clean bill of health?

The answer would seem to lie in a cocktail conference which the ACLU's two general counsel, Morris L. Ernst and Arthur Garfield Hays, had with Representative Dies at the Hay-Adams House in Washington between October 14 and October 23. Telling about this meeting in a recent letter to me Martin Dies, now once more a Congressman, writes:

"It is true that I had a conference with Mr. Morris Ernst, Mr. Arthur Garfield Hays and Mr. Berle ° who represented the Administration. . . . The real purpose of the meeting was to explore the possibility of united action on the part of liberals and conservatives to investigate and expose Communists in the United States. The meeting was called at my instance. I believed that the liberals should take the initiative in a campaign against communism. . . . It was my belief that the liberals would hurt their cause seriously if they continued to collaborate with Communists and evade an all-out denunciation of communism. I felt that we were seriously handicapped in exposing the Communists through a lack of cooperation from the liberals. At the meeting I suggested that if we worked together, we could destroy the Communist apparatus and influence within a few months, and that the liberals would share in the credit. Unfortunately, the meeting was not productive of any fruits."

As we shall see, the facts do not bear out Dies's statement that the talks produced no fruits.

On October 30, 1939, Messrs. Ernst and Hays reported on the conference briefly to the Board of the Civil Liberties Union. They said Mr. Dies had promised to give the Union a hearing, but did not mention his interesting suggestion about liberals helping to track down the Communists.

After the high-level meeting in Washington and Representative

° This refers to Adolf A. Berle, Jr., who in 1939 was an Assistant Secretary of State and represented a diehard anti-Soviet and anti-Communist point of view.

Dies's subsequent white-washing of the ACLU, the projected hearing for the ACLU before the Un-American Activities Committee faded away entirely. What also vanished into thin air was the ACLU plan, relied upon in good faith by Dr. Ward, of challenging the Committee's unconstitutional questions on the basis of the First Amendment. Had the Civil Liberties Union made this important test at that time, the history of Congressional investigations during recent years might have been very different.

The portentous question remains: did Martin Dies promise Ernst and Hays in their Washington interview that he would cease his attacks on the ACLU and withdraw his Committee accusations if the ACLU, on its part, would cleanse itself?

Certainly, very soon after the Hays-Ernst-Dies discussion the Thomas-Ernst group on the Union's Board of Directors started a high-powered anti-Communist cleansing operation that raised havoc in the ACLU for the next fifteen years. This drive was aided at the outset by the rapid growth of anti-Communist sentiment in the United States in the fall of 1939, following the Soviet-Nazi Non-Aggression Pact and the outbreak of the Second World War.

The first move in the purge campaign within the ACLU was an attempt to get rid of Harry F. Ward as Chairman, a position he had held for almost twenty years. The claim was that Dr. Ward was compromising the ACLU because he was also Chairman of the American League for Peace and Democracy. On December 4, 1939, a decisive Board majority rejected the idea of ousting Dr. Ward and stated: "Members of the Union differ sharply in their economic and political views, and all are free to express them without involving the Union."

The answer to this came two weeks later in the form of a biting article on the ACLU by Norman Thomas in *The Call*, official organ of the Socialist Party. This article attacked Dr. Ward as Chairman of the Union, accused alleged Communists and fellow-travelers on the Board of hypocrisy and called for their ousting. It was the first time in the history of the Union that a Board member had discussed internal controversies and attacked fellow-Directors in the public prints. But the Board took no action on a special subcommittee report that the Thomas article was "highly improper."

The purge group's next step was to maneuver the Union's special Nominating Committee so that it went far beyond its function of making nominations and adopted a resolution declaring it inappropriate for supporters of totalitarian dictatorship to serve on the Union's governing committees and staff. The Nominating Committee, with the cooperation of Director Baldwin and his office, then mailed out this resolution to the National Committee of the ACLU for approval. This was in gross violation of the By-Laws, which provided that the National Committee could pass only on matters first acted upon by the Board. Furthermore, when controversial issues were involved, it was the recognized custom to send out to the National Committee the arguments on both sides of the question. On January 18 the Board voted that the Nominating Committee had exceeded its authority and that its action was unconstitutional.

At this same stormy meeting Miss Mary Van Kleeck, in an effort both to end the controversy and to maintain the ACLU's principles, made the following motion: "Resolved, that complete and consistent support of civil liberties as guaranteed in the Bill of Rights of the Constitution of the United States is the one invariable and basic qualification for office or membership in the governing bodies of the American Civil Liberties Union." The Board defeated this sensible motion 7 to 6.

The National Committee voted in favor of the Nominating Committee's resolution 30 to 10; and although this ballot was illegal, it was treated as an "advisory" expression of opinion. The purge group, busily canvassing votes behind the scenes, came to the Annual Meeting of the ACLU on February 5, 1940, able to cite with considerable effect the National Committee's "advisory opinion." After only brief discussion, the members of the National Committee and Board present formally passed, with a few modifications, the original resolution sent out by the Nominating Committee. The final text read:

"While the American Civil Liberties Union does not make any

test of opinion on political or economic questions a condition of membership, and makes no distinction in defending the right to hold and utter any opinions, the personnel of its governing committees and staff is properly subject to the test of consistency in the defense of civil liberties in all aspects and all places.

"That consistency is inevitably compromised by persons who champion civil liberties in the United States and yet who justify or tolerate the denial of civil liberties by dictatorships abroad. Such a dual position in these days, when issues are far sharper and more profound, makes it desirable that the Civil Liberties Union make its position unmistakably clear.

"The Board of Directors and the National Committee of the American Civil Liberties Union therefore hold it inappropriate for any person to serve on the governing committees of the Union or on its staff, who is a member of any political organization which supports totalitarian dictatorship in any country, or who by his public declarations indicates his support of such a principle.

"Within this category we include organizations in the United States supporting the totalitarian governments of the Soviet Union and of the Fascist and Nazi countries (such as the Communist Party, the German-American Bund and others); as well as native organizations with obvious anti-democratic objectives or practices."

The purge group on the Board of the ACLU had carried on a whispering campaign to the effect that this 1940 Resolution was necessary in order to put an end to the Communist machinations of a minority bloc of Directors. This charge of a Communist plot was, of course, utter and complete nonsense. What really happened was that a minority steadily resisted, as contrary to the principles of the organization, repeated efforts to institute a purge in the Union and to drive it into taking a position on political systems and foreign governments. Then the majority, partly to help put across the Resolution and partly to justify its own surrender to the anti-Communist furor, accused the minority of a Communist conspiracy.

That the Resolution was not primarily motivated by the internal situation in the ACLU is shown by the special press release issued by Director Baldwin to explain the Resolution. This release stated in part: "The occasion for raising this issue at this time is the increasing tension which has resulted everywhere from the direction of the Communist international movement since the Soviet-Nazi pact. The abandonment of the struggle against Fascism and the other changes in Communist policy have raised sharp issues which were reflected in the attitude of members of our Board of Directors."

This release also declared, contrary to the facts, that the Resolution did not "change the fundamental policy of the Union" and that "no member of the Communist Party was . . . ever elected or appointed to any position of responsibility in the Union." Actually, William Z. Foster was on the National Committee from the ACLU's founding in 1920 until 1930, and was re-elected three times after he became an open member of the Communist Party in 1921; Miss Anna Rochester was elected to the Board of Directors in 1928 when it was well known she was a member of the Communist Party; and Miss Elizabeth Gurley Flynn was re-elected as a Director in 1939 after she had formally notified the Board that she had joined the Party.

The 1940 Resolution was undoubtedly successful from a public relations standpoint. It received a great deal of newspaper publicity, almost all of it favorable to the Union's new policy. And there is no question that the move gained "respectability" for the organization in influential business and political circles, including the gentlemen who composed the House Committee on Un-American Activities. The Resolution came close, in fact, to that "denunciation of communism" which Representative Dies had suggested to ACLU Directors Ernst and Hays and which he had earlier mentioned in attacking the National Conference of October 13-14, 1939.

Among civil libertarians in general, however, and among members, officers and locals of the ACLU the Resolution aroused strong opposition. Opposing it on the National Committee were such civil liberties stalwarts as Henry T. Hunt of the U.S. Department of the Interior, Professor Robert Morss Lovett and Professor Alexander Meiklejohn. The most effective protest of all came from seventeen prominent liberals who wrote an open letter to the ACLU. They stated:

"We believe that by the purge Resolution the American Civil Liberties Union encourages the very tendencies it was intended to fight. It sets an example less liberal organizations will not be slow to imitate. . . . The phrasing of the purge resolution is so wide as to make the Civil Liberties Union seem a fellow-traveler of the Dies Committee. . . . The Civil Liberties Union has often found it necessary to mobilize public sentiment in order to defend civil liberties. Never before has it been necessary to mobilize public sentiment in order to defend civil liberties within the Civil Liberties Union. The Civil Liberties Union was founded in 1920 to fight postwar hysteria. It would be a great pity if it were now to become the victim of prewar hysteria."

On March 2 Dr. Harry F. Ward, whom John Haynes Holmes had succeeded as Chairman of the Board, publicly issued a letter resigning in protest as a Director and member of the Union. Dr. Ward asserted that the 1940 Resolution set up a test of opinion for officers. "In thus penalizing opinion," he said, "the Union is doing in its own sphere what it has always opposed the government for doing in law or administration. The essence of civil liberties is opposition to all attempts to enforce political orthodoxy. Yet by this Resolution the Civil Liberties Union is attempting to create an orthodoxy in civil liberties, and stranger still, an orthodoxy in political judgment upon events outside the United States, in situations of differing degrees of democratic development. The majority of the Board and of the National Committee, acting under the pressure of wartime public opinion, tells the minority to conform to its views or get out. What kind of civil liberties is this? It is certainly not the kind which has been proclaimed in all our printed matter from the beginning.

"Furthermore, when the Union disqualifies for membership in its governing bodies any person 'who is a member of any political organization which supports totalitarian dictatorship in any country,' it is using the principle of guilt by association which it has always opposed when the government has sought to enforce it. At this point the Resolution becomes concrete only in relation to the Communist Party. The inclusion of other organizations is irrelevant window-dressing."

The Board and the office of the ACLU had carefully prevented any adequate presentation of the minority position from being sent out to the members of the National Committee and of the organization in general. Hence six Board dissenters finally felt impelled to issue a pamphlet entitled *Crisis in the Civil Liberties Union*. Those who signed this statement were Robert W. Dunn, Nathan Greene, A. J. Isserman, William B. Spofford, Mary Van Kleeck and myself. I was in charge of the publication of this pamphlet and wrote the final draft after receiving the suggestions of the other signatories.

In our statement we stressed, first, that the 1940 Resolution threw overboard the traditional policy of the ACLU by forcing the organization to pass judgment on foreign governments and on the twists and turns of foreign politics; second, that the phrase "totalitarian dictatorship" was vague and ambiguous and might well apply to American Catholics as well as Communists; and, third, that the Resolution seriously compromised the work of the ACLU by instituting censorship of opinion, adopting the fatal principle of guilt by association and encouraging government agencies and private organizations to put through similar purges based on the ideas and associations of suspect individuals.

In fact, the Resolution set up an anti-Communist loyalty oath of the sort the Union had long opposed, and it soon became almost the standard formula for the factional splitting of organizations over the Communist issue. Members of Congress cited the Resolution in speaking on behalf of suppressive legislation. In my judgment the ACLU's action was a major turning point in the retrogression of civil liberties in America. Had the Union, with its great prestige in the battle for the Bill of Rights, stood firm for its fundamental principles in those hectic prewar days, I feel sure that the postwar witch-hunt, with its emphasis above all on *guilt by association*, would never have gone so far. What the Civil Liberties Union did, in a time of crisis that everywhere tested men's moral calibre, was to sound retreat and surrender a central bastion of freedom.

It was also disillusioning to me that the purge group acted throughout far more like Tammany Hall politicians than idealistic civil libertarians. The majority which put across the 1940 Resolution used undemocratic methods that violated the By-Laws of the ACLU; they improperly exploited, through the aid of Director Baldwin, the office machinery for their own purposes; and they made a mockery of the mutual fair dealing to be expected of those working together for the Bill of Rights. The truth is that these Directors, who were continually lashing out at the Communists for letting the end justify the means, put into practice this self-same principle in their anti-Communist crusade.

The purge Resolution was quickly brought to bear against Miss Elizabeth Gurley Flynn, a charter member of the Union and also the only member of the Communist Party on the Board of Directors. Mrs. Dorothy Dunbar Bromley, a columnist on the Scripps-Howard newspapers, filed a formal charge for Miss Flynn's expulsion for belonging to the Party. Miss Flynn's hearing before the Board took place on the evening of May 7, 1940, within the respectable walls of the City Club of New York.

It was a heresy trial, pure and simple; an inquisition into an individual's unorthodox opinions, as distinct from overt acts, and conducted by the American Civil Liberties Union, the last organization on earth which should have had anything to do with such a business.

The verbatim record of the Flynn trial,* of which I possess one of the few extant copies, runs to 132 typewritten pages. And it shows that during this long, heated debate not even the most bitter adversaries of Miss Flynn were able to cite one single instance in which she had written, spoken or acted in violation of the Bill of Rights or the civil liberties principles of the ACLU.

*For an excellent detailed account of the Flynn trial see Lucille Milner's *Education of an American Liberal*, pp. 273-294.

The argument against Miss Flynn proceeded solely on the basis that she could no longer serve as a Union officer because of her left-wing views and her guilt by association in being a member of the Communist Party. The final vote on the Bromley charge was nine in the affirmative and nine in the negative. Dr. Holmes as Chairman of the Board broke this tie in favor of the motion that Miss Flynn was ineligible to be a Director because of her political beliefs.

Besides Dr. Holmes, those voting for the expulsion of Miss Flynn on this historic occasion were: Mrs. Bromley, Carl Carmer, Morris Ernst, Ben W. Huebsch, Florina Lasker, William L. Nunn, Elmer Rice, Roger William Riis and Whitney North Seymour. Those who cast their ballot against expulsion were: Robert W. Dunn, John F. Finerty, Osmond K. Fraenkel, Nathan Greene, Arthur Garfield Hays, A. J. Isserman, Dorothy Kenyon, Corliss Lamont and William B. Spofford.

The Board also voted 12 to 8 to sustain two additional motions that Miss Flynn was unqualified to sit as a Board member owing to two articles, published by her after Mrs. Bromley had brought the expulsion charge, attacking the Board majority. Outraged by the ouster proceedings against her and by biased reports in the press, Miss Flynn wrote these pieces in a militant and somewhat intemperate tone. Yet Norman Thomas had done the same sort of thing six months earlier and was not even censured by the Board.

The Flynn trial ended at 2:30 in the morning. I count the six hours of that meeting as one of the most severe ordeals of my life. Everyone went home exhausted. The ACLU office still had to obtain the National Committee's ratification of the Flynn expulsion; and three months later that body duly registered its approval by 27 to 12.

The 1940 Resolution and the Flynn ouster set the tone for ACLU policies during the next fifteen years. And these actions made anti-Communist militancy and purity the main qualifications for the nomination and election of individuals to the Board of Directors and National Committee. It is hardly surprising that the quality of Directors and national committeemen steadily declined. For experience has demonstrated that passionate animosity towards Soviet Russia and communism is no assurance of a man's devotion to civil liberties in America.

From 1940 to 1955 the Civil Liberties Union compromised on many basic issues and often took an apologetic attitude in defending the Bill of Rights. It watered down its criticisms of the House Committee on Un-American Activities, adopted a weak position on the Government's loyalty-security program, boasted of its close and friendly relations with the FBI, approved the Internal Security Act's exclusion of Communists and Fascists as immigrants to the United States, and, worst of all, refused at any time to denounce the compilation and use of the U.S. Attorney General's list of subversive organizations.

Several Directors who had been opposed originally to the Resolution dropped out in disgust; but I remained on the Board and fought for fundamental civil liberties principles as long as I was able to. This was not an easy task. I was fighting a losing battle and my views were constantly voted down. Furthermore, several of the right-wing Directors continually baited me and reveled in making gratuitous personal attacks. Frequently, trying to win votes on a controversial issue, they would attempt to engage me in verbal brawls, through which they hoped to create a tense emotional atmosphere helpful to their side. Even members of the Board friendly to me were reluctant to sit next to me at meetings, lest it compromise them with the other Directors.

During this period the right-wing bloc among the Directors developed the new tactic of bringing public pressure on the Board by leaking, at strategic times, confidential Board matters to the press. They sometimes gave out the precise vote recorded on some Board motion. Most frequently these leaks appeared in stories run by *The New Leader*, the *New York Journal-American* and the *New York World-Telegram*. For example, on January 21, 1950, *The New Leader*, in a column entitled "Heard on the Left" revealed a confidential Board decision and stated, correctly, that "The vote, by hands, was 18 to 2" and that I was one of the two.

It was this item which led John Haynes Holmes, as Chairman of the ACLU Board, to send out three days later a letter to all Directors reading: "There is disturbing evidence of 'leaks' from our Board members to outside sources. In recent weeks, for example, there have been published in *The New Leader*, four separate items that include 'inside information.' I must warn the members of our Board against all carelessness in this important matter." The leaks, however, were not due to carelessness, but to conscious planning; and they were always designed to bolster up in some way the position of the Board's right wing.

In 1950 Patrick Murphy Malin, a Professor of Economics at Swarthmore College, replaced as Executive Director of the ACLU Roger Baldwin, who had reached the usual retirement age of over sixty-five. Mr. Malin did not have wide experience in the field of civil liberties, was overwhelmed by the complexity of his job, and lacked the militant fighting spirit which had characterized Baldwin. Instead of assuming independent leadership and trying to recover lost territory for the ACLU, Malin weakly went along with the right-wing Directors and cooperated with them in taking the Civil Liberties Union further along the road of compromise and political partisanship.

Since the 1940 crisis over the purge Resolution, the Affiliates of the Union had on the whole supported stronger policies on civil liberties than the national body, with the Board of Directors as its executive committee. The excellent locals in Boston, New Haven, Philadelphia, Northern California and Southern California were typical. It was no wonder, then, that the Cold War group * on the Board decided it was time to curb the power of the Affiliates.

Up till 1951 the By-Laws of the ACLU had provided that in matters of new policy or revision of old policy the Board of Directors must act in accordance with the results of a national referendum consisting of the combined vote of the National Com-

* "The Cold War group" is the name I give, for the postwar years, to the bloc on the ACLU Board which I have hitherto referred to as "the purge group."

mittee, the Affiliates and the Board itself. In 1951 the Cold War
group slipped into the By-Laws a new provision, which stated
that the Board should put into effect the majority vote in a referendum, "except where it believes there are vitally important
reasons for not doing so—which it shall explain to the corporation
members." The same provision was adopted in relation to amendment of the By-Laws. What these new provisions meant was that
the Board of Directors had constituted itself, as we shall see, an
inner dictatorship within the ACLU.

The next move of the Cold War group was to initiate, later in
1952, a campaign to have the Board adopt three new policy statements which extended further the apostasy represented by the
1940 Resolution. The Board debated these resolutions back and
forth until May 1953, and kept the national office so busy mimeo-
graphing and distributing endless memoranda and reformulations
that its normal day-to-day work was seriously disrupted. What
the Cold War group really did was to conduct a six months' fili-
buster in which it would not permit the Union to carry on with
its regular activities. Some of the Directors, fatigued and bored
by the whole business, finally voted for the resolutions primarily
in order to make the non-stop talkers cease and desist.

The first of these statements undermined defense of the Bill
of Rights by a long, violent, irrelevant attack on the Communist
Party quite in the spirit of the introductory sections of the Internal
Security Act. It paved the way for the prosecution of Communist
Party members under the Foreign Agents Registration Act, implied that most Communists are guilty of illegal conspiracy, and
gave encouragement to the witch-hunt against so-called Communist fellow-travelers and sympathizers. What the statement did,
in effect, was to enlist the ACLU in the Cold War by deflecting
the organization from its proper business—concentration on civil
liberties—and engaging it in the general battle against world
communism.

The second statement left unchallenged the violation of the
First Amendment and the United Nations Charter by committees
of the United States Congress which interrogated American em-

ployees of the U.N. on matters of personal belief and association. The third statement put the ACLU on record as discarding, in effect, the Fifth Amendment's safeguard against self-incrimination when invoked by teachers, U.N. employees and others before Congressional investigating committees.

After the Board of Directors had finally passed these three statements in May 1953, several Directors, including myself, initiated a national ACLU referendum on the matter. Much to everyone's surprise the Board's position was rejected, by the small margin of 21,271 to 18,995. The vote of the Affiliates was decisive, thirteen of them having voted against the resolutions and only three of the smaller ones in favor. Instead of accepting with good grace this democratic decision, the Cold War group on the Board, abetted by Mr. Malin, immediately started maneuvering to set it aside. And Norman Thomas, with his habitual myopia, muttered ominously about "infiltration by Communists and fellow-travelers."

Executive Director Malin now sent out a letter to the Affiliates asking for further information about their votes; and in this process, although the deadline for the referendum had been October 16, the Chicago Affiliate changed its decision from negative to affirmative. Accordingly, at the next meeting of the Board Malin reported this switch and announced beamingly that the poll had resulted in a victory for the affirmative. I vigorously objected to this procedure on the ground that it was illegal to alter the ballot totals after the referendum had been officially concluded; and that the Chicago switch was in any event improper because it was based chiefly on a hasty and incomplete telephone poll. The Board, however, in a jeering mood, voted me down.

Feeling strongly that the honor of the ACLU was at stake, I telephoned next day the Chairman of the Chicago Affiliate and protested. My protest went before the next meeting of the Chicago group, which then decided that the whole business of a "second vote" was unacceptable, withdrew entirely its second poll and reported its referendum vote again in the negative. Hence Malin, with rueful countenance, was forced to report back to the

Board of Directors that the negative, after all, had won the national referendum.

But the Cold War group, tight-lipped in its fury, was determined to have its way; and shortly afterwards put through a Board resolution (the first one of its kind in the history of the ACLU) to over-ride the referendum under cover of the new veto provision in the By-Laws. The three controversial policy statements stood, adopted officially by the Union. I argued against the over-riding as a violation of democratic procedure particularly to be deplored in an organization dedicated to civil liberties; and stated that the Board's action made a travesty of our complicated machinery for allowing appeals from Board decisions.

Meanwhile, the Cold War bloc had grown increasingly angry over my outspoken opposition to the three policy statements and my drastic criticism of the Board's undemocratic actions. Also they had become fearful that my reputation as a radical and my continued work for American-Soviet cooperation would detract from the Union's respectability. The upshot was that after I had been renominated in November 1953 for a new three-year term, several Directors—including Morris Ernst, Norman Thomas, James Lawrence Fly and Ernest Angell, Chairman of the ACLU Board —threatened to resign if my name went on the ballot and to publicize the controversies in the ACLU as a great Left-Right battle centering around me. At the next meeting of the Board the majority yielded to these bludgeoning tactics and rescinded my nomination.

I had come to the end of the road. Although a number of rank-and-file members of the ACLU in New York City urged that I permit my nomination as a Director through the special section of the By-Laws providing for such nomination by twenty-five regular members, I declined the suggestion. I told my friends that the situation had become too confused and unpleasant for me to continue as a Director, and that I was unwilling to go on working with a group which had forgotten the meaning of fair play.

On November 30 I read a statement to the Board of Directors in which I said: "If I were renominated now, the same high-handed group that forced the withdrawal of my Board nomination would in all probability renew the controversy and create a terrible furor which would again plunge this organization into bitter dissension. I am tired of all this. I believe that I can be more helpful to the cause of civil liberties by giving over my energies directly to the fight against McCarthy and McCarthyism than by endlessly debating my able and eloquent opponents on this Board."

The battle within the ACLU went on, however, after I had left. At the 1954 Biennial Conference of the organization, held in New York over the Lincoln's Birthday week-end, there occurred an all but unanimous revolt of the Affiliates against the conduct of the Board. The Affiliate delegations were able to obtain a temporary withdrawal of the three policy statements and the setting up of a special ACLU subcommittee to redraft them. They also recommended the elimination of the new provision in the ACLU By-Laws permitting the Board of Directors to set aside the results of national referendums and to veto amendments to the By-Laws.

Only a month later, however, the Board of Directors went back on its pledged word and, without waiting for the report of the subcommittee, issued the gist of its original anti-Communist policy statement. This the Board did in order to appease Senator McCarthy, who in a telecast had hurled the old charge of "Communist front" at the ACLU. The Cold War bloc pushed the motion through at a meeting of the Board on March 15 at which Messrs. Ernst, Fly and Thomas again threatened to resign unless the anti-Communist resolution were passed.

In August, after the subcommittee had reported, the Board adopted a somewhat more moderate anti-Communist statement, which read: "In considering the rights of members of the Communist Party, the American Civil Liberties Union recognizes that problems have arisen because of the dual nature of the Communist movement. It is both a political agitational movement and a part of the Soviet conspiracy. Insofar as it is the first, its members have all the rights of members of other parties; to the extent that it is the second, its members may in some particulars be restricted by law." [266]

As to the second policy statement, the Board, following the subcommittee's recommendations, slightly improved it by adding the statement that the Union "opposes inquiry, by the United States or any other member state, into the beliefs or associations of its nationals employed by the United Nations, except in connection with possible subversive activities." [267] The expression "subversive activities" here represents a serious compromise on the part of the ACLU, since a Congressional committee can easily extend the meaning of this undefined phrase to justify all sorts of investigations, in violation of the First Amendment, into beliefs and associations.

The Board's final version of the third policy statement represents little improvement. For the statement opens the door to the dismissal of employees who invoke the Fifth Amendment privilege against self-incrimination by saying that such invocation can be weighed along with other factors in determining that an employee is no longer fit for his job. This provides a hypocritical formula by which employers can pretend they are upholding an employee's right to rely on the Fifth Amendment, and then fire him with the explanation that his refusal to answer questions was the "culmination" of a course of conduct making him unfit for his position.

To sum up, I am convinced that the ACLU's three policy statements of 1954 critically compromise and weaken the organization's defense of the Bill of Rights. These new policies represent a logical culmination of the deterioration of the Union that began with the passage of the 1940 Resolution. While the organization will no doubt continue to do good work in limited sectors, such as the fields of censorship and race relations, it can no longer be depended upon, with its present Board and officers, to wage a militant and principled over-all struggle for civil liberties. The Directors of the ACLU, often sincere, likable and brilliant individuals, have become so wrapped up in the world-wide struggle against communism that they are unable to concentrate on the special task of supporting the Bill of Rights. And they have found it increasingly difficult to think straight on civil liberties issues in the political sphere.

The ACLU Affiliates, however, which are able to exercise a good deal of independence, can be counted on in general to do a far better job than the national organization. An important factor in this picture is that the national headquarters of the ACLU is in New York City and that all Directors must live in the city or near it in order to attend Board meetings regularly. New York is also the headquarters of the American Communist movement, and many of the Directors have had unhappy first-hand experiences with the Communists. This is a major reason for a fanatical anti-Communist spirit on the Board which does not exist on the executive committees of the Affiliates.

A significant commentary on recent developments in the ACLU was provided late in 1955 on a Facts Forum TV panel in which William F. Buckley, Jr., Yale's gift to Senator McCarthy, and Patrick Malin, Executive Director of the Civil Liberties Union, were participants. After some preliminary discussion, Buckley congratulated Malin on the ground that the ACLU had "matured in the past couple of years."

After I left the Board of Directors of the ACLU, I joined the executive committee of the Emergency Civil Liberties Committee and in 1955 became the Vice-Chairman of this organization. Its Chairman is Harvey O'Connor, well-known author convicted in the fall of 1955 for contempt of Congress for refusing to knuckle under to Senator McCarthy; the Director is Dr. Clark Foreman, a Southerner by birth and a prominent official in the Roosevelt Administration; and the General Counsel is Leonard B. Boudin, one of the most experienced and able lawyers in the civil liberties field. The ECLC has a National Council composed of more than sixty eminent citizens and issues a monthly bulletin entitled *Rights*.

The clearcut program of the Emergency Civil Liberties Committee is "to re-establish in full the traditional freedoms guaran-

teed under the Constitution and Bill of Rights. The meaning of
American democracy has always been that these freedoms should
extend to all individuals and groups in the United States. We
stand uncompromisingly for civil liberties for everyone. . . . All
persons of whatever views, race, national origin and religion
properly share in our constitutional liberties, whether as individuals or as collectively grouped in organizations of one kind or
another. Those who make exceptions to the Bill of Rights undermine democracy. . . . We seek the support of all those—and only
those—who believe with us in the all-inclusive application of the
Bill of Rights." [268]

To avoid the fate of the Civil Liberties Union in becoming em-
broiled over extraneous issues, the ECLC states definitely that
"This Committee's sphere of operations is limited to the United
States of America and its possessions. Ours is not an international
organization and does not propose to be drawn into controversies
dealing with American foreign policy and international affairs.
As individuals, our officers and Associates of course have their
opinions about such issues; but the business of our organization
is strictly confined to the defense of the Bill of Rights. Our
strength lies in concentration on this task." [269]

In its four years of existence the Emergency Civil Liberties
Committee has built a country-wide reputation for tireless and
vigilant work on behalf of constitutional freedoms. Through meetings in New York and other cities, it has served to educate the
public on basic civil liberties issues. And Mr. Boudin as its Counsel has successfully fought through a number of legal test cases.
These include several suits against the State Department for passports, and a suit to restrain the U.S. Army in its unjust treatment
of soldiers for pre-induction associations and activities.

In November 1954 there came into existence another civil liberties organization of inclusive national scope—the Bill of Rights
Fund—with myself as Chairman; Miss Edna Ruth Johnson, Man-
aging Editor of the religious journal *The Churchman,* as Secretary; Augustus M. Kelley, a liberal book dealer, as Treasurer; and
Philip Wittenberg, prominent attorney, as Counsel. This Fund is

unique in that it is the first one in the United States whose sole function is to collect money from the general public and to distribute what it raises in defense of the Bill of Rights.

During its first year the Bill of Rights Fund gave financial assistance in more than fifty outstanding court cases involving important constitutional issues. It made grants, for example, towards the legal expenses of defendants prosecuted under the Smith Act, the Internal Security Act, the Immunity Act and two California Acts requiring loyalty oaths or affirmations. It assisted a number of persons indicted for invoking the First or Fifth Amendment in refusing to answer improper questions put by a Congressional committee. The Fund rendered aid to several American citizens illegally denied passports by the U.S. State Department. And it supported two religious groups in their resistance to unconstitutional actions.

There is today such a tremendous amount of work to be done in the preservation of civil liberties that actually little overlapping takes place among the different organizations active in the field. And I cannot envisage a time in this country when some such groups will not be needed to keep alive the spirit of the Bill of Rights, to combat violations of it and to help break new ground in the expansion of intellectual and cultural freedom.

IS THE TIDE TURNING?

The year 1955 saw decided improvement in the civil liberties situation. Court decisions in a number of important cases exhibited a new concern for the Bill of Rights on the part of the Judiciary. The State Department eased up on the granting of passports; the Administration's wire-tapping bill, which the House of Representatives had passed in the previous Congress, could not even get reported out of committee; and the Justice Department's whole system of subsidized informers became widely discredited when Harvey Matusow and other Government witnesses revealed that they had been making lucrative careers out of lying.

The marked decline in the power and prestige of Senator McCarthy has been a large element in the slowing down of the witch-hunt throughout America. The elections of 1954 resulted in a Democratic majority in Congress and brought Democratic control of the Congressional investigating committees. The Permanent Subcommittee on Investigations, after Senator McClellan succeeded McCarthy as chairman, pursued a quite moderate course. This was in sharp contrast with the wild forays still conducted by the Internal Security Committee of the Senate and the Un-American Activities Committee of the House.

In 1955 two Congressional committees, surprising to relate, actually did something on behalf of civil liberties. A Senate subcommittee investigated the Federal loyalty-security program and found that it had grave defects and injustices. More significant, another Senate group, the Subcommittee on Constitutional Rights,° with an appropriation of $50,000, started an inquiry as to whether American civil liberties are being violated, and began with an impressive ceremony in Washington on Constitution Day, September 17, the 168th anniversary of the signing of the U.S. Constitution.

This important Subcommittee, which had been inactive for years, is composed of Senator Thomas C. Hennings, Jr., Democrat of Missouri, Chairman; Senator Joseph C. O'Mahoney, Democrat of Wyoming; and Senator William Langer, Republican of North Dakota. If this Subcommittee proceeds with energy and courage, it could do as fine a job for the Bill of Rights as did the Senate Civil Liberties Committee headed by Senator Robert M. LaFollette, Jr., in the 1930's.

There were other signs during 1955 of growing resistance to the assault on freedom. Books, pamphlets, articles and editorials critical of repressive tendencies came off the press in a steady stream. Commencement speakers lashed out against civil liberties violations. Chief Justice Warren made speeches extolling the Bill of Rights. And ex-Senator Harry Cain, a member of the Subversive Activities Control Board and once a Republican arch-conservative, bitterly assailed the Eisenhower Administration's policies on security, especially the misuse of Attorney General Brownell's list of subversive groups. *Collier's* ran a lead article entitled "The Harry Cain 'Mutiny'," which detailed Mr. Cain's criticisms.

In August the usually restrained Walter Lippmann optimistically wrote in his column "Today and Tomorrow": "We are in the early stages of a great popular reaction against the hysteria and the demagoguery, the lawlessness and the cruel injustices which we quite rightly call the era of McCarthyism. . . . The great majority of the leaders of American opinion are no longer willing to stand for the theory that espionage, sabotage, and subversion can be dealt with only by ignoring the Constitution, and by conniving at what is nakedly and simply lynch law." [270]

° This Subcommittee was formerly called Subcommittee on Civil Rights.

Mr. Lippmann acknowledges that the finally awakened decency of the American people and the fact that McCarthy overplayed his hand have been important in the shift of public opinion. But he states: "The ultimate reason for the change is, I believe, the enormous emotional relief which has come since all the great powers have acknowledged publicly that there is no alternative to peace, that they cannot contemplate war." [271] Undoubtedly the relaxation of international tensions, through the Summit Conference at Geneva and better relations between America and the Communist bloc, has helped greatly in creating a more calm and more tolerant atmosphere within the United States.

Yet no matter how much international affairs improve, we cannot expect that the civil liberties crisis will automatically fade away. For there are certain domestic factors that will in all likelihood continue to have an adverse effect on basic American freedoms.

The unpopularity of dissent, for one thing, is an old story in the United States. As far back as 1835 Alexis de Tocqueville wrote in his *Democracy in America:* "I know of no country in which there is so little independence of mind and real freedom of discussion as in America. . . . In America the majority raises formidable barriers around the liberty of opinion; within these barriers an author may write what he pleases, but woe to him if he goes beyond them. Not that he is in danger of an auto-da-fé, but he is exposed to continued obloquy and persecution. His political career is closed forever, since he has offended the only authority that is able to open it. . . ."

The United States, de Tocqueville went on to say, is one of those democratic republics where the new sovereign (the majority) no longer says: " 'You shall think as I do or you shall die'; but he says: 'You are free to think differently from me and to retain your life, your property, and all that you possess; but you are henceforth a stranger among your people. You may retain your civil rights, but they will be useless to you, for you will never be chosen by your fellow citizens if you solicit their votes; and they will affect to scorn you if you ask for their esteem. You will remain among men, but you will be deprived of the rights of mankind. Your fellow creatures will shun you like an impure being; and even those who believe in your innocence will abandon you, lest they should be shunned in their turn. Go in peace! I have given you your life, but it is an existence worse than death.'" [272]

To what extent America has progressed in democracy since de Tocqueville's time is debatable, but his discerning comment points to a regressive undercurrent which undeniably has always been strong in the life of the country. And his judgment is strikingly relevant to the contemporary situation.

In estimating the future prospects of civil liberties, we must take into consideration other elements deep-rooted in American life. There is, for instance, our persisting political immaturity; the American people's inexperience with radical political groups and ideologies. The English, by way of contrast, have been conditioned to a tolerance of leftist ideas by some fifty years of the British Labor Party and by such outstanding Socialist writers as Sidney and Beatrice Webb, Bernard Shaw and John Strachey. There is the appalling lack of education among most Americans as to the full meaning of democracy and the Bill of Rights—an ignorance which enables demagogues to make headway. There is the growing monopoly control of the twentieth century's potent technological media of mass communication. And there is the powerful influence of the Catholic Church, with its authoritarian principles and practices.

Then we must ask, too, what would happen to the present trend in favor of civil liberties if, while the international situation remained satisfactory, a serious economic depression once more engulfed the United States. In a period of economic crisis, individuals, groups, institutions and the Government are necessarily under severe stress. As pressures increase, fear sweeps the country; patience becomes exhausted; a search for scapegoats begins; and desperate men attempt desperate remedies. It is a time when freedom of expression, though more needed than ever, may get lost in the shuffle. Certainly we can have no assurance that a new depression would result, as during the Presidency of Franklin D. Roosevelt, in *more* freedom for the American people.

Whatever the pertinency of these speculations, I believe that the tide *is* turning in some degree towards the restoration of the Bill of Rights. Yet we have lost so much ground in the past decade that the tide must flow powerfully and for a long time if we are to recover all the freedoms of which we have been deprived. McCarthy the man is in eclipse, but McCarthy*ism* remains strongly entrenched throughout the country.

For example, none of the repressive laws which Congress has passed has been declared invalid by the U.S. Supreme Court; and the Government is still bringing prosecutions under the Smith Act, the Internal Security Act, the Communist Control Act, the Immunity Act and the McCarran-Walter Immigration Act. Furthermore, part of the seeming improvement is owing to the fact that "loyalty screening and the policing of political activities and associations by agencies of the Federal Government is so much taken for granted nowadays that we fail to note the loss or curtailment of formerly well established rights and privileges." [273]

It is too early to determine whether the present turn in the tide represents merely a temporary setback to the forces of reaction or whether it will prove to be a significant trend of considerable duration. Be that as it may, there will never come a time, in my opinion, when the American people can afford to look upon their liberty as permanently established and automatically functioning. Eternal vigilance is the price of transforming an ideal—in this case the Bill of Rights—into a continuing reality.

Whatever advances—or retrogressions—take place in our economic, political and social system, intelligent and democratic-minded Americans will always rank freedom of expression and association as a supreme value. The extent to which the United States maintains that value will be a sure measure of the quality of its civilization.

NOTES *

1—THE IDEAL OF CIVIL LIBERTIES

[1] *West Virginia State Board of Education v. Barnette,* 319 U.S. 624, 642 (1943).
[2] Maxim on title page of *Historical Review of Pennsylvania.*
[3] Address at University of the State of New York, Oct. 24, 1952.
[4] *The Capital Times,* Madison, Wis., July 5, 1951.
[5] Address at Washington University, St. Louis, Mo., Feb. 19, 1955.
[6] In *New York Herald Tribune Book Review,* Dec. 9, 1951, p. 1.
[7] *American Communications Association v. Douds,* 339 U.S. 382, 437-438 (1950).
[8] Gerard Piel in address, "Scientists and Other Citizens," made in Boston, Dec. 29, 1953, before the American Association for the Advancement of Science.

2—CLASH WITH THE UN-AMERICAN ACTIVITIES COMMITTEE

[9] *In re Pacific Railway Commission,* 32 Fed. 241, 263 (1887), quoted in *Jones v. Securities and Exchange Commission,* 298 U.S. 1, 27 (1936).
[10] Brief of the American Civil Liberties Union, as Amicus Curiae, in the case of *Julius Emspak v. United States,* in the U.S. Supreme Court, October Term, 1953, p. 10.

* All references to *The New York Times* will be given simply as *Times.*

[11] *Senate Manual Containing the Standing Rules, Orders, Laws and Resolutions Affecting the Business of the United States Senate*, Washington, D.C., U.S. Govt. Printing Office, 1953, p. 196.

[12] *Congressional Record*, June 26, 1946, p. 7723.

[13] *Quinn v. United States*, 349 U.S. 155, 161 (1955).

3—MY CHALLENGE TO McCARTHY

[14] *Communist Infiltration in the Army*, Hearing before the Permanent Subcommittee on Investigations, 83rd Congress, 1st Session, Sept. 28, 1953, p. 45.

[15] *United States v. Rumely*, 345 U.S. 41, 58 (1953).

[16] *Newsweek* Magazine, Dec. 28, 1953, p. 26.

[17] *Communist Infiltration in the Army, op. cit.*, p. 1.

[18] *New York Herald Tribune*, May 3, 1954.

[19] *Times*, Feb. 7, 1954.

[20] *Ibid.*, Sept. 25, 1953.

[21] Sept. 29, 1953.

[22] Sept. 29, 1953.

[23] *New York Post*, Sept. 2, 1954.

[24] *New York Herald Tribune*, Oct. 16, 1954.

[25] *United States v. Lamont*, 18 F.R.D. 27, 37 (1955).

[26] *United States v. Lamont, supra*, at pages 32, 34.

4—THE CONGRESSIONAL INQUISITION

[27] Quoted by Dan Gillmor, *Fear, the Accuser*, Abelard-Schuman, 1954, pp. 29-30.

[28] *Ibid.*, p. 30.

[29] *New York Herald Tribune*, Jan. 11, 1940.

[30] *Times*, Feb. 23, 1954.

[31] *Ibid.*, Sept. 28, 1954.

[32] Feb. 26, 1954.

[33] *Times*, March 5, 1954.

[34] Speech of Wayne Morse in the United States Senate, Feb. 24, 1954.

[35] Brief of the American Civil Liberties Union in the case of Julius Emspak, *op. cit.*, p. 11.

[36] *Times*, Feb. 26, 1954.

[37] *Ibid.*, July 22, 1953.

[38] *McNabb v. United States*, 318 U.S. 332, 347 (1943).

[39] *New York Herald Tribune*, April 4, 1954.

[40] Henry Steele Commager, *Freedom, Loyalty, Dissent,* Oxford University Press, 1954, pp. 98-99.

[41] *Ibid.,* pp. 121-122.

[42] *Times,* April 10, 1955.

[43] Article I, Section 9, Subsection 3.

[44] *Ibid.*

[45] *Cummings v. Missouri,* 71 U.S. 277, 323 (1866).

[46] *United States v. Lovett,* 90 L.Ed. 1252, 1261, 1259 (1946).

[47] *Times,* May 16, 1953.

[48] Robert K. Carr, *The House Committee on Un-American Activities, 1945-1950,* Cornell University Press, 1952, pp. 168-169.

[49] *Hearings regarding Communist Espionage in the U.S.,* House Committee on Un-American Activities, 80th Congress, 2nd Session, July 31, 1948, p. 561.

[50] *Salt Lake City Tribune,* Nov. 21, 1953.

[51] *New York Post,* March 15, 1954.

[52] Hearing before a Subcommittee of the Committee on Foreign Relations of the U.S. Senate, 81st Congress, 1950, Part I, p. 14.

[53] *Times,* April 26, 1953.

[54] *Ibid.*

[55] *National Guardian,* July 11, 1955.

[56] United Nations Charter, Article 100, Section 2.

[57] *Ibid.,* Section 1.

[58] *Times,* Nov. 14, 1952.

[59] *Ibid.,* March 22, 1954.

[60] *The Daily Compass,* Nov. 25, 26, 28, Dec. 2, 1951.

[61] *Times,* Jan.17, 1954.

[62] *Ibid.,* April 14, 1953.

[63] *Ibid.,* March 7, 1953.

[64] *National Guardian,* May 10, 1954, p. 6.

[65] *New York Post,* April 18, 1954.

[66] *Ibid.*

[67] Abe Fortas, "Outside the Law," *The Atlantic,* August 1953, p. 43.

[68] *Times,* May 8, 1953.

[69] J. B. Matthews, "Reds and Our Churches," *American Mercury,* July 1953, p. 3.

[70] *New York Herald Tribune,* July 10, 1953.

[71] *Annual Report of the Committee on Un-American Activities for the Year 1953,* p. 97.

[72] Letter to William Frauenglass, May 16, 1953, printed in full in Corliss Lamont, *Challenge to McCarthy,* Basic Pamphlets, 1954, pp. 30-31.

5—SUPPRESSION THROUGH LAW

[73] *Dennis v. United States*, 341 U.S. 494, 579 (1951).

[74] *Dennis v. United States*, supra, at page 584.

[75] *Schenck v. United States*, 249 U.S. 47, 52 (1919).

[76] *Whitney v. California*, 274 U.S. 357, 377 (1927).

[77] *Bridges v. California*, 314 U.S. 252, 263 (1941).

[78] *Ex parte Milligan*, 71 U.S. 2, 120 (1866).

[79] *American Communications Association v. Douds*, 339 U.S. 382, 439 (1950).

[80] *Gitlow v. New York*, 268 U.S. 652, 673 (1925).

[81] *Dennis v. United States*, supra, at pages 521, 549.

[82] *Schneiderman v. United States*, 320 U.S. 118, 157 (1943).

[83] Karl Marx, Address at Fifth Congress of the First International, Sept. 8, 1872, printed in *La Liberté*, Brussels periodical, Sept. 15, 1872.

[84] Burton J. Hendrick, *Bulwark of the Republic: A Biography of the Constitution*, Little, Brown, 1937, p. 329.

[85] Zechariah Chafee, Jr., *Free Speech in the United States*, Harvard University Press, 1942, p. 467.

[86] Internal Security Act, Section 13 (f) (4).

[87] *Times*, Nov. 10, 1954.

[88] Internal Security Act, Section 103 (a).

[89] Learned Hand, "A Plea for the Freedom of Dissent," *The New York Times Magazine*, Feb. 6, 1955, p. 33.

[90] *Communist Party v. Subversive Activities Control Board*, 223 F. 2d 531, 544 (1954).

[91] Harvey Matusow, *False Witness*, Cameron & Kahn, 1955, p. 231.

[92] News Release, National Council of American-Soviet Friendship, July 23, 1954.

[93] Communist Control Act of 1954, Section 5.

[94] *Times*, July 29, 1954.

[95] *Congressional Record*, Aug. 4, 1954, p. 12605.

[96] Erwin K. Griswold, *The Fifth Amendment Today*, Harvard University Press, 1955, pp. 7-9.

[97] *Quinn v. United States*, 349 U.S. 155, 161-164 (1955).

[98] Labor Management Relations Act, Section 9 (h).

[99] *National Guardian*, June 6, 1955, p. 7.

[100] Report of the President's Commission on Immigration and Naturalization, *Whom We Shall Welcome*, Washington, U.S. Govt. Printing Office, 1952, p. 263.

[101] President's Commission on Immigration and Naturalization, *Hearings*, U.S. Govt. Printing Office, 1952, p. 60.

[102] Hubert H. Humphrey, Jr., *The Stranger at our Gate*, New York, Public Affairs Committee, Inc., 1954, p. 14.

[103] Milton R. Konvitz, *Civil Rights in Immigration*, Cornell University Press, 1953, p. 22.

[104] President's Commission on Immigration, *Hearings, op. cit.*, p. 239.

[105] *Ibid.*, p. 1597.

[106] *Harisiades v. Shaughnessy*, 342 U.S. 580, 598 (1952).

[107] Laurent B. Frantz, "Deportation Deliriums," *The Nation*, March 26, 1955, pp. 258-264.

[108] *Dennis v. United States, supra*, at pages 555-556.

[109] *Peters v. Hobby et al*, 349 U.S. 331, 338 (1955).

[110] *Parker v. Lester*, No. 14081, C.C.A. 9th, Oct. 26, 1955.

6—THE LOYALTY-SECURITY PROGRAM

[111] Hatch Act, Section 9A.

[112] Commager, *New York Herald Tribune Book Review, op. cit.*, Dec. 9, 1951, p. 1.

[113] *Times*, Nov. 10, 1954.

[114] *Ibid.*, Dec. 14, 1954.

[115] Walter Gellhorn, *Security, Loyalty and Science*, Cornell University Press, 1950, p. 116.

[116] Commager, *Freedom, Loyalty, Dissent, op. cit.*, pp. 141-142.

[117] Quoted by Gellhorn, *op. cit.*, p. 243.

[118] Rowland Watts, *The Draftee and Internal Security*, Workers Defense League, 1955, Appendix C, p. 110.

[119] *Times*, Sept. 13, 1955.

[120] Quoted by Gellhorn, *op. cit.*, p. 152.

[121] *Ibid.*

[122] *Ibid.*, p. 153.

[123] Dissenting Views of Commissioner Clifford J. Durr re Proposed Rules Governing FCC Loyalty Procedure, April 1948.

[124] *Times*, March 3, 1955.

[125] *West Virginia State Board of Education v. Barnette*, 319 U.S. 624, 642 (1943).

[126] Quoted in *An Appeal to Reason*, National Lawyers Guild, 1955, p. 8.

[127] *Joint Anti-Fascist Refugee Committee, National Council of American-Soviet Friendship, Inc., et al, International Workers Order, Inc., et al v. J. Howard McGrath*, 71 S.Ct. 624, 631-633 (1951).

7—POLICE STATE IN THE MAKING

[128] American Civil Liberties Union, *America's Need: A New Birth of Freedom*, 34th Annual Report, 1954, p. 57.

[129] Quoted by Max Lowenthal, *The Federal Bureau of Investigation,* William Sloane Associates, 1950, p. 298.

[130] Robert H. Jackson, *The Supreme Court in the American System of Government,* Harvard University Press, 1955, p. 197.

[131] *The Churchman,* March 1, 1954, p. 6.

[132] *National Guardian,* Aug. 2, 1954.

[133] Quoted by Richard H. Rovere, "The Kept Witness," *Harper's* Magazine, May 1955, p. 33.

[134] Respondent's Brief *In the Matter of Jacob Burck,* A.R. No. 4,587,587, Before the Board of Immigration Appeals, Malkin Appendix, p. 11.

[135] *The Churchman,* Sept. 1954, p. 10.

[136] *Times,* Oct. 19, 1954.

[137] Quoted from letter reproduced in Matusow, *op. cit.,* p. 201.

[138] *Times,* March 17, 1955.

[139] *Ibid.,* May 10, 1955.

[140] *Ibid.*

[141] *Ibid.*

[142] *Ibid.,* Dec. 17, 1952.

[143] *Ibid.,* Oct. 8, 1954.

[144] *Ibid.,* Oct. 24, 1954.

[145] *Ibid.,* Jan. 19, 1955.

[146] Letter from Attorney General Brownell to Senator William Langer, July 7, 1954, p. 6.

[147] *Joint Anti-Fascist Refugee Committee v. McGrath,* 71 S.Ct. 624, 651-653 (1951).

[148] *Journal of the American Medical Association,* Nov. 25, 1950, p. 1094.

[149] *New York Herald Tribune,* April 20, 1950.

[150] *Times,* May 13, 1955.

[151] *The Daily Compass,* July 10, 1952.

[152] Code of Federal Regulations, Title 22, Chapter 1, Part 51, 135 (b).

[153] *Chicago Tribune,* July 18, 1954.

[154] *Ibid.*

[155] *Times,* June 24, 1955.

[156] *I. F. Stone's Weekly,* Oct. 17, 1955.

[157] Walter Gellhorn (ed.), *The States and Subversion,* Cornell University Press, 1952, p. 391.

8—THE STATES ON THE TRAIL OF SUBVERSION

[158] Quoted by Lawrence H. Chamberlain, *Loyalty and Legislative Action: A Survey of Activity by the New York State Legislature, 1919-1949,* Cornell University Press, 1951, p. 200.

[159] *Adler v. Board of Education of New York City*, 342 U.S. 485, 508-509 (1952).

[160] Quoted in *Cummings v. Missouri*, 71 U.S. 277, 330-331.

[161] *Green v. Schumway*, 39 N.Y. 418, 421 (1868).

[162] *Minneapolis Sunday Tribune*, May 1, 1955.

[163] Louisville *Courier-Journal*, Sept. 17, 1954.

[164] Chamberlain, *op. cit.*, p. 187.

[165] Walter Gellhorn (ed.), *The States and Subversion, op. cit.*, p. 373.

[166] Quoted by Edward L. Barrett, Jr., *The Tenney Committee: Legislative Investigation of Subversive Activities in California*, Cornell University Press, 1951, p. 257.

[167] Quoted, *ibid.*, p. 173.

[168] *Ibid.*, p. 175.

[169] *Ibid.*

[170] *Ibid.*

[171] *Monthly Review*, August 1954, p. 146.

[172] *United States ex rel. Santo Caminito v. Murphy*, 222, F.2d 698, 700-704.

9—THE DRIVE AGAINST CULTURAL FREEDOM

[173] *Times*, Sept. 13, 1950.

[174] *The New Yorker*, Feb. 21, 1948.

[175] *Times*, March 29, 1952.

[176] *New York Post*, May 26, 1955.

[177] *Joseph Burstyn, Inc. v. Wilson et al*, 72 S.Ct. 777, 781 (1952).

[178] *Times*, Jan. 3, 1954.

[179] Quoted, *ibid.*

[180] *Times*, March 27, 1953.

[181] *Ibid.*, March 1, 1953.

[182] *Ibid.*

[183] *Ibid.*

[184] *Peekskill Evening Star*, Sept. 6, 1955.

[185] Quoted by Matthew Josephson, "The Vandals Are Here," *The Nation*, Sept. 26, 1953, pp. 245-246.

[186] *Ibid.*, p. 245.

[187] Quoted by Scrutineer in "Secret Blacklist: Untold Story of the USIA," *The Nation*, Oct. 30, 1954, p. 377.

[188] *Times*, June 15, 1953.

[189] *Ibid.*, Nov. 14, 1953.

[190] *New York World-Telegram*, Nov. 14, 1953.

[191] *Times*, Nov. 14, 1953.

[192] Quoted by Ben H. Bagdikian, "Girl Scouts in Retreat," *Christian Register*, Feb. 1955, p. 12.

[193] *Weekly Bulletin*, American Civil Liberties Union, Feb. 28, 1955.

[194] George Sokolsky, "Open Letter to the Post Office," *The Saturday Review*, April 23, 1955, p. 9.

[195] David J. Dallin, "Post Office Folly," *The New Leader*, Oct. 20, 1952.

[196] *Times*, Nov. 12, 1952.

[197] Quoted in *American Civil Liberties Union News*, San Francisco, June 1955, p. 2.

[198] *Times*, June 15, 1955.

[199] U.S. House of Representatives, *Report of the Select Committee on Current Pornographic Materials*, Dec. 31, 1952, p. 2.

[200] *Ibid.*, p. 6.

[201] *Times*, June 23, 1953.

[202] *Ibid.*, July 25, 1954.

[203] *Tax Exempt Foundations*, Hearings before Special Committee to Investigate Tax-Exempt Foundations and Comparable Organizations, House of Representatives, 83rd Congress, 2nd Session, Part 1, June 9, 1954, pp. 604-607.

[204] *Ibid.*

[205] *Times*, Dec. 20, 1954.

[206] *Ibid.*

[207] *Ibid.*

[208] *Ibid.*

[209] Quoted in *I. F. Stone's Weekly*, Feb. 7, 1955.

[210] Vashti Cromwell McCollum, *One Woman's Fight*, Doubleday, 1951, pp. 82-83.

[211] *Ibid.*, p. 95.

[212] *Ibid.*, p. 97.

[213] *Illinois ex. rel. McCollum v. Board of Education of Champaign County, Ill., et al*, 333 U.S. 203, 212 (1948).

[214] *Zorach et al v. Board of Education of the City of New York*, 343 U.S. 306, 316, 318 (1952).

[215] *Zorach v. Board of Education, supra*, at page 325.

[216] Samuel A. Stouffer, *Communism, Conformity and Civil Liberties*, Doubleday, 1955, pp. 32-33.

10—THE ASSAULT ON ACADEMIC FREEDOM

[217] *Times*, May 10, 1951.

[218] *New York Herald Tribune*, June 14, 1951.

[219] *Times*, June 29, 1952.

[220] *Ibid.*, Oct. 25, 1953.

[221] Quoted in *The Saturday Review*, Feb. 19, 1955, p. 23.

[222] *Times*, Nov. 16, 1954.

[223] *Ibid.*

[224] Quoted in *Weekly Bulletin*, American Civil Liberties Union, May 9, 1955.

[225] *Times*, April 4, 1953.

[226] *The New Leader*, Oct. 6, 1952.

[227] *The Denver Post*, Sept. 20, 1954.

[228] Matusow, *op. cit.*, p. 89.

[229] *Ibid.*, p. 91.

[230] *Subversive Influence in the Educational Process*, Hearings before Subcommittee to Investigate the Administration of the Internal Security Act and Other Internal Security Laws, Committee on the Judiciary, U.S. Senate, 83rd Congress, 1st Session, March 19, 24, and 25, 1953, Part 5, p. 607.

[231] Letter to *The New York Times*, published April 28, 1953.

[232] Robert M. Hutchins, "Are Our Teachers Afraid to Teach?" *Look* Magazine, March 9, 1954, p. 28.

[233] Transcript of Testimony before the Board of Public Education of Philadelphia in the matter of Goldie Watson, a Professional Employee, Philadelphia, Pa., June 4, 1954, p. 79a.

[234] *Ibid.*, p. 12a.

[235] Quoted by Horace M. Kallen, "Behind the Bertrand Russell Case," in *Twice A Year*, Issue V-VI, 1940.

[236] *Weekly Bulletin*, American Civil Liberties Union, Feb. 21, 1955.

[237] Quoted in *The Denver Post*, "Faceless Informers," Sept. 23, 1954.

[238] *Adler v. Board of Education*, 342 U.S. 485, 509-510 (1952).

[239] *Adler v. Board of Education, supra*, at pages 496-497.

[240] *New York Herald Tribune*, Dec. 15, 1953.

[241] *Harvard Alumni Bulletin*, June 25, 1949, pp. 732-733, 736.

[242] Alexander Meiklejohn, "Should Communists Be Allowed to Teach?" in *The New York Times Magazine*, March, 27, 1949, p. 65.

[243] *Ibid.*, p. 64.

[244] Broadus Mitchell, "Witch Hunt at Hunter: Triumph of the Primitives," *The Nation*, Nov. 6, 1954, p. 402.

[245] *The Liberal*, Philadelphia, April 1955, p. 2.

[246] *Ibid.*

11—CONFORM—OR LOSE YOUR JOB

[247] Associated Press dispatch, Sept. 18, 1953.

[248] *Ibid.*

[249] Merle Miller, *The Judges and the Judged*, New York, Doubleday, 1952, p. 9.

[250] *New York Herald Tribune*, June 15, 1955.

[251] Jay Nelson Tuck, "On the Air," *New York Post*, May 26, 1955.

[252] Resolution passed 197-149 by New York Local of AFTRA, May 24, 1955.

[253] *Barsky v. Board of Regents of the University of the State of New York*, 347 U.S. 442, 470 (1954).

[254] *Barsky v. Board of Regents, supra*, at pages 472-473.

[255] Quoted in *American Civil Liberties Union News*, San Francisco, Feb. 1955.

[256] *Ibid.*

[257] *Weekly Bulletin*, American Civil Liberties Union, Aug. 9, 1954.

[258] Walter P. Reuther, *Annual Report to the CIO*, December 1954, p. 21.

[259] *Ibid.*, p. 22.

[260] Quoted by Murray Kempton, *New York Post*, June 14, 1955.

[261] Steve Nelson, *The 13th Juror*, Masses & Mainstream, 1955, p. 119.

12—THE DECLINE OF THE CIVIL LIBERTIES UNION

[262] Lucille Milner, *Education of an American Liberal*, Horizon Press, 1954, pp. 124-125.

[263] American Civil Liberties Union, Annual Report, *The Bill of Rights—150 Years After*, 1939, p. 24.

[264] *Report of the Special Committee on Un-American Activities*, Jan. 6, 1939, p. 122.

[265] Hearings before a Special Committee on Un-American Activities, House of Representatives, 76th Congress, 1st Session, on H. Res. 282, Volume 10, October 16-21, 23-25, 28, 1939, p. 6309.

[266] American Civil Liberties Union, *America's Need: A New Birth of Freedom*, 34th Annual Report, 1954, p. 26.

[267] *Ibid.*, p. 27.

[268] A Statement of Principles, adopted by the Emergency Civil Liberties Committee, May 15, 1954.

[269] *Ibid.*

13—IS THE TIDE TURNING?

[270] *New York Herald Tribune*, Aug. 25, 1955.

[271] *Ibid.*

[272] Alexis de Tocqueville, *Democracy in America*, Alfred A. Knopf, 1945, Vol. I, pp. 263-264.

[273] *The Nation*, Aug. 27, 1955.

SELECTED BIBLIOGRAPHY

BALDWIN, ROGER N., and RANDALL, CLARENCE B. *Civil Liberties and Industrial Conflict.* Cambridge: Harvard University Press, 1938.

BARRETT, EDWARD L., JR. *The Tenney Committee.* Ithaca: Cornell University Press, 1951.

BARTH, ALAN. *The Loyalty of Free Men.* New York: The Viking Press, 1951.

BENET, WILLIAM ROSE, and COUSINS, NORMAN (eds.). *The Poetry of Freedom.* New York: Modern Library, 1945.

BLANSHARD, PAUL. *American Freedom and Catholic Power.* Boston: The Beacon Press, 1949.

———. *The Right to Read.* Boston: The Beacon Press, 1955.

CARR, ROBERT K. *Federal Protection of Civil Rights: Quest for a Sword.* Ithaca: Cornell University Press, 1947.

———. *The House Committee on Un-American Activities, 1949-1950.* Ithaca: Cornell University Press, 1952.

CHAFEE, ZECHARIAH, JR. *Free Speech in the United States.* Cambridge: Harvard University Press, 1954.

———. *Thirty-five Years with Freedom of Speech.* New York: Roger N. Baldwin Civil Liberties Foundation, 1952.

CHAMBERLAIN, LAWRENCE H. *Loyalty and Legislative Action.* Ithaca: Cornell University Press, 1951.

CHENERY, WILLIAM L. *Freedom of the Press.* New York: Harcourt, Brace and Company, 1955.

COMMAGER, HENRY STEELE. *Freedom, Loyalty, Dissent.* New York: Oxford University Press, 1954.

COUNTRYMAN, VERN. *Un-American Activities in the State of Washington.* Ithaca: Cornell University Press, 1951.

CUSHMAN, ROBERT E. *New Threats to American Freedoms.* (Public Affairs Pamphlet No. 143) New York: Public Affairs Committee, Inc., 1948.

DAVIS, ELMER. *But We Were Born Free.* New York: Bobbs-Merrill Company, Inc., 1954.

DOUGLAS, WILLIAM O. *An Almanac of Liberty.* Garden City: Doubleday & Company, Inc., 1954.

EDMAN, IRWIN, with SCHNEIDER, HERBERT W. (eds.). *Fountainheads of Freedom: The Growth of the Democratic Idea.* New York: Reynal & Hitchcock, 1941.

EMERSON, THOMAS I. and HABER, DAVID. *Political and Civil Rights in the United States, A Collection of Legal and Related Materials.* Buffalo, New York: Dennis & Co., Inc., 1952.

ERNST, MORRIS, and SEAGLE, WILLIAM. *To the Pure: A Study of Obscenity and the Censor.* New York: The Viking Press, 1928.

FRAENKEL, OSMOND. *Our Civil Liberties.* New York: The Viking Press, 1944.

———. *The Supreme Court and Civil Liberties.* New York: American Civil Liberties Union, 1952.

GELLHORN, WALTER. *Security, Loyalty, and Science.* Ithaca: Cornell University Press, 1950.

——— (ed.). *The States and Subversion.* Ithaca: Cornell University Press, 1952.

GILLMOR, DAN. *Fear, the Accuser.* New York: Abelard-Schuman, 1954.

GRISWOLD, ERWIN N. *The Fifth Amendment Today.* Cambridge: Harvard University Press, 1955.

HAIGHT, ANNE LYON. *Banned Books: Informal Notes on Some Books Banned for Various Reasons at Various Times and in Various Places.* New York: R. R. Bowker Company, 1955.

HAND, LEARNED. *The Spirit of Liberty.* New York: Alfred A. Knopf, 1952.

HAYS, ARTHUR GARFIELD. *Let Freedom Ring.* New York: Boni and Liveright, 1928.

HULBURD, DAVID. *This Happened in Pasadena.* New York: The Macmillan Company, 1951.

JACKSON, ROBERT H. *The Supreme Court in the American System of Government.* Cambridge: Harvard University Press, 1955.

KAHN, GORDON. *Hollywood on Trial.* New York: Boni and Gaer, 1948.

KONVITZ, MILTON R. *Civil Rights in Immigration.* Ithaca: Cornell University Press, 1953.

LATTIMORE, OWEN. *Ordeal by Slander.* New York: Bantam Books, 1951.

LOWENTHAL, MAX. *The Federal Bureau of Investigation.* New York: William Sloane Associates, Inc., 1950.

MACIVER, ROBERT M. *Academic Freedom in Our Time*. New York: Columbia University Press, 1955.

MATUSOW, HARVEY. *False Witness*. New York: Cameron & Kahn, 1955.

MCCOLLUM, VASHTI CROMWELL. *One Woman's Fight*. Garden City: Doubleday & Company, Inc., 1951.

MEIKLEJOHN, ALEXANDER. *Free Speech and Its Relation to Self-Government*. New York: Harper & Brothers, 1948.

MILLER, MERLE. *The Judges and the Judged*. Garden City: Doubleday & Company, Inc., 1952.

MILNER, LUCILLE. *Education of an American Liberal*. New York: Horizon Press, 1954.

NATIONAL LAWYERS GUILD. *Civil Liberties Docket* (Published five times annually). New York.

O'BRIAN, JOHN LORD. *National Security and Individual Freedom*. Cambridge: Harvard University Press, 1955.

OXNAM, G. BROMLEY. *I Protest*. New York: Harper & Brothers, 1954.

PRESIDENT'S COMMISSION ON IMMIGRATION AND NATURALIZATION. *Whom We Shall Welcome*. Washington: U.S. Government Printing Office, 1953.

PRESIDENT'S COMMITTEE ON CIVIL RIGHTS. *To Secure These Rights*. Washington: U.S. Government Printing Office, 1947.

RICE, ELMER. *The Supreme Freedom*. Whitestone, N. Y.: The Graphics Group, 1949.

ROGGE, O. JOHN. *Our Vanishing Civil Liberties*. New York: Gaer Associates, 1949.

STOUFFER, SAMUEL A. *Communism, Conformity, and Civil Liberties*. Garden City: Doubleday & Company, Inc., 1955.

TAYLOR, TELFORD. *Grand Inquest*. New York: Simon & Schuster, 1955.

VAN DOREN, MARK. *Man's Right to Knowledge and the Free Use Thereof*. New York: Columbia University, 1954.

WARD, HARRY F. *Democracy and Social Change*. New York: Modern Age Books, 1940.

WECHSLER, JAMES A. *The Age of Suspicion*. New York: Random House, 1953.

WHIPPLE, LEON. *The Story of Civil Liberties in the United States*. New York: Vanguard Press, Inc., 1927.

INDEX

EPILOGUE: 1981

A large proportion of the American people tend to forget that the worst civil liberties crisis in the history of the United States occurred during the decade 1946-55, following the end of the Second World War. Those years marked the high point of McCarthyism, when the witchhunt led by the Senator from Wisconsin penetrated well-nigh every sector of political, economic, and cultural life.

I think that reprinting *Freedom Is As Freedom Does* twenty-five years after its original publication is relevant and important because it makes available a history and summary of postwar repression in America. Reading this book can both strengthen the determination to help prevent another such calamitous period and provide knowledge and perspective concerning the present state of American democracy.

In the last chapter of my book, I stated that, as of late 1955, the tide was turning in favor of civil liberties. I personally found this to be true when in August of 1956 a United States appeals court unanimously upheld the decision of a district court that had dismissed my indictment for contempt of Congress. That indictment had come from my refusal to answer certain loaded questions, which I regarded as unconstitutional, put to me by Senator McCarthy at a session of his Subcommittee on Government Operations. The Government did not appeal the ruling of the appeals court. (See Chapter 3, "My Challenge to McCarthy.")

The Establishment had also borne down on me heavily in 1951, when the Passport Division of the State Department refused to grant an extension of my passport because of my criticisms of U.S. Government policy in both domestic and foreign affairs. In 1957, I finally brought suit for a passport against Secretary of State Dulles, lost my case in a federal district court, and promptly appealed to a U.S. circuit court. My appeal was argued in May, 1958, but a month later the United States Supreme Court ruled in the joint case of artist Rockwell Kent, and Dr. Walter Briehl, that American passports could not be denied on account of a citizen's beliefs or associations. This decision automatically gave me victory, and, after a delay of eight years, I received my passport two weeks later.

The tide was still running in my favor seven years later in 1965 when the Supreme Court unanimously upheld, 8-0, my suit attacking as unconstitutional a Congressional statute that had directed the United States Postmaster General to screen second- and third-class mail from foreign countries in order to detain or destroy "Communist political propaganda." The addressee could obtain his mail only if he returned a reply card to the Post Office Department requesting the item in question. When the Post Office held up a magazine, *The Peking Review*, addressed to me from Communist China, I sued the Postmaster General on the basis that this procedure contravened the Bill of Rights. In *Lamont* v. *Postmaster General* the Supreme Court, for the first time in its history, declared a federal law invalid on the grounds that it directly violated the First Amendment. My case definitely established the right of the people to know and has been widely cited as a precedent in civil litigation involving this principle.

My legal victories underscore the fact that the courts, especially the U.S. appeals courts and the Supreme Court, have in general lent support to the Bill of Rights in recent decades. Indicative of the Supreme Court's stance on civil liberties was its 1971 decision that the *New York Times* and the *Washington Post* could not be restrained by the United States Government from publishing the Pentagon Papers on the Vietnam war. This was a major triumph for freedom of the press. It is significant that one of the attorneys arguing on behalf of the *Times* stressed *Lamont* v. *Postmaster General* in support of the public's right to know what was in the Pentagon Papers.

The 1970's turned out to be a favorable period for American civil liberties, especially because of the passage of the Freedom of Information Act in 1974. This Act gave every American citizen the right to know what data Government institutions such as the Federal Bureau of Investigation and Central Intelligence Agency were keeping about him. The FBI admitted that it had a file on me of 2,739 pages, of which it released to me all except about 773. These it held back "in the interest of national security and foreign policy." I forced myself to read most of the FBI file; it was boring because they had monitored my radio and TV speeches, and copies of my articles and pamphlets.

A lot of the material was downright absurd. For instance, in 1961 Professor John Kenneth Galbraith was appointed Ambassador to India by President Kennedy and had to have a security clearance by the FBI. One of the questions they asked was: "Professor Galbraith, why were you living fourteen years ago in the same apartment house in New York City as Corliss Lamont?" The fact is that when Galbraith and I were teaching at Columbia University, we both lived at 450 Riverside Drive. Galbraith fielded the question with scorn and affronted dignity. This ridiculous episode cemented my friendship with him.

I also discovered that the CIA kept an extensive file on me of over 1,000 pages, including copies of 155 letters, mailed first-class, to and from the Soviet Union. This correspondence was mostly with an old Russian friend, Vladimir Kazakevich, who had been a brilliant economics instructor at Columbia. The CIA admitted that its opening of these letters was illegal. I sued the CIA for $150,000 damages for the violation of my right of privacy under the Fourth Amendment.

After a trial held in February, 1978, the presiding Federal Judge, Jack B. Weinstein, condemned the behavior of the CIA, awarded me $2,000 in damages and directed the United States Government to send me an adequate letter of regret for the CIA's unconstitutional actions. Judge Weinstein was especially incensed over two "love letters" to my wife Helen from Moscow and stated: "Illegal governmental prying into the shared intimacies of husband and wife is despicable." Had I only written additional "love letters" from the Soviet Union, the Judge might have awarded me larger damages!

He said: "The sums being awarded are in large measure symbolic. They probably substantially underestimate the deep sense of personal affront and the psychic loss suffered... But the court must be practical; the number of possible plaintiffs runs into the thousands and the possible damages, even at the modest level fixed by the court, into the millions. These damages will not be paid by the bunglers responsible for the wrongs, but by the taxpayers who were unaware of the program."

Still another triumph for civil liberties had taken place two years earlier. The American Civil Liberties Union in 1976—long after the death of Elizabeth Gurley Flynn—reversed the decision it had made in 1940 to oust her from its Board of Directors merely because she was a member of the Communist Party,* although she had so informed the Board before she was unanimously re-elected in the previous year. That action had violated the ACLU's own position that guilt by association was contrary to the basic principles of civil liberties.

The sweeping victory of President Ronald Reagan and the Republican Party in the November, 1980, elections indicates that we shall have to work harder for civil liberties and the Bill of Rights. Whatever the political climate in the United States, that struggle must go on unabated, whether we are fighting for civil liberties in the courts or trying to prevent repressive legislation. With a Republican majority in control of the U.S. Senate, such legislation is a real danger, as well as the degree of tension in U.S. foreign relations under the Reagan Administration which will affect American civil liberties for better or for worse. However, a conservative Administration in Washington does not mean that the anti-Communist hysteria of the McCarthy years will be repeated. In any case, past experience gives reason to believe that America's democratic institutions are going to survive and in the end attain greater strength than ever before.

February, 1981   Corliss Lamont

*See pages 276-277

Books Edited by Corliss Lamont

Dialogue on John Dewey, Horizon Press, New York, NY, 1981. (Write Author)

Dialogue on George Santayana, Horizon Press, New York, NY, 1981. (Write Author)

Man Answers Death, Philosophical Library, New York, NY, 1954.

Collected Poems of John Reed, Lawrence Hill Books, Brooklyn, NY, 1985.

The Trial of Elizabeth Gurley Flynn by the American Civil Liberties Union, Horizon Press, New York, NY, 1969.